GOVERNING MOTIONS

Vote required?	Applies to what other motions?	Can have what other motions applied to it?[5]	Renewable?
Majority	None	Amend, close debate, limit debate	Yes
Majority	None	Amend, close debate, limit debate	Yes[6]
None	None	None	Yes
2/3	Main motion	None	No
2/3	Debatable motions	None	Yes
2/3	Debatable motions	Amend, close debate	Yes[6]
Majority	Main motion	Amend, close debate, limit debate	Yes[6]
Majority	Main motion	Amend, close debate, limit debate	Yes[6]
Majority	Rewordable motions	Amend, close debate, limit debate	No[6]
Majority	None	Subsidiary	No
Majority	None	Subsidiary	No
Same Vote	Adopted main motion	Subsidiary	No
Same Vote	Adopted main motion	Subsidiary	No
Majority	Referred main motion	Close debate, limit debate	No
Majority	Vote on main motion	Close debate, limit debate	No
Same Vote	Adopted main motion	Subsidiary, except amend	No

MOTIONS

Vote required?	Applies to what other motion?	Can have what other motions applied to it?[5]	Renewable?
Majority[7]	Ruling of chair	Close debate, limit debate	No
2/3	Procedural rules	None	Yes
Majority	Main motion or subject	None	Yes
None	Procedural error	N	
None	All motions	N	
None[8]	All motions	N	
None[8]	Main motion	N	
None[8]	Indecisive vote	I	

[5] Withdraw may be applied to all motions.

[6] Renewable at the discretion of the presiding officer.

[7] A tie or majority vote sustains the ruling of the presiding officer; a majority vote in the negative reverses the ruling.

[8] If decided by the assembly, by motion, requires a majority vote to adopt.

American Institute

OF

Parliamentarians

—— STANDARD CODE OF ——

PARLIAMENTARY PROCEDURE

New York   Chicago   San Francisco   Lisbon   London
Madrid   Mexico City   Milan   New Delhi   San Juan
Seoul   Singapore   Sydney   Toronto

CONTENTS

INTRODUCTION

Meeting procedures are sometimes seen as esoteric, complicated, baffling, and irritating. Some people view them as a waste of time. Yet, they are only a tool to be used in meetings to ensure fairness, justice, and consistency in making decisions in an environment in which people have different opinions and are not shy about expressing those opinions. This book is written to untie what is complicated, to enlighten and simplify the procedures, and to make the procedure accessible, not just to the few, but to all members of an organization who are willing to take the time to read the book. The book is extremely readable, strips away unneeded and overly complex procedures, and does not burden the meeting attendee with archaic and obtuse language. Overall, the book provides a simplified, yet complete, set of procedural rules that can be used by organizations of all sizes.

Alice Sturgis, in 1950, produced a book on procedures called the *Sturgis Standard Code of Parliamentary Procedure*, which dramatically simplified meeting procedures with the intent of making the rules understandable by all. The procedure was simple, used plain language, dropped archaic procedure and terminology, and yet was complete and usable by most organizations. The American Institute of Parliamentarians (AIP) continues Alice Sturgis's philosophy through this book titled *American Institute of Parliamentarians Standard Code of Parliamentary Procedure*.

This book has many legal citations that support the underlying philosophy of specific concepts and rules. Two fundamental principles—the right of association and the right of assembly—have been introduced. Of course, these two principles are always with us in a democracy but are explained in the context of meeting procedures.

Two motions are new. The first removes an unwanted main motion by a two-thirds vote with no discussion allowed. This is the motion to table. The second new motion, adopt in-lieu-of, is to be used mainly at conventions, where the assembly may adopt a single main motion, even though other main motions on the same subject are known to be coming before the assembly. This single main motion will be adopted in lieu of all other named main motions on the same subject. Adopt in-lieu-of is intended to improve significantly the efficiency of conducting business in large conventions by removing the need to process all main motions on the same subject.

Additional information, innovations, and changes from prior parliamentary books are introduced in the hope of providing a useful reference that is consistent with modern meeting needs and practices. These include appendices on flag etiquette and on meeting protocol; a ninth basic rule concerning renewing a motion; a complete explanation of the motion to recall a motion from a committee or board; information on the use of the important concept of informal discussion; elucidation on the topic of election challenges; a thorough explanation of different types of organizations; appendices on proxy forms, minutes, tellers reports, and bylaws; the use of the term "specific main motion" for some main motions; and up-to-date information on finances. The motions to postpone temporarily and resume consideration are not used in this modern book.

The authorship team, composed of members of AIP, includes Barry Glazer, James N. Jones, James Lochrie, Michael Malamut, Mary Randolph, Ann Rempel, Mary Remson, and Thomas Soliday. All team members are certified parliamentarians, are well-respected professionals in the field, and have a wide range of experience through their clients and the American Institute of Parliamentarians. They are eminently qualified as individuals and as a team to have written this book.

The advisors listed below have provided specific, detailed guidance on some of the chapters and have provided support for the efforts of the team.

Alan Bromstein obtained his law degree from Osgoode Hall Law School in Toronto, Ontario. His practice includes providing general legal as well as legislative advice to self-regulatory bodies, appearing as counsel at administrative hearings, and acting as independent legal counsel at administrative tribunals. He practices as a sole practitioner in Toronto.

Robert Dove is a former parliamentarian of the U.S. Senate having served from 1981 to 1987 and from 1995 to 2001. Since 2001, he has served as parliamentary consultant to a number of foreign legislatures, including the State Duma of Russia, National Assembly of Bulgaria, Assembly of Representatives of Yemen, and National Assembly of Kuwait. He is currently a professor of political science at George Washington University, specializing in congressional leadership.

Patricia Friend served as the international president for the Association of Flight Attendants—Communication Workers of America from 1995 to 2010, where she presided over the union's governing bodies. She also served as vice president of the AFL-CIO Executive Council from 1995 to 2010. She is currently serving on the boards of the U. S. National Endowment for Democracy, the United Way Worldwide, and EmergeAmerica.

Dr. Roger Keen, is a certified general accountant in Ottawa, Ontario, where he operates Roger Keen Consulting Ltd. He is former board member of Certified General Accountants—Ontario. He provided advice to the team on matters related to finances.

Leah Raye Mabry is long-time speaker of the Congress of Delegates of The American Academy of Family Physicians (AAFP) and brings her expertise on large conventions to the book. She contributed extensively to the chapter on reference committees. Dr Mabry is a recognized leader in family medicine. She continues to practice medicine, saving time to serve national, state, and local family medical professional organizations and the Texas State Board of Medical Examiners.

Helen T. McFadden currently practices law in Lake City, South Carolina. She has served as an attorney for the General Assembly of South Carolina, where she developed expertise in legislative parliamentary practice (1982–1986). She teaches in this area for the South Carolina County Association and other governmental organizations in South Carolina. Ms. McFadden has served the Democratic National Committee as parliamentarian since 1998. She serves as chair of the Board of Voter Registration in Williamsburg County. She has represented many local governing bodies as legal counsel.

Donald Lee Nickles served as U.S. senator from Oklahoma from1981 to 2005. Prior to the U.S. Senate, he served in the Oklahoma State Senate. At various times he served as the U. S. Senate majority whip and minority whip for the Republican Party. He founded the Nickles Group, a government consultant group in Washington, DC.

Michael Keith (Mike) Simpson, is a U.S. congressman, serving Idaho's second congressional district since 1999. He served in the Idaho House of Representatives for fourteen years, seven of those years as speaker of the house. By profession, he is a dentist.

Ronald Stinson is a businessman in South Texas and a past president of the National Association of Parliamentarians, serving with the organization as president from 2009 to 2011. He is a professional registered parliamentarian with that organization and serves national and international clients. He served simultaneously on the boards of the American Institute of Parliamentarians and the National Association of Parliamentarians for ten years.

Many organizations will want to adopt this book as their parliamentary authority. To do so will require a statement in their bylaws, such as the following:

> The *American Institute of Parliamentarians Standard Code of Parliamentary Procedure* shall govern the Association in all cases to which it is applicable and is not inconsistent with the bylaws and standing rules of the Association.

Chapter 1

PARLIAMENTARY LAW

Mr. Onslow, the ablest among the Speakers of the House of Commons, used to say "… it was a maxim … from old and experienced members, that nothing tended more to throw power into the hands of administration and those who acted with the majority of the House of Commons, than a neglect of, or departure from, the rules of proceeding: that these forms, as instituted by our ancestors, operated as a check and controul on the actions of the majority; and that they were in many instances, a shelter and protection to the minority, against the attempts of power."

2 Hats. 171, 172.

The above quote is from Jefferson's *Manual on Parliamentary Practice* quoting John Hatsell, quoting Arthur Onslow, quoting old and experienced members.

These three eminent historical persons, the honorable Arthur Onslow (1691–1768), longest-serving speaker in the English parliament, John Hatsell (1733–1820), clerk of the House of Commons and a world renowned authority, in his time, on parliamentary procedure, and Thomas Jefferson (1743–1826), the third president of the United States and author of the *Manual of Parliamentary Practice*, all recognized, taught, and documented the historic need for safeguarding the rights of members of parliament or congress through rules of procedure. The maxim stated in the first paragraph was established and understood well before the seventeenth century, and it formed one of the fundamental principles of democratic practices in parliament.

Procedural Rights in a Democratic Organization

One need look to the law in every state in the United States, every province in the Dominion of Canada, and indeed in every other democratic nation on earth to see that the law is infused with procedural safeguards insisting on such matters as the right to be informed, the right to attend hearings and meetings, the right to speak out, the right to due process, the right to complain when process is not followed, and finally the right to take civil action. All these rights and more make up our noisy democracies, but all with the intention of procedural fairness and hopefully, in the end, justice.

Organizations and their meetings are a microcosm of larger society. Meeting rules insist on protecting the rights of the members of an organization through well-defined processes (rankings of the motions). Members may complain when the process is not followed (point of order) and further complain when they believe the presiding officer is unfair or perhaps just simply wrong in making rulings (appeal). Debate is to be orderly, courteous, fair, and available to all members except in very unusual circumstances (if the member is under suspension). Members can aspire to the highest offices in the organization, which are attained through procedural processes (nominations and elections) that are rigidly followed to ensure fairness. Members may run afoul of the organization thus leading to sanctions, perhaps suspensions and expulsion, but again in these procedures rigidly follow the rules contained in a disciplinary process adopted by the organization.

It is very difficult to imagine anything happening in an organization without the need for rules. Even organizational social events may require a master of ceremonies, a head table, seating arrangements, introduction of guests in the right order, and perhaps even customary rituals and protocols to follow. Even in the simplest of social events with none of these formalities necessary, someone will still need to be in charge of the event to avoid confusion, with such a person having enough authority and employing customary practices to ensure that the event goes smoothly.

Meeting Procedures

The purpose of meeting procedures is to allow members to reach informed business decisions in an effective, efficient, orderly, courteous, and fair manner. Meeting procedures allow the members making the decisions to work as a cohesive group, respectful of the other members, and to reach decisions through debate and majority vote. Meeting procedures facilitate group decisions and help members attain the organization's objectives.

Procedures in meetings can be found in statutes, regulations, the charter of a parent organization, bylaws, special and standing rules adopted by the organization, and in an adopted parliamentary authority, such as this book. In some cases, the rules may be customary, based on usage, and not written down. Written rules have precedence over customary rules when brought to the attention of the meeting. The statutes and regulations may be federal, state, or local. They may contain general procedural rules that cover many organizations and industries, including for-profit and nonprofit corporations. However, in some cases they may apply to a specific class of organization such as labor unions. When applying such rules, it is incumbent on the leaders of an organization to know the rules and to consult legal counsel for matters involving statutory law and governmental regulations.

While the above brief description of meeting procedures probably covers most of the rules that an organization will use, other procedural rules may derive from the common law of parliamentary procedure, itself derived from judicial decisions and custom.

All these rules together are called *parliamentary law*. Parliamentary law applies in meetings generally; in processes concerning meetings, such as elections of officers and disciplinary matters; in committees; to products of meetings such as minutes and reports; and to all other processes concerning organizational governance, because the will of a body (such as the membership, an assembly of delegates, a board, or a committee) can generally be expressed only through meetings.

Abuse of Parliamentary Law

In some cases members may use meetings to gain an improper personal advantage. For example, a member may use information gained in meetings, perhaps even in a closed meeting where the information is to be protected, at least for a time, to ensure that the organization is not harmed by premature disclosure of the information. A member may gain a private pecuniary interest through this information. While a member may have a right to information, that information cannot be used for private gain, and using it for that purpose is an abuse of the meeting rules. This type of behavior is not allowed, and the sanctions against such behavior should be swift and direct.

A member or group of members may use specific procedural rules to thwart the will of the assembly, even though the use of the rules may, on the face of it, appear to be proper. Continual use of the rules, for example, for no other reason than to delay the meeting is an abuse of the rules. It is important that such tactics not be tolerated by the presiding officer and the other attendees of the meeting.

Organizations That Use Parliamentary Law

Government at its highest level (such as the U.S. House of Representatives and Senate), state legislatures, national parliaments (such as the UK Parliament), and most nations around the world that have such governmental structures use parliamentary procedure suited specifically to their needs. Governments rely on the general principles of democracy, and have evolved their rules over the centuries into complex sets of procedures governing mainly two levels of legislatures that deal with hundreds, if not thousands, of pieces of business in any year and where decisions are often highly politicized. This complex type of procedure would have no place in most organizations.

Associations, boards, commissions, and labor unions and lower-level government bodies such as school boards, municipal council, and government commissions all use parliamentary law. These organizations define which deliberative bodies within their own structure make decisions for the organization. The two main deliberative bodies within an organization are the meeting of members (the assembly) and the board of directors (governing board). While a meeting of members is generally the highest governing body in an organization, the members, in their wisdom, often confer on the governing board substantive powers to carry on the work of the organization between meetings of members. In addition, in most cases, there are continuing committees and special committees that are mostly advisory to the two main bodies.

The meetings of these organizations must use parliamentary law, which might be imposed on them by statute, common law, or a superior body, but is often deliberately chosen. Voluntary organizations usually set up their own rules to complement their adopted parliamentary authority and to ensure that their organization operates democratically. In small organizations the procedure can be minimal but must conform to the fundamental principles contained in the parliamentary authority. In large organizations, especially where hundreds may attend an annual membership meeting, the rules will be much more formal and will be rigidly applied. An organization must find its own level of formality in its meetings.

The Parliamentary Authority

A parliamentary authority is a written set of principles and specific procedural rules that can be adopted by motion or stated in bylaws that determine the rules to be followed in all meetings of the organization. The parliamentary authority can be superseded by other rules adopted by the organization. These are variously called *standing rules* or *special rules*. These rules are often small in number compared to the thousands of rules contained in the parliamentary authority.

This book, *American Institute of Parliamentarians Standard Code of Parliamentary Procedure*, is a comprehensive parliamentary authority that can be adopted by any organization. Special procedural rules, which differ from those in this book or that perhaps augment the rules contained in this book, can then be adopted separately to cover the specific needs of the organization.

Chapter 2

FUNDAMENTAL PRINCIPLES OF PARLIAMENTARY LAW

Knowledge of the fundamental principles of parliamentary law enables you to reason out the answers to most questions about parliamentary procedure. An understanding of these principles clarifies the subject of parliamentary procedure. When you understand the basic principles of parliamentary law, it is easier to become familiar with the rules because most of them follow logically from the principles.

The principles are simple and so familiar that we sometimes fail to recognize their importance. They are the same principles on which democracies are based.

Some fundamental principles are based on law and others on centuries of democratic practice. While an organization may choose to adopt a rule that is contrary to the fundamental principles, consideration should be given to whether such a rule is permissible under applicable law. If permissible, such a rule should be adopted only with serious consideration of the fundamental principles and the basis for their broad historical acceptance. The most appropriate placement of such rules is usually in the bylaws.

Occasionally, the fundamental principles, which have no order of precedence, may seem to conflict with one another. Often, when this is the case, the parliamentary authority (such as this book) will provide a specific rule to resolve the apparent conflict. An example of this is when the majority, which has a right to decide matters, wishes to end debate, while the minority wishes to exercise the right to full and free discussion. This book resolves the conflict of these principles by requiring a two-thirds vote to close debate.

Some of the important principles of parliamentary law are given below. These basic principles serve as a foundation for the framework of democratic group procedures.

The Purpose of Parliamentary Law

The purpose of parliamentary procedure is to facilitate the orderly transaction of business and to promote cooperation and harmony. The philosophy of parliamentary law is constructive. Parliamentary law makes it easier for people to work together effectively and is designed to help organizations and members accomplish their purposes.

Parliamentary procedure should not be used to awe, entangle, or confuse the uninitiated.[1] The rules should be used only to the extent necessary to observe the law, to expedite business, to avoid confusion, and to protect the rights of members.

Some basic procedural rules have been developed to ensure that simple and direct procedures for accomplishing a purpose are observed. For example, some classes of motions have a definite order of precedence, each motion having a fixed rank for being introduced and considered. Another example of this basic principle is the rule that only one question is considered at a time. When one motion is under consideration, it can be superseded by a motion having a higher rank, but each motion is considered separately and in turn so that only one question is before the assembly at one time.

Right of Association

Individual persons have the right to associate with other persons to promote and pursue their common interests and aspirations.[2] In forming or joining such associations, the members choose the terms of their relationship with each other by agreeing, through democratic processes, to a set of bylaws and other governing documents. The governing documents form a contract between each member and the association. This contract may be amended from time to time as the common requirements of the association and the members change. Members of the association have equal rights (see below) and are expected to be loyal to the association. They are also expected to promote and defend their common interest and aspirations and to pay any membership fees as required. Members also have a right not to associate and may resign at any time subject to the association's rules at that time.

Right of Assembly

Individual persons or groups have a right to assemble to promote their common interest. The right of assembly is inherent in the right to associate.

Associations may protect this right to assemble by securing their assembly location and environment from interference from others, including their own members, to ensure privacy, quiet enjoyment, and security of property and person. In addition, the assembly controls those who may and may not attend, whether the person is a regular member, a delegate, or a nonmember, such as a guest or observer. This protection can be enforced through rules of the association and, as a last resort, through outside agencies such as law enforcement.

Equality of Rights

All members have equal rights, privileges, and obligations. Every member has an equal right to propose motions, speak, ask questions, nominate, be a candidate for office, vote, or exercise any other privilege of a member. Every member has equal obligations, including the obligation to insist on the protection of the rights of all members. The rights of members present and the rights of members who are absent must be safeguarded.

The presiding officer should be strictly impartial and should act promptly to protect the equality of all members in the exercise of their rights and privileges. The general rule that the presiding officer does not take part in debate while presiding, except on small boards and committees, is based on the principle of the presiding officer's impartiality.

Majority Decision

The majority vote decides. The ultimate authority of an organization is, as a general matter, vested in a majority of its members.[3] This is a fundamental concept of democracy.

A primary purpose of parliamentary procedure is to determine the will of the majority and to see that it is carried out. By the act of joining a group, a member agrees to be governed by the vote of its majority. Until the vote on a question is announced, every member has an equal right to voice opposition or approval and to seek to persuade others. Unanimous agreement is seldom possible. After the vote is announced, the decision of the majority becomes the decision of every member of the organization, and it is the duty of every member to accept and abide by that decision.

When the members of an organization select officers, boards, or committees and delegate authority to them, this selection and delegation should be by the democratic process of majority vote.

Minority Rights

The rights of the minority must be protected. Democratic organizations always protect certain basic rights of all members. The right to present proposals, to be heard, and to oppose proposals are valued rights of all members, although the ultimate decision rests with a majority, except when a higher vote is required. The members who are in the minority on a question are entitled to the same consideration and respect as members who are in the majority.

The minority of today is frequently the majority of tomorrow. A member of the majority on one question may be in the minority on the next. The protection of the rights of all members, minority and majority alike, should be the concern of every member.

The Right of Discussion

Full and free discussion of every proposition presented for decision is an established right of members. Each member of an assembly has the right to express his or her opinion freely without interruption or interference provided that the rules of debate and decorum, which are applicable to all members, are observed. This right to speak freely is as important as the right to vote. The democratic concept of freedom of speech is so important that a two-thirds vote is required to supersede that right by adopting motions to limit or close debate, thus providing a balance between the rights of the minority and the principle of majority rule.

The Right to Information

Every member has the right to know the meaning of the question before the assembly and what its effect will be. The presiding officer should keep the pending motion clearly before the assembly at all times and, when necessary, explain it or call on a member to do so. Any motion and its effect should be explained if there are members who do not understand it. Members have the right to request information from or through the presiding officer on any motion they do not understand so that they may vote intelligently. This principle underlies a member's right to rise to a parliamentary or factual inquiry. Members are entitled to information that will facilitate good decision making.

Fairness and Good Faith

All meetings must be characterized by fairness and by good faith. Trickery, overemphasis on minor technicalities, dilatory tactics, indulgence in personalities, and "railroading" threaten the spirit and practice of fairness and good faith. If a meeting is characterized by fairness and good faith, a minor procedural error will not invalidate an action that has been taken by an organization. But fraud, unfairness, or absence of good faith may cause a court to hold any action invalid.

Parliamentary strategy is the art of using legitimately the parliamentary principles, rules, and motions to support or defeat a proposal. It includes, for example, such important factors as timing, wording of proposals, choice of supporters, selection of arguments, and manipulation of proposals by other motions. Strategy, ethically used, is constructive; however, if it involves deceit, fraud, misrepresentation, intimidation, railroading, or denial of the rights of members, it is destructive and actually illegal.

In 1776 John Hatsell, the famous chief clerk of the House of Commons, wrote, "Motives ought to outweigh objections of form." The interpretations of the courts make it clear that the intent and overall good faith of the group are more important than the particular detail of procedure used in a given instance.[4] The effectiveness and, in fact, often the existence of an organization are destroyed if its officers or members condone unfairness or lack of good faith.

Chapter 3

CLASSIFICATION OF MOTIONS

Motions are classified into five groups according to their purposes and characteristics:

1. Main motions
2. Specific main motions
3. Subsidiary motions
4. Privileged motions
5. Incidental motions

Main Motions

Main motions are the most important and most frequently used kind of motion. The main motion is the foundation for conducting business. Its purpose is to bring substantive proposals before the assembly for consideration and action. After it is stated to the assembly by the presiding officer, the main motion becomes the subject for deliberation and decision.

Specific Main Motions

There are six main motions that have specific names and are governed by somewhat different rules. They are referred to as specific main motions because they perform unique and specific functions. They do not present a new proposal, but they concern actions that were previously taken. The specific main motions are:

1. Adopt in-lieu-of
2. Amend a previous action
3. Ratify
4. Recall from committee (or board)
5. Reconsider
6. Rescind

Subsidiary Motions

Subsidiary motions alter the main motion, or delay or hasten its consideration. Subsidiary motions are usually applied to the main motion, but some of them may be applied to certain other motions. As a result, they are subsidiary to the motion to which they are applied.

The six subsidiary motions are listed in their order of precedence (from highest to lowest in rank):

1. Table
2. Close debate and vote immediately
3. Limit or extend debate
4. Postpone to a certain time
5. Refer to a committee
6. Amend

Privileged Motions

Privileged motions have no direct connection with the main motion before the assembly. They are emergency motions of such urgency that they are entitled to immediate consideration. They relate to the members, to the organization, and to the meeting as a whole rather than to particular items of business. Privileged motions would be main motions but for their urgency. Because of their urgency, they are given the privilege of being considered ahead of other motions that are before the assembly.

The three privileged motions are listed in their order of rank (from highest to lowest):

1. Adjourn
2. Recess
3. Question of privilege

Incidental Motions

Incidental motions arise incidentally out of the business before the assembly. They do not relate directly to the main motion or to specific main motions but usually relate to matters incidental to the conduct of the meeting. Because of their nature, they may interrupt business and may sometimes interrupt the speaker. Incidental motions may be offered at any time, have no order of rank, and are disposed of prior to the business out of which they arise.

Some of the frequently used incidental motions include:

- Appeal from a decision of the chair
- Suspend the rules
- Consider informally
- Point of order
- Inquiry
- Withdrawal of a motion
- Division of a question
- Division of the assembly

Classification of Unlisted Motions

The motions within each class—main, specific main motion, subsidiary, privileged, and incidental—differ somewhat from each other, but they have similar purposes and characteristics. Only the more commonly used motions in each class are listed in charts and classifications. There are many other motions that may be proposed, and the presiding officer must know how to classify them in order to determine whether they are in order and what rules govern them. Therefore, it is essential to understand the purposes and characteristics of each class in order to classify the less-used motions.

For example, while a main motion is being considered, a member might move "that the vote on the motion be taken by roll call." This might appear to be a main motion. It is, however, an incidental motion because it arises incidentally out of the business before the assembly. It would therefore be in order and would be decided immediately. Or a member might move "that the article in today's newspaper explaining the reason for a city sales tax increase be procured and read to the assembly before we vote on the question under consideration." This would be a privileged motion because of its urgency and would be considered immediately. Without an understanding of the classification of motions, the presiding officer might mistakenly think that the examples just cited are main motions and rule them out of order on the grounds that another main motion is pending.

The name given a motion by its proposer is not the determining factor in classifying the motion because the proposer may name the motion incorrectly. For example, someone might move "to table the motion until ten o'clock." This is a motion to postpone to a certain time, not a motion to table, since a time is specified.

Changes in Classification of Motions

A motion that usually is listed in one classification may belong in another if it is proposed in a different situation. The classification of a motion is usually based on the relationship of that motion to the main motion. The main motion is the foundation motion that determines the classification of other motions.

Usually a main motion is already pending when a subsidiary, privileged, or incidental motion is proposed. However, certain of the subsidiary, privileged, or incidental motions may be proposed when no main motion is pending. In this situation the subsidiary and privileged motions are classified as main motions. An incidental motion moved when no business is pending is not a main motion but simply retains the same governing rules as the incidental motion moved when business is pending.

The following sections provide examples of subsidiary, privileged, and incidental motions that may be proposed when no business is pending (with an example of a possible form in which each might be proposed).

Subsidiary Motions as Main Motions

- *Limit debate.* I move that debate on the bylaws amendments be limited to 45 minutes.
- *Postpone to a certain time.* I move to postpone reports of officers until after the mayor's speech.
- *Refer to committee.* I move that the president appoint a committee of three to review the condition of all office equipment and report its recommendations for any upgrades that may be needed at the May meeting.

Privileged Motions as Main Motions

- *Adjourn.* I move we adjourn, *or* I move that we adjourn this evening at 6 p.m. so that everyone can attend the auction.
- *Recess.* I move that we recess for 20 minutes, *or* I move that after the report of the nominating committee, we recess the meeting until tomorrow morning at 8 a.m.
- *Question of privilege (presented as a motion).* I move that we move into a closed meeting to hold an informal discussion on marketing our services and possibly employing consultants.

Incidental Motions Moved When No Business Is Pending

- *Appeal.* Presider: Your demand to discuss the reserve funds is not in order because no motion is pending. Member: I appeal from the decision of the chair.
- *Suspend rules.* Member: For the next two agenda items, I move that we suspend the rules prohibiting members from speaking more than once on a question so that we can have a more thorough exchange of ideas when the strategic plan and the budget are considered next.

Chapter 4

RANKING OF MOTIONS

The rank or precedence of various motions is important. The rank of a motion determines its priority when it is proposed and the sequence in which it must be considered and disposed of. The purpose of the rank of a motion is to ensure that each motion is dealt with consistently and without confusion. The precedence of motions is logical and is based on the relative urgency of each motion.

From the highest ranking to the lowest ranking, the order of the rank of motions is:

Privileged Motions

1. Adjourn
2. Recess
3. Question of privilege

Subsidiary Motions

4. Table
5. Close debate
6. Limit or extend debate
7. Postpone to a certain time
8. Refer to committee
9. Amend

Main Motions

10. The main motion and specific main motions

Basic Rules of Ranking

There are two basic rules of ranking:

1. *When a motion is being considered, any motion of higher rank may be proposed, but no motion of lower rank may be proposed.* For example, when a main motion (10) is pending, a member may move to refer the motion to a committee (8). Another member may move to recess (2). There will then be three motions pending at the same time. Since the proper order of rank was followed in proposing them, there will be no confusion in considering and disposing of them.
2. *Motions are considered and voted on in reverse order of their proposal. The motion last proposed, and which is the highest ranked motion pending, is considered and disposed of first.* For example, if motions (10), (8), and (2) are proposed in that order and are pending, they are considered and decided in the reverse order, which is (2), (8), and (10).

Motions without Rank

Incidental motions have no order of ranking. They can arise incidentally out of the immediately pending business at any time. Incidental motions must be decided as soon as they arise. For more information on incidental motions, see Chapter 11.

Example of Ranking

Suppose that a member proposes a main motion (10) "that the club sponsor 10 students attending the summer music camp." While this motion is pending, another member moves to amend it by striking out 10 and replacing it with 15 (9). While the amendment is being discussed, another member moves to "limit debate on the amendment to one speech per member for no more than two minutes per speech" (6).

Another member now moves to postpone the motion until the next meeting (7). Immediately, still another member rises to a point of order (an incidental motion, which can be made whenever necessary) and states that the motion to postpone to a certain time (7) is not in order because it is of lower rank than the immediately pending motion—limit debate (6). The presiding officer rules that the member's point is "well taken" and declares the motion to postpone to a certain time to not be in order, stating that the immediately pending motion is "to limit debate." A member then moves "that we take a recess for 20 minutes" (2).

All these motions, except the one ruled out of order, have followed the correct ranking and are therefore in order. The four motions shown in Table 4.1 are pending.

Table 4.1

Motions Pending	Rank
Recess	2
Limit debate	6
Amend	9
The main motion	10

The presiding officer first takes a vote on the motion to recess. If the motion to recess is defeated, the presiding officer then calls for a vote on the motion to limit debate. If, however, the motion to recess is adopted, the motion to limit debate will be pending when the members return from recess. After the motion to limit debate has been adopted or defeated, the motion to amend is the immediately pending question. After it has been discussed and voted on, the presiding officer calls for discussion on the main motion.

While the assembly is considering any of the four motions in their order of rank, a member may present another motion, provided that it has a higher rank than the one that is currently being considered. For example, while the motion to limit debate is pending, a motion to close debate would be in order, but a motion to refer to committee would not.

Complicated problems in regard to the ranking of motions should rarely occur. Quite frequently, however, two or three motions are awaiting decision by the assembly. All motions that have been proposed and stated to the assembly but are not yet decided are called *pending questions* or *pending motions.*

The particular motion being considered by the assembly at any particular time is called the *immediately pending motion* (or *question*).

It is the duty of the presiding officer, with assistance from the secretary or parliamentarian, to keep the assembly informed as to what motion is immediately pending. This is most readily accomplished by repeated statements from the presiding officer concerning which motion is immediately pending as he or she calls for debate and again immediately prior to taking the vote.

Chapter 5

RULES GOVERNING MOTIONS

Orderly procedure requires that basic motions be strictly and uniformly applied. Understanding the basic rules of motions begins with understanding the purpose and logic of the rules. Nothing is more essential to procedure, in which full justice is accorded each member, than applying all rules with uniformity and certainty.[1]

The basic questions that must be answered to fully understand each motion are:

1. Can the motion interrupt a speaker?
2. Does the motion require a second?
3. Is the motion debatable?
4. Can the motion be amended?
5. What vote does the motion require?
6. What is the ranking of the motion?
7. To what other motions can the motion apply?
8. What other motions can be applied to the motion?
9. Can the motion be renewed?

Can the Motion Interrupt a Speaker?

There are two types of motions that, because of their urgency, can interrupt a speaker: those that are subject to a time limit to move the motion and those that present a question requiring immediate attention.

The first are those motions that must be proposed and decided within a specific time limit: to reconsider, to appeal, division of the assembly, and request to withdraw a motion. The motion to reconsider must be made during the same meeting or convention at which the vote to be reconsidered was taken and may be moved by any member.[2] An appeal and a call for division of the assembly must be made before another item of business is taken up by the assembly. A proposer who wishes to withdraw his or her motion may interrupt the presiding officer who is stating, or is about to state, the motion. After the motion has been stated by the presiding officer, the proposer may interrupt another speaker to request the withdrawal of the motion. The withdrawal must occur before the motion is voted on.

The second are those motions that relate to the immediate rights and privileges of a member or of the assembly: question of privilege, point of order, factual inquiry, and parliamentary inquiry.

A question of privilege involving the immediate convenience, comfort, or rights of the organization or of its members may be so urgent that it justifies interrupting a speaker; an example is noise that prevents the member from hearing the speaker. A point of order involving a mistake, error, or failure to comply with the rules may interrupt a speaker if the point relates to the speaker or to some error that cannot wait for the completion of the speech.

To justify interrupting a speaker, a factual inquiry or parliamentary inquiry must relate to the speaker, to the speech, or to some other matter that cannot be delayed until the completion of the speech. A factual inquiry may be appropriate if it directly relates to an error in the presentation of information, which would create a substantive problem with the question being debated. A parliamentary inquiry is similar to a point of order in that it may raise a question about procedure that may be immediately taken.

Does the Motion Require a Second?

Motions normally require a second except in meetings of committees, boards, or some government bodies.[3] To justify the consideration of the assembly, a proposal should have the support of at least two members: one who makes the motion and another, the seconder, who indicates willingness for the motion to be considered. The seconder indicates only that the member believes the motion should be considered and does not mean that he or she agrees with the proposal.

A few actions do not require seconds because, although technically classified as motions, they are *requests* that are decided, or must be granted, by the presiding officer. These are: point of order, factual and parliamentary inquiries, withdrawal of a motion, division of a question, division of the assembly, and question of privilege. Questions of privilege, division of a question, and withdrawal of a motion are sometimes presented as motions instead of as requests. If they are presented as motions, they require seconds.

Is the Motion Debatable?

Some motions are open to full debate, others are open to restricted debate, and still others are undebatable. The only motions that are *fully debatable* are: main motions, amendments to fully debatable main motions, and motions to ratify, adopt in-lieu-of, amend a previous action, rescind, and appeal. They are fully debatable because they all require the members to be well informed before making a decision.

Main motions are debatable because they present substantive propositions requiring the consideration of the organization. Amendments to debatable motions involve a part of the motion itself and are therefore debatable. An appeal from a decision of the chair is debatable because the presiding officer should give reasons for his or her decision, and the member appealing has a right to present reasons for appealing that decision. The motions to amend a previous action and rescind a main motion that was previously passed are debatable because they change or repeal an action taken earlier, and members need to understand the action that is being taken. The motion to ratify is fully debatable because members must fully understand what is being ratified. Adopt in-lieu-of is fully debatable because the members need to understand the main motion that is being presented in lieu of other main motions.

Eight motions are open to *restricted* debate: the subsidiary motions to amend a motion for which debate is restricted, to postpone to a certain time, to refer to a committee or board, and to limit debate; the privileged motions to recess and to adjourn; and the specific main motions to recall a motion or subject from a committee or board, and to reconsider. Restricted debate confines discussion to a few specific points relative to the purpose of the motion itself. Thus debate on the motion to postpone to a certain time is restricted to discussion of the advisability of postponing and of the time to which the matter would be postponed. Debate on the motion to refer to a committee is restricted to the advisability of referral and to the selection, membership, and duties of the committee, or instructions to it. Debate on the motion to limit debate is restricted to the need for limitation and the type and time of limitation. Debate on the motion to recall a motion or subject from a committee is restricted to the reasons for the removal from a committee's (or board's) consideration. Debate on the motion to reconsider is restricted to the reasons for reconsidering. Debate on the privileged motion to recess is restricted to a brief discussion on the advisability of the recess and its length. Debate on the privileged form of the motion to adjourn is limited to the advisability of amending it to continue the meeting at a later time and to the time at which the meeting will be continued. Debate is restricted on any amendments applied to the motions with restricted debate.

Debate is not permitted on the subsidiary motion to table because the sole purpose of the motion is to remove the main motion from consideration without further debate. Debate is not permitted on other motions because they deal with simple procedural questions, which can be decided without discussion.

Can the Motion Be Amended?

A simple test determines whether a motion can be amended. If the motion contains wording that can be varied, then it is amendable. For example, the motion, "I move we recess for 10 minutes" could have been stated, "I move we recess for 30 minutes." The motion, "I move that we limit debate on this question to one more speech on each side" could have been stated, "I move that we limit debate to two more speeches on each side." Such motions therefore are amendable.

On the other hand, if a change in the wording would make the motion a different kind of motion, it would not be amendable. For example, to try to amend the motion to table by saying, "I move to strike out the word 'table' and insert the word 'postpone,'" would make it a different kind of motion (to postpone to a certain time), so the amendment is not in order.

The only motions that can be amended freely are main motions and amendments of main motions; some motions can be amended with restrictions, and some other motions cannot be amended at all.

Five motions can be amended only within restrictions: recess, limit debate, postpone to a certain time, refer to a committee, and adjourn. Recess, limit debate, and postpone to a certain time can be amended only as to time or manner of restriction, and refer to a committee can be amended only as to the method of selection, size, duties of, or instructions to the committee. The motion to adjourn can be amended to change it to continue the meeting at a later time.

What Vote Does the Motion Require?

The foundation of parliamentary procedure rests upon decisions made by the majority. For this reason, most motions require a majority vote. Motions that affect the rights of members may require a two-thirds vote. These motions limit the rights of members to propose, discuss, and decide proposals and include motions to close debate, limit debate, table, and suspend the rules. An organization's bylaws may provide that certain other motions require a two-thirds vote. For example, most bylaws require a two-thirds vote to amend the bylaws, and in some states statutory law requires a two-thirds vote for a nonprofit membership corporation to buy, sell, or lease real estate or to mortgage substantially all of its property.[4]

What Is the Ranking (Precedence) of the Motion?

To avoid confusion, each motion is assigned a definite rank or priority. This rank is based on the urgency of the motion. The ranking of motions is discussed in Chapter 4. When a motion is before the assembly, any motion is in order if it has a higher rank than the immediately pending motion, but no motion having a lower rank is in order. Motions are considered and decided in reverse order to that of their proposal.

The general order of rank gives privileged motions the highest rank, subsidiary motions second, and the main and specific main motions the lowest. Incidental motions have no order of rank among themselves. Incidental motions may be proposed at any time they are needed and are decided upon immediately.

To What Other Motions Can the Motion Apply?

A motion is said to apply to another motion when it is used to alter or dispose of or affect the original motion in some way. For example, if a main motion is being considered and a member moves "to postpone the consideration of the motion until Friday at three o'clock," the motion to postpone *applies to* the main motion. All specific main motions apply to main motions in some way. Subsidiary motions apply to main motions and other applicable motions. The subsidiary motions to close debate and to limit debate apply to all debatable motions. The subsidiary motion to amend applies to a main motion; to the specific main motions to ratify, amend a previous action, and adopt in-lieu-of; to the subsidiary motions to amend, refer, postpone to a certain time, and limit debate; and to the privileged motions to recess and adjourn.

Privileged motions relate to the organization and to the welfare and rights of its members rather than to particular items of business and therefore do not apply to any other motion.

Incidental motions do not apply to other motions, except that the motion to withdraw applies to any motion, and division of the question applies to main motions. Division of the assembly applies to *votes* on motions.

What Other Motions Can Be Applied to the Motion?

When a motion is being considered, it is important to know what other motions can be applied to it. The following rules determine what motions may be applied to each individual motion:

1. Every motion can have the motion to withdraw applied to it.
2. All debatable motions can have the motions to close debate and vote immediately and to limit or extend debate applied to them.
3. All motions that may be worded in more than one way thereby producing different results can have the motion to amend applied to them.
4. The main motion can have all the subsidiary motions applied to it.
5. Applying subsidiary motions to specific main motions varies according to the nature of the specific main motion. Three of the specific main motions—amend a previous action, ratify, and adopt in-lieu-of—can have all subsidiary motions applied to them. Recall a motion or subject from a committee, reconsider, and rescind cannot be amended but can have the motions to limit debate and close debate applied to them. Rescind may also have the motions to refer and postpone applied to it.
6. Privileged motions can have no other motion applied to them, except that the motions to recess and adjourn may be amended and may have the motions to close debate and vote immediately and to limit or extend debate applied to them.
7. Incidental motions can have no other motions applied to them, except the motion to appeal may have the motions to close debate and vote immediately and to limit or extend debate applied to it.

Can a Motion Be Renewed?

As a general rule, when a main motion has been voted on and has lost, the same, or substantially the same, motion cannot be proposed again at the same meeting or convention. Parliamentary law recognizes, however, that an assembly may change its mind, just as an individual may, and that some method must be provided for changing a decision that has been made. In the case of a main motion (one which presents a substantive proposal to the assembly), the matter can be brought before the assembly again at the same meeting or convention by the motion to *reconsider*, which is discussed in Chapter 8. Approval of the motion to reconsider cancels the earlier vote and enables the assembly to discuss and amend the motion, if desired, and to take another vote.

If the motion in question was adopted at an earlier meeting or convention, it cannot be reconsidered. It may be *repealed*, however, by the motion *to rescind*, which nullifies the earlier decision. Unlike the motion to reconsider, the motion to rescind (or to repeal) has no time limit.

If a main motion was *rejected* at an earlier meeting or convention, it may be renewed by being introduced as a new main motion at a subsequent meeting or convention.

All motions that are procedural rather than substantive may be renewed at the discretion of the presiding officer. The presiding officer should judge the likelihood of a different outcome if the procedural motion is renewed. This is often based on a change in the parliamentary situation, which may occur by amending the main motion so that the procedural motion now applies to a somewhat different question, or which may occur by progress in debate. For example, a defeated motion to refer may now be more likely to be adopted if the underlying motion has changed, or if further debate or repeated attempts to amend have made it apparent that the motion may be more complex than previously realized and that referral may have merit now, in spite of the assembly's earlier decision not to refer.

In addition to the nine questions about each motion that have been summarized in this chapter, there is one additional procedural question that should be understood: "How does a main motion that is currently pending affect previous main motions that are on the same subject and that are still in effect?" This is explained through the concept of repeal by implication, below.

Repeal by Implication

A main motion that has been adopted can be affected by a new main motion that has been introduced at a later meeting. *Repeal by implication*[5] automatically results from the adoption of a motion that conflicts in whole or in part with another motion or motions previously adopted. The first motion is repealed only to the extent that its provisions cannot be reconciled with those of the new motion.

Members may be unaware of related motions previously adopted, or they may have overlooked them. Before a member proposes a new main motion, it is good procedure to search the records for adopted main motions, which may still be in effect but with which the new motion might conflict. Such motions that are still in effect should be rescinded before a new motion is adopted. Repeal by implication is intended to correct *inadvertent* conflicts, not to be a blanket method for disposing of previously adopted main motions without voting directly on their repeal.

Repeal by implication applies to any previously adopted motion, rule, or bylaw that is in conflict with a newly adopted motion, rule, or bylaw. If the new motion conflicts with a provision in a source of higher authority, for example, a charter or the bylaws, it is out of order.

Table 5.1 provides a synopsis of the motions and processes that can be used to change main motions that have been adopted, or the case of a defeated main motion, how to renew or reconsider the defeated motion. It shows when the motion or process can be used and what other motions it can be applied to.

Table 5.1   Changing Main Motions Already Voted On

	May Be Used:	**Applies To:**
Motion to reconsider	Only at same meeting or convention	Any main motion adopted, lost, or tabled
Motion to rescind	At any meeting or convention	Any main motion adopted at an earlier meeting or convention
Amend a previous action	At any meeting or convention	Any main motion previously adopted
Renew by new main motion	At any meeting or convention	Any main motion lost at a prior meeting or convention
Repeal or amend by implication	At any meeting or convention	Any main motion previously adopted that conflicts with a current main motion

Chapter 6

PROCESSING OF MOTIONS

A *motion* is a formal statement of a proposal or question to an assembly to take action or express certain sentiments. A main motion brings a new item of business before the meeting. However, most business conducted during a meeting will be in the form of motions relating to pending business. Once stated, a motion may be referred to as a "question" or "proposition," depending on the context. If the motion expresses a sentiment or expression of the assembly, it is usually presented in the form of a written resolution.

Steps in Presenting a Motion

Motions may take many forms, but the initial presentation follows a generally accepted procedure. Presenting a motion usually requires the following steps:

1. A member rises and addresses the presiding officer.
2. The member is recognized by the presiding officer.
3. The member proposes a motion.
4. Another member seconds the motion.
5. The presiding officer states the motion to the assembly.

Addressing the Presiding Officer

Any member has the right to present a motion. Addressing the presiding officer indicates that the member wishes to obtain the floor, that is, to have the right to present a motion or to speak. To do this, the member rises and addresses the presiding officer by his or her official title. If the member does not know the official title of the presiding officer, the terms "Mister Chairman" and "Madam Chairman" are always correct unless the organization has adopted a different style of address. After addressing the presiding officer, the member waits for recognition.

In large assemblies, if a microphone system is used, members follow the following procedure. They form a line at the appropriate microphone, and the presiding officer recognizes the members based on the microphone number or location. This is done instead of rising and addressing the presiding officer from the members' seated locations.

Recognition by the Presiding Officer

The presiding officer should recognize all members in the same manner to avoid the perception of favoritism. For instance, if the presiding officer does not know every member by name, then another form of recognition must be used. This may include, "Speaker at microphone A," or, "The member in row 4," or even, "The member in the red jacket."

Except in very small assemblies, members, when recognized, should identify themselves by name and, if appropriate, the state, district, or other unit they represent. They should then state the purpose for which they rise. For example, "Bill Brown, delegate from Wyoming. I rise to speak in favor of the motion."

Having received formal recognition from the presiding officer, a member is said to have the floor and is entitled to present a motion or to speak. Other members who were also seeking recognition should be seated as soon as one member is recognized. If a microphone system is being used, members in line may keep their places in line, but they should step back to avoid crowding the member who has the floor.

Proposal of a Motion by a Member

The correct form for stating a motion is, "I move that …" followed by a statement of the proposal the member wishes to bring before the assembly; for example, "I move that this organization have a fundraiser for the community park." The enacting clause "I move …" gives notice to the presiding officer and to the assembly that the speaker is submitting a proposal. Members should avoid forms such as, "I move you" or, "I make a motion that." Statements beginning "I propose" or "I suggest" should be recognized as debate and not as motions. However, the presiding officer may inquire whether the member wishes to put the statement in the form of a motion. The presiding officer may assist members in clarifying the wording of motions. Aside from an occasional brief explanatory remark, no discussion is permissible until the presiding officer states the motion to the assembly.

It is critically important that the presider and the assembly understand the exact wording of every motion. If the motion is not initially clear, the presiding officer has the responsibility to assist the proposer in clarifying the motion. In doing so, the presiding officer must take care not to propose any substantive changes to the motion or otherwise suggest that he or she might have an opinion on the matter being proposed. The presiding officer may require that any but the simplest motions be submitted in writing if he or she finds it essential for understanding the wording of the motion. A lengthy, complicated, or important motion, such as a resolution, should always be prepared in writing and given to the presider and to the secretary. Many assemblies provide triplicate forms for submitting motions in writing; one copy is provided to the presiding officer, one is kept by the member making the motion, and the third may be given to the secretary, parliamentarian, or a staff member who will arrange for its projection on a screen for all to see.

Seconding a Motion

After proposing a motion, the member sits down or steps back from the microphone. Another member may, without waiting for recognition, say, "I second the motion," or, "Second." Seconding a motion is not necessarily an endorsement of the motion. It merely indicates that the member wishes the motion to be considered by the assembly.

If the motion is not seconded, the presiding officer asks, "Is there a second to this motion?" If the meaning of the motion is not clear to the members, the presiding officer should ask the proposing member to state the motion more clearly. The presiding officer should ask again if there is a second. If there is no response, the presiding officer may say, "There is no second. The motion is not before the assembly." The presiding officer then proceeds to other business.

Seconds may be assumed by the presiding officer on routine items of business if that is the custom of the organization. If any member objects to the lack of a second, the presiding officer must call for one, unless debate by more than one member has already occurred, in which case the purpose of the second—indication that more than one member wishes the motion to be considered—has been fulfilled.

A second is not required for motions when they are submitted by a committee to the superior body. When a motion is presented in a committee or small board, it does not require a second.

Statement of a Motion by the Presiding Officer

When a motion has been properly moved and seconded, the presiding officer states the motion to the assembly as correctly and clearly as possible. If the presiding officer makes an error in stating a motion, the proposer should immediately raise a point of order to correct the error. If there is a difference of opinion as to what the exact wording of a motion should be, the motion as stated by the member is the legal motion.

The presiding officer states the motion as follows: "It has been moved and seconded that this organization establish a scholarship fund for the local swim team," or, "It has been moved and seconded that the following resolution be adopted: *Resolved:* That this service organization commit each member to providing four days a month to community activities with young people for the next six-month period."

In large assemblies or conventions, it is useful to have written copies of motions submitted to an assistant or a staff member who will project the motion, or amendment, on a large screen for all members to see. In such situations, the presiding officer may ask permission of the assembly to dispense with restating the entire motion and direct the assembly to the written version on the screen. If this is done, the presiding officer should first confirm that the wording of the projected motion is correct and that all members can read the screen.

After a motion has been stated to the assembly by the presiding officer, it is open for discussion if it is debatable. From the time a motion is stated by the presiding officer until it is disposed of, it is called a "pending question" or "pending motion."

Example of the Presentation of a Motion

MEMBER A: (rising and addressing the presiding officer): Mr. President.

PRESIDER: Member A.

MEMBER A: I move that this organization undertake a campaign to raise funds for equipment for the community park.

MEMBER B: (remaining seated): I second the motion.

PRESIDER: It has been moved and seconded "That this organization undertake a campaign to raise funds for equipment for the community park." Is there any discussion?"

Addressing Members during Discussion or Debate

In meetings that follow formal parliamentary procedure, members should address each other by last name, or in the third person, even though they may ordinarily be on a first-name basis. In a large group, this adds a note of formality, which keeps the discussion at a higher level. In recent years, however, with the trend toward greater informality, this practice is often ignored, especially in small groups and in social organizations where all members are on a first-name basis. Under no circumstances, however, should the presiding officer call some members by their first names and others by their last, as this may create a perception of an in-group composed of close friends of the presiding officer.

In very large assemblies, it is often the custom to avoid the use of names completely by referring to members by such terms as "the previous speaker," "the maker of the motion," or "the delegate from Arizona." This helps to keep discussion impersonal and is especially recommended in conventions where people speak not as individuals but as representatives of a chapter or other constituency. Another purpose for this formality is to create an atmosphere that is conducive to respectful behavior among the members.

Steps in Voting

The final step in the processing of a motion is to formally determine the action to be taken. After debate on a motion has concluded, it is necessary to take final action on the motion by voting on it. Main motions must be disposed of, for that meeting, by adoption, or defeat, or by adoption of a subsidiary motion to refer to a committee, to postpone to a certain time, or to table. Whether it is the vote on the main motion or the vote on the subsidiary motion, at least one vote must occur for the motion to be disposed of. Voting on a motion usually requires the following steps:

1. The presiding officer restates the pending question.
2. The presiding officer takes the affirmative vote.
3. The presiding officer takes the negative vote.

4. The presiding officer announces which side prevailed.
5. The presiding officer announces whether the motion was adopted or defeated.
6. The presiding officer announces what will be done as a result of the vote.
7. The presiding officer introduces the next item of business or calls for further business.

Restating the Question

Prior to the vote, the presiding officer should restate the motion as it is pending at the time. The presiding officer must be sure that the members understand the effect of adoption or defeat of the motion prior to voting.

Taking the Affirmative Vote

The presiding officer takes the affirmative vote in the following manner: for a voice vote, the presiding officer says, "All in favor, say aye." For a vote by division or for a two-thirds vote, the presiding officer says, "All in favor, rise. Be seated." In small groups, the presiding officer may ask members to raise their hands instead of rising. For a vote by other methods, the presiding officer clearly instructs the members how to indicate their preference. For more information on methods of voting, see Chapter 18.

It is a common practice to make an exception to taking a formal vote in motions honoring or thanking members, in which case it is not unusual for the assembly to demonstrate its approval by applause.

Taking the Negative Vote

Following the completion of the affirmative vote, the presiding officer must always take the negative vote even if it appears that the affirmative vote is unanimous. The method used should parallel the procedures used for the affirmative vote. For example, for a voice vote, the presiding officer says, "All opposed, say no." The presiding officer, in taking the negative vote, must ensure that there is no perception that he or she has a preference as to how members should vote. The language should never discourage members who wish to vote against a proposal from doing so; for example, "Anybody opposed?" is unacceptable.

Announcing Which Side Prevailed

The presiding officer determines which side prevailed and announces this; for example, "The ayes have it." If the presiding officer is uncertain which side prevailed, the vote should be repeated using a more definitive method; for example, a division or a counted vote. It is essential that the result of the vote be certain and that the members have confidence in the announcement concerning which side prevailed. There is nothing more damaging to an organization and its meetings than a feeling by some members that the outcome of one or more votes was determined incorrectly.

Announcing Whether the Motion Was Adopted or Defeated

The presiding officer announces the effect of the vote on the motion; for example, "The motion is adopted," or "The motion is defeated."

Announcing What Will Happen

The presiding officer explains what will happen as a result of the vote; for example, "This organization will (*or* will not) undertake a campaign to raise funds for the scholarship for the local swim team."

Introducing the Next Business

It is the responsibility of the presiding officer to keep the assembly informed of the item of business that is pending and what will be considered next. If a subsidiary or other motion has been voted on, the presiding officer presents the next pending motion, in order of precedence, for consideration by the assembly; for example, "The motion to refer is defeated; is there further discussion on the main motion, which is ...?" Of course, if referral is adopted, the next business would be another main motion or the introduction of the next agenda item.

If a main motion has been voted on and an adopted agenda designates the next item of business, the presiding officer places that item of business before the assembly; for example, "The next item of business is ... "

Skipping Steps in Processing Motions

While all the steps in processing a motion should ordinarily be followed, there are often circumstances in which either the rules or the circumstances allow steps to be skipped.

For example, if the rules applicable to a motion allow the proposer to interrupt, the steps by which a member seeks and is granted recognition might be skipped. For a motion that does not require a second, the seconding step would be skipped.

In routine matters, almost all the steps in processing a motion might be skipped. As an example, if the minutes have been distributed, the presiding officer might say, "Are there corrections to the minutes as distributed? (Pause) There being no corrections, the minutes are approved as distributed." In this example, the presiding officer *assumes* the motion to approve the minutes. That is, no one seeks recognition, no one is recognized, no one makes the motion, and the motion is not seconded; even the statement of the motion by the presiding officer is implied rather than explicit. In taking the vote, general consent is presumed, and all of the steps are compressed into the indicated statements by the presiding officer.

While more significant actions would skip fewer or no steps, it is also not uncommon to combine steps. For example, after taking the vote on an amendment to the main motion, the presiding officer might say, "The ayes have it, and the amendment is adopted; the main motion now reads . ... Is there discussion?" Thus the presiding officer will have combined the last four steps of voting into a concise but clear and complete statement.

If any member finds the omission of steps confusing, that member should feel free to raise a point of order, and the presiding officer can either correct the omissions or explain how steps have been combined. While it can be tedious to follow every step in processing every motion, at no time should steps be omitted to rush business through the assembly, nor should steps be omitted if it will create an impression that such rushing is occurring.

Chapter 7

MAIN MOTIONS

A *main motion* is a substantive proposal presented to the assembly for consideration, discussion, decision, and action. It is usually originated by an individual member or a committee. It is the basic motion for the transaction of business. Because it is a fundamental principle of parliamentary law that only one subject can be considered at one time, the main motion can be proposed only when no other motion is before the assembly.[1] While the main motion is the most important kind of motion, it is also the lowest ranking motion in the precedence of motions. Following are some examples of main motions

MEMBER: I move that we organize a campaign to elect our president to the national board.

or

MEMBER: I move the adoption of the following resolution:

"*Whereas,* the president of this organization has been shown to be an effective leader,

"*Whereas,* the president of this organization is eligible to serve as an officer at all levels of the organization, and

"*Whereas* the national board will be elected at the national convention in July, therefore, be it

"*Resolved,* that we organize a campaign to elect our president to the national board."

or

MEMBER: I move that we organize a campaign to elect our president to the national board and that we ask our members to contribute to a fund to finance the campaign at the national convention.

PRESIDER: (after the motion is seconded): It has been moved and seconded that we organize a campaign to elect our president to the national board and that we ask our members to contribute to a fund to finance the campaign at the national convention. Is there any discussion?

Phrasing the Main Motion

The main motion is a proposal of action that a member presents for consideration by the assembly. Because of the many kinds of actions that can be taken, the wording of main motions varies greatly, and wide latitude is permitted. However, all motions must be introduced by the words "I move." A motion should be concise and clear. If a member presents a confusing motion that is longer or more complicated than necessary, the presiding officer should ask the proposer to rephrase the motion or be willing to assist a member in the proper phrasing of a motion. The presiding officer cannot change the intent of the motion, and any suggested rephrasing by the presiding officer must be acceptable to the member who proposed the motion.

If a motion is long, complicated, or controversial, it is wise to submit it in writing. The presiding officer has a right to insist that any motion be submitted in writing.

The proposer of a main motion may rephrase or withdraw the motion at any time before it is stated by the presiding officer to the assembly. After the motion is stated by the presiding officer, it may be changed or withdrawn only with the permission of the assembly. The motion is then owned by the assembly.

The main motion should be stated in the affirmative, because the negative form often confuses members in voting. If a motion is presented in the negative, the presiding officer may request that the proposer rephrase the motion, or the presiding officer may rephrase it with the consent of the proposer. For example, the motion, "That we do not permit any member to stay on the Hospitality Committee after not attending three consecutive meetings," is more clearly stated affirmatively as, "That any member of the Hospitality Committee who misses three consecutive meetings be discharged from the committee."

The Main Motion in Resolution Form

Main motions that express sentiments or are a formal statement of the opinions of the assembly are usually presented in the form of resolutions. Resolution form is also used when the proposal is highly important or is long and involved. A resolution should be in writing and is usually introduced in a form such as:

I move the adoption of the following resolution:
"Resolved: That this organization express its appreciation for the outstanding service rendered by our executive director during the past 10 years, and be it further

"Resolved: That we give the executive director a $5,000 bonus at a reception held in her honor during our annual convention."

Often a resolution is prefaced by statements, each introduced by the word "whereas." The statements give the background to or the reasons for the resolution. This part of a resolution is called the *preamble*. The statements contained in the "whereas" clauses are of no legal effect and sometimes are the source of disagreement. Members frequently attempt to debate and amend these prefacing statements, often to the neglect of the substantive "resolved" clauses. The "whereas" clauses are useful mainly when the organization plans to publish the resolution and wishes the background and reasons for its adoption to be read with it.

Discussion of the Main Motion

As soon as the main motion has been formally stated to the assembly by the presiding officer, it is open for debate. It cannot be debated before this formal statement unless a motion has been adopted to discuss it informally. For more information on this form of discussion, see "Informal Consideration" in Chapter 16. Discussion on the main motion must conform to the rules governing debate. For additional information on rules of debate, see Chapter 16.

Disposition of the Main Motion

Whenever the main motion has been stated to an assembly by the presiding officer, some action must be taken on it and recorded in the minutes. The main motion may be decided by a vote approving or defeating it, or it may be disposed of by some other motion such as a motion to refer. A main motion cannot be ignored; definite action of some kind must be taken on it.

A motion on the same subject may be offered as a substitute amendment to the main motion. For more information on this method of amending a main motion, see "Amendment by Substitution of a New Motion" in Chapter 9.

A single main motion may be presented by a reference committee which combines or rewords similar proposed resolutions under the concept of adopt in-lieu-of as referenced below and in Chapter 24.

When a main motion has been acted on and defeated, it cannot be renewed in the same or substantially the same wording at the same meeting or convention, but it may be reconsidered at the same meeting or convention or presented as a new main motion at a later meeting or convention. Likewise, an adopted main motion may not be revisited at the same meeting except by the use of reconsideration, or at a subsequent meeting except by the use of motions to amend a previous action or to rescind a motion.

The Effect of Adopting the Main Motion

The effect of the adoption of the main motion is to commit the organization to the proposed action stated by the motion and approved by vote of the assembly.

Basic Rules Governing the Main Motion

The basic rules governing the main motion are:

1. Cannot interrupt a speaker
2. Requires a second
3. Is debatable because it presents a substantive proposal for consideration
4. Can be amended
5. Requires a majority vote
6. Does not take precedence over other motions
7. Applies to no other motion
8. Can have applied to it all subsidiary motions and incidental motions to withdraw, to divide the question, and to be considered by paragraph
9. Cannot be renewed at the same meeting or convention, but can be reconsidered

Chapter 8

SPECIFIC MAIN MOTIONS

There are main motions that permit an assembly to revisit motions that have been disposed of by adoption, defeat, or referral (amend a previous action, recall from committee, reconsider, and rescind); to ratify action previously taken or about to be taken (ratify); and to adopt a single main motion in place of a number of similar main motions (adopt in-lieu-of). These six main motions are called *specific main motions*. They have specific names, perform a unique function in the meeting, have somewhat different rules, but all are main motions. They are explained below.

Motion to Adopt In-Lieu-Of

Under special circumstances, a main motion may be introduced with the intent that its adoption will also dispose of one or more other main motions that are known to be coming before the assembly, such as when main motions are required to be submitted in advance of a meeting. Such a main motion is the motion to adopt in-lieu-of and would be moved in the following manner:

> I move that the following motion be adopted in lieu of (indicating the proposed motions that will be disposed of) ... (followed by the main motion proposed for adoption).
>
> *or*
>
> I move the adoption of Resolution X in lieu of Resolutions A, B, and C.

The adopt in-lieu-of motion has the following two features:

1. If adopted, a main motion introduced in lieu of one or more main motions not only enacts the motion itself, but also defeats the other main motion or motions named.

2. If the main motion is defeated, any of the other in-lieu-of motions named may be introduced by a member for consideration and vote by the assembly.

Other than the above two unique features, the adopt in-lieu-of motion is a specific main motion and has all the same characteristics of a main motion.

For a detailed explanation of the use of the motion to adopt in-lieu-of in reference committees, see Chapter 24.

Motion to Amend a Previous Action

The purpose of a motion to amend a previous action is to modify (amend) a main motion that has already been adopted. For example:

MEMBER: I move to amend the motion, which was adopted at the previous annual meeting, to create a scholarship fund for youth, by striking out "youth" and inserting "students enrolled at least half-time in an accredited college or university." (Seconded by another member.)

PRESIDER: It has been moved and seconded that the motion, which was adopted at the previous annual meeting, to create a scholarship fund for youth, be amended by striking out "youth" and inserting "students enrolled at least half-time in an accredited college or university." If the amendment is adopted, the previously adopted scholarship fund for youth will be a scholarship fund for students enrolled at least half-time in an accredited college or university." Is there any discussion of the proposed amendment?

Those in favor of the amendment, say aye. Those opposed, say no. The motion is adopted, and the scholarship fund for youth has been changed to a scholarship fund for students enrolled at least half-time in an accredited college or university.

What Previous Actions Can Be Amended?

A main motion adopted at a previous meeting or convention can be amended without notice by majority vote, unless the adopted motion required notice or a higher vote for its original adoption. In this case the same notice and vote are required to amend the motion. Since a motion amending a previous action is a specific main motion, it is subject to primary and secondary amendments, as is any other main motion.

The motion to amend a previous action, if adopted, affects the present and future only and is not retroactive. For example, if a contract has been signed, a motion to change the terms of that contract would not be in order, since a signed contract cannot be changed by one party alone, but a motion to attempt to renegotiate the terms of the contract could be considered. As another example, if a motion has been adopted to assess members a fine for missing meetings, the motion to amend a previous action could be used to change the amount of the fine or the number of meetings missed before a fine is owed. However, any fines already owed or paid would remain properly owed or collected. A separate motion (or a motion combined with the motion to amend the previous action) could be considered to forgive or refund some or all of the previously owed or paid fines.

Basic Rules Governing the Motion to Amend a Previous Action

The rules governing the motion to amend a previous action are as follows:

1. Cannot interrupt a speaker
2. Requires a second
3. Is debatable
4. Can be amended
5. Requires the same vote (and notice, if any) that was required for adoption of the original motion
6. Does not take precedence over other motions
7. Applies to main motions previously approved or actions taken at a previous meeting
8. Can have applied to it subsidiary motions and the incidental motions to withdraw, division of a question, and consider by paragraph
9. Cannot be renewed at the same meeting or convention, but can be reconsidered

Motion to Ratify

The purpose of a motion to ratify is to confirm and thereby validate an action that was taken in an emergency or when a quorum was not present, or to confirm the action or decision of another body. For example:

> MEMBER: I move to ratify the action taken by the director of facilities and the president on January 6 to spend $1,500 to install security lighting in our clubhouse after the break-in on New Year's Day.

> *or*

> I move to ratify the decision made at the April meeting, where a quorum was not present, to establish August 1 as our rollout date for our long-planned upgrade to our website.

> *or*

> I move to ratify the new advertising and communication strategy as adopted by the International Association.

Need for Ratification

The officers of an organization sometimes have to make emergency decisions when it is not possible to obtain the permission of the body that has the authority to take the action. A committee sometimes may have to take action that exceeds its authority, and in a meeting that lacks a quorum, it is sometimes necessary to take action that cannot be delayed until a special meeting can be called or until the next regular meeting. These actions may be challenged if they are not formally approved. They should be ratified as soon as possible at a meeting with a quorum present, by the body with authority to approve the otherwise improper action.

Another form of ratification occurs when organizations require that specific actions taken by one body be approved by another level of the organization. For example, this may be a ratification by a parent body or by a subsidiary body before an action becomes official.

Basic Rules Governing the Motion to Ratify

The rules to follow for the motion to ratify include:

1. Cannot interrupt a speaker
2. Requires a second
3. Is debatable
4. Can be amended
5. Requires a majority vote, unless the action requiring ratification would regularly require a higher vote

6. Does not take precedence over other motions
7. Applies to actions taken without proper authority or in the absence of a quorum, or to another body's actions that require ratification before taking effect
8. Can have applied to it all subsidiary motions and the incidental motions to withdraw and division of the question
9. Cannot be renewed at the same meeting or convention, but can be reconsidered

Motion to Recall a Motion or Subject from a Committee (or Board)

The purpose of a motion to recall a motion or subject from a committee or board is to enable an assembly to remove a motion or subject from a committee or board and present it before the assembly for consideration. For example:

MEMBER: I move to recall the motion to create new standards for accreditation from the education committee. (Seconded by another member.)

PRESIDER: It has been moved and seconded to recall the motion to create new standards for accreditation from the education committee. Is there any discussion on the motion to recall the referred motion?

Those in favor of recalling the referred motion, say aye. Those opposed, say no.

The motion to recall the referred motion is adopted. The motion to create new standards for accreditation is again open for discussion.

or

MEMBER: I move to recall the matter concerning Bill 2012–43 concerning money laundering which had been referred to our PAC committee for study and recommendation. (Seconded by another member.)

PRESIDER: It has been moved and seconded to recall the matter involving Bill 2012–43 concerning money laundering, which had been referred to our PAC committee for study and recommendation. If this motion is adopted, the matter concerning money laundering will immediately come before the assembly for consideration. Is there any discussion?

Those in favor of recalling the referred subject, say aye. Those opposed, say no.

The motion to recall the referred subject is adopted. The subject is the matter concerning money laundering. Is there a motion on this subject?

Need for a Motion to Recall a Motion or Subject

An assembly that has referred a pending main motion or subject to a committee or board may have reasons to remove the motion or subject from the committee or board for consideration and action by the assembly or to refer the motion or subject to a different committee.

Effect of Adopting a Motion to Recall a Motion or Subject

The effect of adopting a motion to recall is to place the original main motion and any adhering amendments before the assembly again or to place the subject matter before the assembly for consideration.

Rules Governing the Motion to Recall a Motion or Subject from a Committee (or Board)

The rules governing the motion to recall include:

1. Cannot interrupt a speaker
2. Requires a second
3. Debate is restricted to the reasons for recalling the motion or subject
4. Cannot be amended
5. Requires a majority vote
6. Does not take precedence over other motions
7. Applies to any main motion or subject that has been referred to a committee or board
8. Can have applied to it the motions to limit debate, close debate, and withdraw
9. Cannot be renewed at the same meeting or convention

Motion to Reconsider

The purpose of a motion to reconsider is to enable an assembly to set aside the vote on a main motion taken at the same meeting or convention and to consider the motion again as though no vote had been taken on it. For example:

MEMBER: I move to reconsider the vote on the motion, which was adopted earlier in the meeting, to donate $500 from our reserve funds to the Community Relief Fund. (Seconded by another member.)

PRESIDER: It has been moved and seconded to reconsider the vote on the motion, which was adopted earlier in the meeting, to donate $500 from our reserve funds to the Community Relief Fund. Is there any discussion on the motion to reconsider the vote on this motion?

Those in favor of reconsidering the vote, say aye. Those opposed, say no. The motion to reconsider is adopted. The motion to donate $500 from our reserve funds to the Community Relief Fund is again open for discussion.

What Votes Can Be Reconsidered?

Main motions are occasionally adopted, defeated, or tabled by the assembly because of a misunderstanding or lack of adequate information. In addition, sometimes later events at the meeting or convention cause the assembly to change its mind.

The vote on a main motion can be reconsidered at the same meeting or convention, except when, as a result of the vote, something has been done that cannot be undone. For example, when an affirmative vote has resulted in a contract, when money has been paid, or when a time limit has passed, the vote cannot be reconsidered.

The motion to reconsider can be applied only to the vote on the main motion, some specific main motions, and main motions that have been tabled. A motion to reconsider cannot be applied to itself. In addition, an adopted motion to recall a motion referred to a committee or board cannot be reconsidered because the recalled motion can be recommitted, but a defeated motion to recall a referred motion from a committee or board can be reconsidered. The same result is accomplished for all other motions by more simple and direct means. Procedural motions that have been defeated can be proposed again or renewed as soon as, in the judgment of the presiding officer, the vote might result differently. (For more information on renewal of motions, see Chapter 5.) Amendments to main motions may be further amended if, in the judgment of the presiding officer, the assembly seems to want additional changes.

Proposal of a Motion to Reconsider

The motion to reconsider is a specific main motion and can be proposed at any time during a meeting. It is unusual in that, unlike a general main motion, it may be proposed when other business is under consideration. Proposal of the motion to reconsider the vote suspends any action provided for in the motion targeted to be reconsidered until the motion to reconsider is decided. When a motion to reconsider is proposed and seconded while other business is pending, the presiding officer directs the secretary to record its proposal, but the motion to reconsider is not considered until the pending business has been handled. The motion to reconsider is then considered and decided immediately. If the motion to reconsider is offered when no other business is pending, it is considered immediately.

Who Can Move to Reconsider?

Some parliamentary authorities allow the motion to reconsider to be proposed only by a member who voted on the prevailing side when the main motion was originally adopted or defeated. The limitation has always led to deceitful maneuverings, and, as far back as 1856, Luther Cushing, the eminent lawyer and parliamentarian, wrote, "... a motion to reconsider may be made at any time or by any member, precisely like any other motion."

This book upholds Cushing's position, and in the absence of a provision to the contrary in the organization's bylaws or in its parliamentary authority, the motion to reconsider may be offered by any member.

The proponents of restricting the proposal of the motion to reconsider to those who voted on the prevailing side argue that this prevents the dilatory use of the motion. The purpose of this limitation, however, is defeated because under such a rule:

1. Any member can vote on the prevailing side for the sole purpose of being eligible to move to reconsider.
2. Even if a member fails to vote with the prevailing side, a vote can be changed just prior to the final announcement of the vote, making the member eligible to move for reconsideration.
3. Except in the case of a roll call, it is impossible to determine accurately how anyone has voted.

4. In a ballot vote, no one can be asked how he or she voted because the inquiry would violate the fundamental principle of the secret vote.

This book permits any member to propose the motion to reconsider when it appears justified. The motion to reconsider is useful when new information becomes known, a decision should be changed, and when errors have been made by hasty decisions. The presiding officer can rule a motion to reconsider out of order if he or she finds it to be dilatory. If members disagree with the presiding officer's ruling, the decision can be appealed, and the final decision will rest with the assembly.

Debate on the Motion to Reconsider

The motion to reconsider is debatable, but debate is restricted to reasons for reconsidering the motion. Debate on the main motion must wait until the assembly has voted to reconsider it.

Since the proposal of the motion to reconsider suspends action on a motion that has already been voted on, the motion to reconsider should be decided immediately and cannot be postponed to a later meeting.

Effect of Adopting the Motion to Reconsider

The adoption of a motion to reconsider cancels a vote on a motion as completely as though it had never been taken and brings that motion before the assembly for consideration as though it had never been voted on.

Basic Rules Governing the Motion to Reconsider

The rules governing the motion to reconsider include:

1. Can interrupt proceedings, but not a speaker
2. Requires a second
3. Debate is restricted to the reasons for reconsideration
4. Cannot be amended
5. Requires a majority vote
6. Does not take precedence over other motions

7. Applies to votes on main motions taken at the same meeting or convention
8. Can have applied to it the motions to close debate, to limit debate, and to withdraw
9. Cannot be renewed at the same meeting or convention

Motion to Rescind

The purpose of a motion to rescind is to repeal (cancel, nullify, void) a main motion approved at a previous meeting. For example:

MEMBER: I move to rescind the motion, which was adopted at last month's meeting, stating that the club would host a golf tournament for youth each September. (Seconded by another member.)

PRESIDER: It has been moved and seconded to rescind the motion, which was adopted at last month's meeting, stating that the club would host a golf tournament for youth each September. Is there any discussion?

Those in favor of rescinding the motion, say aye. Those opposed, say no. The motion to rescind is adopted. The motion that the club would host a golf tournament for youth each September is rescinded.

What Motions Can Be Rescinded?

Any main motion that was adopted, no matter how long before, may be rescinded, but the rescission does not include action taken before adoption of the motion to rescind.

The motion to rescind, if adopted, affects the present and future only, since it is not retroactive.[1] For example, if a motion to assess special fees from members were rescinded, those fees would no longer be imposed; however, the fees already collected would be retained and fees that were assessed before the motion was rescinded would still be collectible.

If a member believes that the existing policy should be continued with some revisions, as an alternative to rescinding it, the member can state the intent to move to amend the policy (through the motion to amend a previous action) if the motion to rescind is defeated or withdrawn.

Vote and Notice Required to Rescind

A main motion approved at a previous meeting can be rescinded by a majority vote, unless the adopted motion required notice or a higher vote, in which case the same notice and vote are required to rescind the action.

Effect of Adoption of a Motion to Rescind

Adoption of a motion to rescind repeals, cancels, nullifies, or voids a motion from the time of the adoption of the motion to rescind.

Basic Rules Governing the Motion to Rescind

The rules governing the motion to rescind include:

1. Cannot interrupt a speaker
2. Requires a second
3. Is debatable and opens to debate the motion it proposes to rescind
4. Cannot be amended
5. Requires the same vote (and notice, if any) that was required for adoption of the original motion
6. Does not take precedence over other motions
7. Applies to main motions adopted at a previous meeting or convention
8. Can have applied to it all subsidiary motions, except the motion to amend, and the incidental motion to withdraw
9. Cannot be renewed at the same meeting or convention, but can be reconsidered

Chapter 9

SUBSIDIARY MOTIONS

Subsidiary motions apply to the main motion and help change the main motion, dispose of the motion, and help control the debate on the motion. Some subsidiary motions also apply to other motions as described in the sections below. The six subsidiary motions are amend, refer to a committee, postpone to a certain time, limit or extend debate, close debate, and table.

Motion to Amend

The purpose of the motion to amend is to modify a motion that is being considered by the assembly so that it will express more satisfactorily the will of the members.

There are four types of amendments:

1. Amendment by inserting (addition)
2. Amendment by striking out (deletion)
3. Amendment by striking out and inserting
4. Amendment by substitution

For example, there is a pending main motion stating that the chapter use its reserve funds to purchase a headquarters building and hire an executive director.

Here is an example of an amendment by inserting (addition):

MEMBER: I move to amend the main motion by inserting the words "half of" before the word "its." (Seconded by another member.)

PRESIDER: It has been moved and seconded to amend the main motion by inserting the words "half of" before the word "its." The main motion, *if amended*, would read: "That the chapter use half of its reserve funds to purchase a headquarters building and hire an executive director." Is there any discussion on the amendment?

Those in favor of the amendment, say aye. Those opposed to the amendment, say no. The amendment is adopted, and the main motion as amended now reads: "That the chapter use half of its reserve funds to purchase a headquarters building and hire an executive director."

Is there any discussion on the main motion as amended?

Following is an example of an amendment by striking out (deletion):

MEMBER: I move to amend the main motion by striking out the words "and hire an executive director." (Seconded by another member.)

PRESIDER: It has been moved and seconded to amend the main motion by striking out the words "and hire an executive director." The main motion, if amended, would read: "That the chapter use its reserve funds to purchase a headquarters building." Is there any discussion on the amendment?

Now we look at an example of an amendment by striking out and inserting:

MEMBER: I move to amend the main motion by striking out the word "purchase" and inserting in its place the word "lease." (Seconded by another member.)

PRESIDER: It has been moved and seconded to amend the main motion by striking out the word "purchase" and inserting in its place the word "lease." The main motion, if amended, would read: "That the chapter use its reserve funds to lease a headquarters building and hire an executive director." Is there any discussion on the amendment?

Now we examine an example of an amendment by substitution:

MEMBER: I move to amend the main motion by substituting for it the following motion: "That our chapter hire a management company and dismiss our employees at the expiration of the current office rental agreement." (Seconded by another member.)

PRESIDER: It has been moved and seconded to amend the main motion "That the chapter use its reserve funds to purchase a headquarters building and hire an executive director" by substituting for it a new motion "That our chapter hire a management company and dismiss our employees at the expiration of the current office rental agreement." Is there any discussion on the amendment?

What Motions May Be Amended?

The only motions that may be amended without restriction are main motions (including the two specific main motions to ratify and amend a previous action) and the subsidiary motion to amend.

Five motions are open to restricted amendment. The motions to postpone to a certain time, to limit debate, and to recess may be amended as to time. The motion to refer to a committee may be amended concerning such details as name, number of members, method of selection of the committee or the instructions to the committee, and such details as the time the motion is to be reported back to the assembly. The privileged motion to adjourn may be amended to change the time of adjournment or to set a time for a continued meeting.

Amendments Must Be Germane

The most important principle concerning amendments is that they must be germane to the pending motion; that is, they must be relevant to and have direct bearing on the subject of the pending motion that the amendment seeks to change.[1] For example, a motion, "That the association contract with a national Internet service provider to obtain leased equipment for a five-year period." could be amended by adding the words, "not to exceed $12,000 for the contract period." These additional words relate closely to a lease and would therefore be germane to the motion.

However, an amendment to add the words, "and that we contract with an employment agency to provide 20 hours of secretarial work per week," would not be germane to the subject of the motion. The presiding officer should immediately rule this amendment not in order, stating: "The chair rules the amendment not in order as it is not germane to the pending main motion."

An amendment that would change one type of motion into another type of motion is never in order. For example, if a member moves, "That the main motion be referred to the board of trustees," it would not be in order for a member to move, "That the motion to refer be amended by striking out the words "referred to the board of trustees" and inserting the words "postponed until next month's meeting." This would change the motion from a motion to refer to a motion to postpone to a certain time, which has a different rank in the order of precedence. This type of amendment is therefore not in order. However, instead of moving to amend the motion to refer, a member could move to postpone to a certain time, since that motion is higher ranking than the motion to refer.

Amendments May Be Hostile

An amendment may be hostile.[2] This means that it may be directly opposed to the actual intent of the original motion. It may even nullify or change completely the effect of the motion. For example, the motion "that we write a letter to the city council condemning its stance on denying employees the right to organize as a labor union" might be amended by striking out the word "condemning" and inserting the word "endorsing." Thus the intent of the original motion would be reversed by a hostile amendment. This amendment would be germane to the subject of the main motion, which is to express the organization's attitude toward the action of the city council, and therefore is in order.

An amendment that merely changes an affirmative statement of a motion to a negative statement of the same motion is not in order. For example, a motion, "That we write a letter to city council," cannot be amended by inserting the words "do not" before the word "write." Such a motion is not in order because the same result can be attained by voting against the main motion. It also provides for an ambiguous result if the motion with the words "do not" is defeated. The negative wording of the motion can also confuse members who are casting votes.

Limitations on Pending Amendments

Amendments are of two ranks.: Those applied to the original motion are amendments of the first rank, or primary amendments, and they must relate directly to the motion to be amended.

Amendments to a pending amendment are amendments of the second rank, or secondary amendments, and must relate directly to the pending amendment. Amendments of the third rank are not in order.

Only one amendment of each rank can be pending at a time. When a primary amendment to a motion is pending, another primary amendment is not in order, but a secondary amendment (an amendment to the primary amendment) is in order. Whenever a secondary amendment is pending, another secondary amendment is not in order.

After an amendment of either rank is adopted or defeated, another amendment of the same rank is in order. Several amendments and amendments to amendments may be offered in succession, but only one amendment of each rank may be pending at the same time. If the motion, "That the chapter sponsor a drive to raise funds for the City Youth Club" is pending, and someone moves to amend it by adding the words, "during the month of September," this is an amendment to the motion or an amendment of the first rank (primary amendment). If, during discussion on this amendment, someone proposes that the amendment be amended by inserting the words "first week of" before the words "the month," this is an amendment of the second rank or an amendment to the amendment. It is a secondary amendment and is in order. However, while the primary amendment is pending, if a member proposes an amendment to strike out the words "sponsor a drive" and insert the words "hold an auction," this is not in order at this time because it is another primary amendment—an amendment of first rank. When an amendment of the first rank is pending, no other amendment of that same rank is in order until the pending amendment is disposed of.

A proposed amendment to the bylaws (amend a previous action) or to a motion already adopted is a specific main motion and amendments of both ranks are in order.

Debate on Amendments

Amendments to debatable motions are debatable. Amendments to undebatable motions are not debatable. When an amendment to a motion is proposed, discussion is limited to that amendment until it is disposed of. When an amendment to the amendment is proposed, discussion is limited to the amendment of second rank until it is disposed of.

Reference to the main motion is permissible only for the purpose of explaining the amendment or its effect. When opposing an amendment, it is in order to say that if the amendment is rejected or withdrawn, the speaker will propose another amendment, which may be stated briefly.

Amendment by Substitution of a New Motion

When the wording or effect of a motion as proposed is not satisfactory, it is sometimes better, instead of proposing several amendments, to reword the motion and propose it as an amendment by substitution. Such an amendment must be germane to the subject of the original motion, but it may differ completely from the original motion in wording, purpose, and effect. The amendment by substitution of a new or reworded motion follows the usual rules governing amendments and is subject only to a secondary amendment to the substitute amendment (which is the primary amendment).

If a pending main motion is to approve the funding of a New Year's Day parade float in support of military veterans in the organization's city, a member might move a substitute amendment as follows: "I move to substitute for the pending main motion the following: That we donate $ 3,000 to the Veterans' Hospital."

The motion would be germane since it concerns the same general subject—that is, showing support for veterans. The substitute motion is a primary amendment and therefore is subject only to a secondary amendment. In other words, an amendment to a substitute motion cannot be amended because amendments of both first rank and second rank are already pending.

Filling Blanks

Motions or resolutions are sometimes submitted with blank spaces for names, dates, or numbers, with the blank spaces to be filled allowing members, without seconds, to propose suggestions. Sometimes the presiding officer creates a blank by general consent or assumes a blank based on the parliamentary situation. A member may also move to strike out a variable part of a motion to create a blank. The motion to create a blank requires a second and is not debatable. The words that have been stricken to create the blank become a suggestion for consideration in filling the blank.

Filling blanks is not a form of amendment, but it is a system that allows for alternative proposals and is therefore similar to amending.

Members call out suggestions for filling the blank, and when no more suggestions are offered, the presiding officer opens discussion on the suggestions followed by a vote on each suggestion in the order in which each was proposed. Each member can vote for or against each suggestion, casting as many votes as there are suggestions. For example, if five names have been proposed to fill a vacancy in an office, a member who prefers three of the people suggested could vote for each of those three and against the other two.

The suggestion receiving the highest vote, provided that it is a majority, is inserted in the blank. If the highest vote is tied or if no suggestion receives a majority, the voting on all suggestions is repeated, unless the assembly adopts a motion to follow another procedure. A motion can be offered to reopen suggestions in order to reach a compromise. After the blank has been filled, further discussion of the motion or resolution is allowed, and then a vote is taken on the motion as a whole.

Ballot voting can be used for filling blanks, but write-ins are inappropriate in such a case. Each ballot contains every suggestion, and a member may vote for as many of the suggestions as the member chooses. The highest affirmative vote, provided that it receives a majority of the votes cast, fills the blank.

Withdrawing and Accepting Amendments

The proposer of a motion or an amendment has the right to modify or withdraw the motion or amendment at any time before the presiding officer has presented it to the assembly for consideration. As soon as it has been stated to the assembly by the presiding officer, it belongs to the body, and the proposer of the amendment can withdraw it only by vote of the assembly or by general consent.

If another member proposes an amendment that the maker of the motion wishes to accept, the maker of the original motion may save time by saying, "Madam President, the mover accepts the amendment." The consent of the seconder is not necessary. If the original motion has not yet been stated by the presiding officer, the proposed amendment becomes part of the original motion by this acceptance, and the presiding officer should state the motion, as amended, to the assembly. If the original motion has already been stated by the presiding officer, then the presiding officer asks if there is an objection to this acceptance. If no objection is made, the presiding officer states that the motion is amended by general consent. If anyone objects, the amendment must be formally stated by the presiding officer, debated, and voted on in the usual manner.

Adhering Amendments

When a main motion that has amendments pending is referred to a committee or postponed to a certain time, all pending amendments adhere to it and go with it. When the main motion comes before the assembly again, the amendments still adhere and are also before the assembly for consideration.

Voting on Amendments

Amendments are voted on in the reverse order of their proposal. An amendment to an amendment (the secondary amendment) is voted on first. The vote is then taken on the amendment to the motion (the primary amendment) and, finally, on the motion.

If a debatable motion, an amendment to it, and an amendment to the amendment are pending, the procedure for disposing of them is as follows:

1. Discussion is called for on the amendment to the amendment, and when discussion is complete or debate is closed, a vote is taken on it.
2. Discussion is then called for on the primary amendment, either as amended if the amendment to the amendment has been adopted, or as originally proposed if the secondary amendment was not adopted. When discussion of the primary amendment is complete or debate is closed, a vote is taken on it.
3. Discussion is called for on the motion, either as amended if the primary amendment has been adopted, or as originally proposed if the primary amendment is not adopted. When discussion on the motion is complete or debate is closed, a vote is taken on the motion. A vote adopting an amendment to a motion—even an amendment that substitutes an entirely new motion—does not adopt the motion, and a final vote on the adoption of the motion itself is required.

Vote Required on Amendments

An amendment to any pending motion or amendment requires only a majority vote, even though the motion requires a higher vote for adoption.[3] This is because the subsidiary motion to amend requires only a majority vote for adoption.

An amendment to the bylaws requires whatever vote the bylaws provide, but amendments to proposed bylaw amendments, or to a pending revision of the bylaws, require only a majority vote.

Amending Actions Previously Taken

Amending actions previously taken is a specific main motion and is not to be confused with the subsidiary motion to amend. The motion to amend a previous action can itself be amended by primary and secondary amendments.

Effect of Adoption of a Motion to Amend

The adoption of a motion to amend changes the original motion as the amendment provides.

Basic Rules Governing the Motion to Amend

The rules governing the motion to amend are as follows:

1. Cannot interrupt a speaker
2. Requires a second
3. Is debatable, unless applied to an undebatable motion
4. Can be amended
5. Requires a majority vote, even if the motion to which it applies requires a higher vote
6. Takes precedence over the main motion; when applied to other motions, it takes precedence over the motion it proposes to amend
7. Applies to motions that may be stated in different ways: main motions; motions that amend a previous action; and motions to ratify, amend, refer to committee, postpone to a certain time, limit debate, recess, and adjourn
8. Can have applied to it the motions to close debate, to limit debate, to amend, and to withdraw
9. Can be renewed at the discretion of the presiding officer

Motion to Refer to Committee

The purpose of a motion to refer to committee is to transfer a motion that is pending before the assembly to a committee for one of the following reasons:

1. To investigate or study the proposal, make recommendations on it, and return it to the assembly

2. To conserve the time of the assembly by delegating the duty of deciding the proposal, and sometimes of carrying out the decision, to a smaller group
3. To ensure privacy in considering a delicate matter
4. To provide a hearing on the proposal

For example:

MEMBER: I move to refer the motion to the standing committee on certification with instructions to report at the annual meeting. (Seconded by another member.)

or

MEMBER: I move to refer the motion to a committee composed of Members X, Y, and Z with instructions to report at the annual meeting. (Seconded by another member.)

or

MEMBER: I move to refer the motion to a special committee of five members to be appointed by the president with instructions to report at the annual meeting. (Seconded by another member.)

PRESIDER: It has been moved and seconded to refer the motion to the standing committee on certification with instructions to report at the annual meeting. Is there any discussion on the motion to refer the motion to the committee on certification?

Provisions Included in the Motion to Refer

A member may propose the motion in the simple form, "I move to refer this motion to a committee," or the member may include provisions such as the type of committee, the number of members and how they are to be selected, the committee chair, or instructions to the committee. If the committee is to have power to act on behalf of the organization, the wording of the motion to refer must provide for this power. Empowering the committee is important if the committee is expected to take action. If these provisions are not specified in the motion, the presiding officer may put the motion to refer to a vote and, if adopted, may use his or her judgment in deciding on the membership of the committee, assigning its work, and giving instructions to it. If the presiding officer does not wish to take this responsibility, he or she may ask the assembly to determine the detailed provisions either before or after the motion to refer to committee is voted on. These provisions may be included in the motion to refer if the proposer of the motion accepts them before the motion to refer is stated by the presiding officer. They may also be proposed as amendments to the motion to refer to a committee or in a motion proposed after the motion to refer has been adopted.

If the pending motion is concerned with a subject that is within the scope of a particular standing or reference committee, that committee is the one to which any referral is ordinarily made.

When the assembly has voted that a committee be appointed, without further provisions, the presiding officer may appoint and announce the committee members at once or may take a reasonable time to consider the appointments and announce them later.

Debate on the motion to refer, or on amendments to it, is restricted to a brief discussion on the advisability of referring or to such details as the selection, membership, or duties of the committee or instructions to it. Similarly, an amendment is restricted to these same details.

Instructions to a Committee

Instructions from the assembly or from the presiding officer may be given to a committee as a part of the motion to refer, or by a separate motion, or by oral directions from the presiding officer, or in a memorandum from the secretary. Additional instructions may be given to the committee at any time before its report is submitted to the assembly. After the report is submitted, the motion or committee assignment may be referred to the committee again, with or without additional instructions.

An assembly that has referred a motion or a matter to a committee may, by use of a motion to recall, vote at any time to return the motion or matter to the assembly, after which the assembly may refer the motion to another committee, give more or different instructions to the committee, or decide the question itself.

If no main motion is pending and a member moves to refer a subject or problem to a committee or moves to create a new committee, or to give instructions to an existing committee, this motion is a main motion.

Effect of Adoption of a Motion to Refer

The adoption of a motion to refer transfers the main motion and its amendments (if any) to the designated committee immediately.

Basic Rules Governing the Motion to Refer

The rules governing the motion to refer include the following:

1. Cannot interrupt a speaker
2. Requires a second
3. Debate restricted to brief discussion on the advisability of referring, and to the committee selected, membership, or duties of the committee, or instructions to it
4. Amendments restricted to such details as the committee selected, membership, or duties of the committee, or instructions to it
5. Requires a majority vote
6. Takes precedence over the main motion and a motion to amend the main motion
7. Applies to main motions only
8. Can have applied to it the motions to close debate, to limit debate, to amend, and to withdraw
9. Can be renewed after change in the parliamentary situation

Motion to Postpone to a Certain Time

The purpose of a motion to postpone to a certain time is to put off consideration, or further consideration, of a pending main motion and to fix a definite time for its consideration.

For example:

MEMBER: I move to postpone the motion until after the presentation by the management consultant who will arrive later in this meeting. (Seconded by another member.)

or

MEMBER: I move to postpone the motion until after the recess that has been scheduled for mid-morning. (Seconded by another member.)

or

MEMBER: I move to postpone the question until the next regular meeting. (Seconded by another member.)

or

MEMBER: I move to postpone the motion to the next regular meeting and make it a special order for 7:30 p.m. (Seconded by another member.)

or

MEMBER: I move to set aside (postpone) the pending motion until the treasurer arrives. (Seconded by another member.)

PRESIDER: It has been moved and seconded that the motion be postponed until after the presentation by the management consultant who will arrive later in this meeting. (This should refer specifically to the motion presented.)

Limitations on a Motion to Postpone to a Certain Time

A main motion cannot be postponed:

1. To a meeting that is not already scheduled—for example, to a special meeting that has not been established.
2. To any time that would be too late for the proposed motion to be effective, if adopted. For example, a motion "That the chapter participates in the senior citizens' annual talent show to raise funds for the City Youth Club" cannot be postponed to a meeting that will occur after the talent show.
3. By delegates at one convention or members at an annual meeting to the next convention or annual meeting.

Postponing as a General or Special Order

Any main motion that is postponed to a certain time becomes a general order for that time. When that time arrives, the presiding officer states the postponed motion to the assembly for consideration immediately unless another item of business is pending. If another item of business is pending, the presiding officer states the general order to the assembly as soon as the pending item of business has been disposed of.

When a main motion is postponed within the same meeting or convention depending on an event occurring, such as the arrival of a member or another agenda item having been disposed of, the main motion comes automatically to the floor when the event occurs unless another item of business is pending. If another item of business is pending, the presiding officer states the main motion immediately after the pending item of business is disposed of.

To postpone a main motion and designate it as a general order for a particular time requires a majority vote. A motion postponed to a certain time as a general order may again be postponed to a later time or day by a majority vote.

Instead of designating a postponed motion as a general order, the assembly may vote to make it a special order. This means that when the specified time arrives, the matter must be taken up immediately, regardless of whether something else is pending at that time. Any motion or proceeding that is interrupted by the special order is simply put aside until the special order is disposed of, at which point consideration of the interrupted motion is resumed.

Because a special order interrupts pending business, a two-thirds vote is required to postpone a main motion and make it a special order.

If the assembly does not want to take up consideration of a special order at the prescribed time, it may order further postponement, but only by a two-thirds vote.

Types of Postponement

A main motion may be postponed:

1. To a later time in the same meeting or convention as a general or special order.

2. To a later meeting within the official year as a general or a special order or as an item of business to come up under unfinished business at the specified meeting. If a motion is postponed to a particular meeting but not to a specified time, it comes up under unfinished business at the meeting to which it was postponed.

A main motion may be postponed as a general or special order to a time that is not stated but that is dependent on some other item of business. For example, a main motion might be postponed "until after the report of the special committee appointed to plan the chapter's centennial celebration is presented."

A pending motion cannot be postponed to the next annual meeting or a later convention. The next annual meeting or convention will be composed of different members or delegates who can begin anew any consideration of the matter, instead of dealing with motions developed by a meeting or convention body that no longer exists. An annual meeting or convention may defer action to a future annual meeting or convention by referring the matter to a committee, which is ordered to submit a report on its study at the next annual meeting or convention. In such a case, it is the subject that is being referred to a committee.

Consideration of Postponed Motions

If a motion that was postponed to a certain time or until an event occurs (or set as a general or special order) is not taken up at the meeting for which it was set, it comes up as unfinished business at the next meeting.

When a motion that has been postponed to a certain time is stated to the assembly for consideration, it may again be postponed to a later time or day.

If no main motion is pending and a motion is proposed to postpone a motion or subject to a certain time, the motion to postpone is a main motion.

Effect of Adoption of the Motion to Postpone to a Certain Time

When a motion to postpone to a certain time is adopted, it puts off consideration of the pending main motion until a certain time, event, date, meeting, or position on the agenda.

When a main motion is postponed, any pending subsidiary motions (for example, an amendment or a motion to refer) adhere to the main motion and are also postponed. When the main motion and any adhering subsidiary motions come up again before the assembly, the question is considered in the same form it was in at the time of postponement.

Basic Rules Governing the Motion to Postpone to a Certain Time

The rules governing the motion to postpone to a certain time include the following:

1. Cannot interrupt a speaker
2. Requires a second
3. Debate restricted to brief discussion on reasons for, or time of, postponement

4. Amendments restricted to time of postponement, or to making the postponement a special order
5. Requires a majority vote unless proposed as a special order, which requires a two-thirds vote
6. Takes precedence over refer to a committee and amend the main motion
7. Applies to main motions only
8. Can have applied to it the motions to amend, to close debate, to limit debate, and to withdraw
9. Can be renewed after change in the parliamentary situation

Motion to Limit or Extend Debate

The purpose of a motion to limit or extend debate relates to the time that will be devoted to discussion of a pending motion or motions. Such a motion may also modify or remove limitations already imposed on the discussion. For example:

MEMBER: I move to limit the time of each member speaking on this motion to two minutes. (Seconded by another member.)

or

MEMBER: I move to limit debate on this bylaw amendment to a total time of 15 minutes. (Seconded by another member.)

or

MEMBER: I move that the time of the speaker be extended by two minutes. (Seconded by another member.)

PRESIDER: It has been moved and seconded that the time of each member speaking on this motion be limited to two minutes (or whatever has been presented in the motion). The motion to limit debate can be debated or amended only in terms of the nature of the limitations. Is there discussion?

Those in favor of the motion, please rise. Be seated. Those opposed, please rise. Be seated. The vote is two-thirds in the affirmative, and the motion to limit debate is adopted.

Types of Limitations on Debate

A motion to limit debate on a pending question or to modify limitations already set up usually relates to the number of speakers who may participate, the length of time allotted to each speaker, the total time allotted for discussion of the motion, or some variation or combination of these limitations. The most common example of a motion extending limitations on debate is one that extends the time allowed a particular speaker.

If one form of the motion to limit or extend debate is pending before the assembly, another form that does not conflict with the first may be moved as an amendment; for example, if a motion to limit each speaker to a specified number of minutes is pending, an amendment may be proposed to include a limit on the number of speakers on each side of the debate.

How Limiting or Extending Debate Affects Pending Motions

The motion to limit or extend debate may be applied to all pending debatable motions or to only the immediately pending motion. To illustrate, if a main motion, an amendment, and an amendment to the amendment are pending and the proposer of the motion to limit debate does not specify the motion or motions to which the limit is to apply, only the immediately pending question—in this case, the amendment to the amendment—is affected.

Termination of the Effect of the Motion to Limit or Extend Debate

A motion limiting or extending debate is in force only during the meeting or convention at which it was adopted. If the main motion is postponed until another meeting or referred to a committee, the motion limiting or extending debate is no longer in effect when the motion is taken up again.

If no main motion is pending and a motion is made to limit or extend debate on a motion or motions that are to come up later, this is a main motion and not a subsidiary motion to limit or extend debate.

Effect of Adoption of the Motion to Limit or Extend Debate

The adoption of a motion to limit or extend debate limits discussion on a pending question or extends or removes limitations already adopted.

Basic Rules Governing the Motion to Limit or Extend Debate

Rules governing the motion to limit or extend debate include:

1. Cannot interrupt a speaker
2. Requires a second
3. Debate restricted to type and time of limitations.
4. Amendments restricted to limitations, extensions, or removal of limitations on debate
5. Requires a two-thirds vote because it limits freedom of debate or modifies already adopted limitations on debate
6. Takes precedence over to postpone to a certain time, to refer to committee, to amend the main motion, and the main motion
7. Applies to debatable motions only
8. Can have applied to it the motions to close debate, to amend, and to withdraw
9. Can be renewed after change in the parliamentary situation

Motion to Close Debate and Vote Immediately

A motion to close debate and vote immediately prevents or stops discussion on the pending question or questions. Such a motion is made to prevent the proposal of other subsidiary motions except to table the main motion, and to bring the pending question or questions to an immediate vote. For example:

MEMBER: I move to close debate and vote immediately on the motion. (Seconded by another member.)

or

MEMBER: I move to vote immediately. (Seconded by another member.)

or

MEMBER: I move to close debate. (Seconded by another member.)

or

MEMBER: I move to close debate and vote immediately on all pending motions. (Seconded by another member.)

PRESIDER: It has been moved and seconded to close debate and vote immediately on the pending motion. Those in favor of closing debate and voting immediately, please rise. Be seated. Those opposed, please rise. Be seated. There are two-thirds voting in the affirmative, and the motion to close debate and vote immediately is adopted. We will now vote on the pending motion, which is the main motion as amended. (Presider restates the motion that will be voted on.)

Proposing the Motion to Close Debate and Vote Immediately

The motion to close debate is a powerful tool for expediting business. It may be proposed at any time after the motion to which it applies has been stated to the assembly. It cannot be combined with the motion to which it applies. For example, the motion "I move that we install an Internet portal in our head office lobby area and that we close debate on this motion" is out of order. Similarly, it is out of order for a member to debate the issue and end the remarks with a motion to close debate.

If the motion to close debate is proposed as soon as a main motion has been stated to the assembly, its adoption prevents any discussion of the question and the vote is taken immediately.

How Closing Debate and Voting Immediately Affects Pending Motions

If the motion to close debate and vote immediately is unqualified— "I move that we close debate," for example—it applies to the immediately pending motion only.

If more than one motion is pending, the motion to close debate should specify the pending motions to which it applies. For example, suppose a main motion, an amendment, and an amendment to that amendment are all pending. If the proposer of the motion to close debate wishes it to apply to both the amendment and the secondary amendment, but not to the main motion, this qualification should be stated. If the motion is to apply to all pending motions, this should also be stated. If the motion to close debate on all pending motions is adopted, an immediate vote must be taken on the amendment to the amendment, then on the amendment, and then on the main motion. The motion to close debate may be applied only to successive pending motions and must include the immediately pending motion.

Termination of the Effect of a Motion to Close Debate and Vote Immediately

The effect of a motion to close debate and vote immediately terminates with the adjournment of the meeting or convention at which it is adopted. For example, assume a main motion and the motion to postpone the main motion are pending; a member then moves to close debate on all pending motions, and the motion to close debate is adopted. If the assembly then adopts the motion to postpone the main motion to a later time within the meeting and takes up consideration of the main motion at that time or later in the meeting, the effect of the motion to close debate still applies, no debate is permitted on the main motion, and it is voted on immediately. However, if a motion to postpone to the next meeting has been adopted after the motion to close debate has been adopted in this same example, then at the next meeting the postponed main motion is fully debatable.

Two-Thirds Vote Required

A motion to close debate is the most drastic of the motions that seek to control debate. Common parliamentary practice requires a two-thirds vote to terminate debate.

Call the Question

The correct way to bring a matter to an immediate vote is to obtain the floor and move to close debate and vote immediately. A common practice, however, is to call out, "Call the question!" or even, "Question!" without obtaining the floor.

Calling out "question" is an informal way to move to close debate and vote immediately, but the practice is not in order if it interrupts a speaker or if other members wish to speak. In those situations, the presiding officer should ignore the member calling out "question" or should call the member to order. The vote on the motion to close debate may be taken by general consent or by formal vote. When a formal vote is taken, the closing of debate requires a two-thirds vote.

Effect of Adoption of a Motion to Close Debate and Vote Immediately

Adoption of a motion to close debate and vote immediately prevents or stops debate on the motion (or motions) to which it is applied and brings it (them) to an immediate vote.

Basic Rules Governing the Motion to Close Debate and Vote Immediately

Rules governing the motion to close debate and vote immediately include:

1. Cannot interrupt a speaker
2. Requires a second
3. Is not debatable
4. Cannot be amended
5. Requires a two-thirds vote because it prevents or cuts off debate
6. Takes precedence over all subsidiary motions except to table
7. Applies to debatable motions only
8. Can have no motion applied to it except the motion to withdraw
9. Can be renewed after change in the parliamentary situation

Motion to Table (Dispose without Direct Vote)

When adopted, a motion to table disposes of a main motion without a direct vote on the main motion. It suppresses or kills a main motion, without further debate, with the intention of avoiding any further action on the main motion in the meeting. For example:

MEMBER: I move that the main motion be tabled. (Seconded by another member.)

or

MEMBER: I move to table the main motion. (Seconded by another member.)

PRESIDER: It has been moved and seconded to table the main motion currently before the assembly. Those in favor of tabling, please rise. Be seated. Those opposed, please rise. Be seated. The vote is 95 to 17. Since there is a two-thirds affirmative vote, the motion to table the main motion is adopted.

Reasons for Tabling

On occasion, an assembly may wish to dispose of a main motion without any debate or without further debate and without a direct vote on the main motion. The main motion could be seen by some members as extremely objectionable, divisive, or clearly unwanted. This may occur even after some debate has taken place and when members may come to realize the consequences of further discussion on the matter. It permits the assembly to sidestep an unwelcome issue quickly and decisively.

Adhering Motions Also Tabled and Disposed Of

When a main motion is tabled, all pending amendments and other adhering motions are also tabled and disposed of.

In the event that the main motion is brought before the assembly again through the motion to reconsider the vote, only the main motion becomes pending at that time, and the subsidiary motions that were pending when the main motion was tabled are not before the assembly.

Use of the Term "to Table"

The practice of killing a motion by tabling it is used frequently by the U.S. Congress and by most voluntary organizations, although it is frowned upon in some other parliamentary manuals. The manuals argue against it because the motion, being undebatable, permits a bare majority to kill a proposal without discussion. This violates the principle that debate can be ended only by a two-thirds vote. However, the motion is so convenient a means of ending discussion and setting a motion aside that it continues to be widely used for that purpose, despite efforts to discourage its use. In this book, the motion to table requires a two-thirds vote to adopt.

The motion to table does not kill the main motion immediately; by the use of the motion to reconsider the vote, a majority of the members, at any time before the end of the meeting or convention, can return the main motion to the assembly for further consideration. The main motion can also be renewed at a future meeting or convention.

Effect of Adoption of a Motion to Table

Adoption of a motion to table stops debate on the main motion and removes it, with amendments and other adhering motions, from the consideration of the assembly during the current meeting or convention.

Basic Rules Governing the Motion to Table

The rules governing the motion to table include the following:

1. Cannot interrupt a speaker
2. Requires a second
3. Is not debatable
4. Cannot be amended
5. Requires a two-thirds vote to be adopted
6. Takes precedence over all other subsidiary motions
7. Applies to main motions only
8. Can have no motion applied to it except the motion to withdraw
9. Cannot be renewed (and cannot be reconsidered, but the main motion that has been tabled can be reconsidered)

Chapter 10

PRIVILEGED MOTIONS

Privileged motions deal with basic member rights, actions requiring immediate attention, and actions of the assembly as a whole. These motions affect the comfort or convenience of the assembly or one of its members. Privileged motions do not relate to pending business but when moved take priority over any main motion or pending subsidiary motions.

Question of Privilege

The purpose of a question of privilege is to allow a single member to request of the presiding officer immediate action that might affect the safety, health, security, comfort, and integrity of the members of the assembly. This could include the rights and privileges of a member or members or of the assembly. In some instances the request may be to make a motion to take immediate action even when other business is pending. There are three kinds of questions of privilege.

The first is a question of privilege of the assembly (request). For example:

MEMBER (without waiting for recognition): Mr. President, I rise to a question of privilege of the assembly.

PRESIDER (no second required): State your question of privilege.

MEMBER: May we have the members use a microphone during debate?

PRESIDER: Yes, the request is granted. The members will use the floor microphone when speaking to the assembly.

The second question of privilege is a question of personal privilege (request). For example:

MEMBER (without waiting for recognition): I rise to a question of personal privilege.

PRESIDER: (no second required): State your question of privilege.

MEMBER: May I be excused from serving on the election committee since I must leave the meeting early today?

PRESIDER: Yes, your request is granted. The chair will appoint another member to serve on the committee.

The third kind of question of privilege is a motion of privilege. It is used when a member believes that immediate action by the assembly is required to protect the privileges of the assembly or of a member or members, and states the action required in the form of a motion for the assembly to decide, rather than the presiding officer deciding. For example:

MEMBER: (without waiting for recognition): I rise to a question of privilege to present a motion.

PRESIDER: State your motion.

MEMBER: I move that the meeting go into executive session to consider the personnel issues. (Seconded by another member.)

PRESIDER: As a motion of privilege, it has been moved and seconded that the meeting go into executive session to consider the personnel issues.

Member's Right to Request Privilege

A member has the right to request a decision or action by the presiding officer or by the assembly on urgent questions involving the immediate convenience, comfort, rights, or privileges of the assembly, or of another member, or of himself or herself. A question of privilege may be in the form of a request to be decided by the presiding officer or a motion to be decided by the assembly. The presiding officer may decide that a particular motion is not a proper question of privilege and rule it not in order.

Interruption by a Question of Privilege

The importance or emergency nature of a question of privilege allows its proposer to interrupt a speaker. When interrupted by a question of privilege, a speaker should relinquish the floor temporarily, sitting down until the matter is settled. The presiding officer must rule immediately on the question of privilege by granting or denying it. Any member may appeal this decision.

If the presiding officer decides that the request is a proper question of privilege and of sufficient urgency, the privilege is granted, and the request is carried out immediately. If the presiding officer decides that it is a proper question of privilege but that it can wait, the presiding officer explains that the privilege will be granted when the speaker who was interrupted has finished. If the presiding officer decides that the question of privilege is not a proper request, it is denied. As soon as the question of privilege has been handled, the speaker who was interrupted is again assigned the floor.

Privilege of the Assembly

Questions relating to a privilege of the assembly have to do with the rights, safety, integrity, comfort, or convenience of the whole assembly. They frequently are concerned with the heating, lighting, or ventilation of the hall, the seating of members, or the control of noise. A question of privilege relating to the assembly takes precedence over a question of privilege relating to a member.

Personal Privilege

Questions of personal privilege pertain to an individual member or a small group of members and usually relate to their rights, reputation, conduct, safety, or convenience as members of the body.

Motions as Questions of Privilege

Sometimes when one main motion is pending, it is necessary to propose another main motion to take care of an emergency. The emergency motion can interrupt only as a question of privilege. The presiding officer will usually grant the member the right to state an urgent motion. If, after hearing the motion, the presiding officer believes that it needs an immediate decision, the question is stated to the assembly and opened for debate, thus setting aside the pending business temporarily. If the presiding officer believes that the motion is not urgent or is not a question of privilege, it is ruled not in order until the pending business is disposed of.

For example, if during a convention an embarrassing discussion arises that should not be made public, the presiding officer might allow a member to move, as a question of privilege, "That guests and observers be required to leave the room," or, "That the assembly move into a closed meeting."

When a question of privilege is presented as a motion, it is a main motion which is given special privilege. It follows all the rules of a main motion except that it may interrupt and has the precedence (rank) of a question of privilege. If it is noncontroversial, as it often is, it will usually be handled by general consent.

Effect of Proposing a Question of Privilege

Proposing a question of privilege secures appropriate action by the presiding officer on a request, or by the assembly on a motion, in order to meet an immediate need or emergency. If stated as a request, the presiding officer, after permitting the request, may state the request as a motion to permit the assembly to decide the requested action.

Basic Rules Governing a Question of Privilege (Request)

The rules governing a question of privilege include:

1. Can interrupt a speaker if it requires immediate decision and action
2. Requires no second because it is a request
3. Is not debatable because it is decided by the presiding officer
4. Cannot be amended
5. Requires no vote
6. Takes precedence over all motions except to adjourn and to recess
7. Applies to no other motion
8. Can have no motion applied to it except the motion to withdraw
9. Can be renewed after change in the parliamentary situation

Note: When the question of privilege is stated as a motion and is permitted by the presiding officer, the motion has all the characteristics of a main motion and is treated in all ways as a main motion.

Motion to Recess

A motion to recess permits a break in a meeting and sets a definite time for resuming the meeting. For example:

MEMBER: I move that we recess for 20 minutes. (Seconded by another member.)

or

MEMBER: I move to recess until 2:45 p.m. (Seconded by another member.)

or (in a convention or meeting lasting more than a day)

MEMBER: I move that we recess until tomorrow morning at 8:30 a.m. (Seconded by another member.)

PRESIDER: It has been moved and seconded that we recess for 20 minutes. Brief discussion on the amount of time is in order. Is there discussion on or amendment to the amount of time? Those in favor, say aye. Those opposed, say no. The motion is adopted. The meeting is recessed for 20 minutes.

Difference between Recess and Adjourn

A motion to recess *interrupts* the current meeting until a later time. An unqualified motion to adjourn *terminates* the meeting. When an assembly reconvenes following a recess, it resumes the meeting at the point at which it was interrupted by the motion to recess. When an assembly reconvenes following an adjournment, it begins an entirely new meeting, starting with the first step in the regular order of business. The only exception to this procedure is when an assembly adjourns to a continued meeting. For more information on this type of meeting, see "Adjournment to a Continued Meeting" below and in Chapter 12. This type of adjournment is, in fact, similar to a recess.

Conventions often transact business for several days, and the series of periods for the transaction of business are actually a series of business meetings. A convention, therefore, may move to recess to the next period for transacting business and then adjourn at the end of the convention.

Limitations and Restrictions on a Motion to Recess

The duration of a recess is usually brief, but there is no definite limitation on its length except that a recess cannot extend beyond the time set for the next regular or special meeting or, in a convention, beyond the time set for the next business meeting or for adjournment of the convention.

It is usually desirable to set a definite time for reconvening rather than moving to recess "upon the call of the chair." This avoids the anxiety members feel about leaving the immediate vicinity for a few minutes and perhaps missing the resumption of the meeting.

The motion to recess may be amended only as to the time or duration of the recess, and debate on it is restricted to the time, duration, or need for a recess.

As with all privileged motions, the motion to recess is privileged only if it is proposed when a main motion is pending. If it is proposed when no main motion is pending, it is a main motion.

Effect of Adoption of a Motion to Recess

Adopting a motion to recess suspends the meeting until the time stated for reconvening.

Basic Rules Governing the Motion to Recess

The rules governing the motion to recess include:

1. Cannot interrupt a speaker
2. Requires a second
3. Debate restricted to brief discussion on the time, duration, or need for a recess
4. Amendments restricted to the time or duration of the recess
5. Requires a majority vote
6. Takes precedence over all motions except to adjourn
7. Applies to no other motion
8. Can have applied to it the motions to amend, to withdraw, to limit debate, and to close debate
9. Can be renewed after change in the parliamentary situation

Motion to Adjourn

The purpose of a motion to adjourn is twofold:

1. To end a meeting or convention
2. To end a meeting or convention and to set a time to continue the meeting or convention

Following is an example of a motion to adjourn:

MEMBER: I move that we adjourn. (Seconded by another member.)

or

MEMBER: I move that the Annual Meeting of the American Institute of Parliamentarians adjourn. (Seconded by another member.)

or (to set a continued meeting and to adjourn immediately)

MEMBER: I move that we adjourn to resume this meeting on Friday, February 25, as a continued meeting, at 7 p.m. in this room. (Seconded by another member.)

or (making adjournment conditional—
only moved as a main motion)

MEMBER: I move that if the electricity is not turned on again in one hour, we adjourn at that time. (Seconded by another member.)

or (fixing a time for a future adjournment—
only moved as a main motion)

MEMBER: I move that we adjourn in twenty minutes. (Seconded by another member.)

or

MEMBER: I move that we adjourn at 11.00 a.m. (Seconded by another member.)

PRESIDER: It has been moved and seconded that we adjourn. Those in favor say, say aye. Those opposed, say no. The motion is adopted. The meeting is adjourned.

The Privileged Motion to Adjourn

When a main motion is pending, the motion to adjourn is a privileged motion that takes precedence over all other ranked motions. Adoption of a privileged motion to adjourn requires that adjournment take place immediately. The privileged motion to adjourn is subject to restricted debate and may be amended to establish the time when the current meeting will end or will continue. If a main motion is not pending, the motion to adjourn is a main motion and is open to full debate and amendment—it is subject to all the rules of a main motion.

Completion of Business Before Adjournment

When a motion to adjourn is made, it is the duty of the presiding officer to see that no important business is overlooked before putting the motion to a vote. If the presiding officer knows of any important matter that has not been considered and that requires action before adjournment, it should be called to the attention of the assembly. If the presiding officer fails to do this, any member may call attention to the oversight. For example, if decisions have not been made for an event that is to be held before the next meeting, it is important that this be done before adjournment.

When attention is called to some action that must be taken before adjournment, the presiding officer usually asks the proposer of the motion to adjourn to withdraw the motion until the essential business has been completed. If the member refuses to do so and if the assembly chooses to disregard the warning of the presiding officer, the assembly has the right to vote to adjourn.

Adjournment to a Continued Meeting

When an assembly cannot consider all its important business in the time available for a meeting, it may be desirable to continue the meeting at a later time. No exact form is required in stating such a motion to adjourn, but it must be clear that the meeting is to continue at a later date, and the time and place of the continued meeting must be specified. The setting of the time to continue the meeting can be done through a main motion to adjourn, a privileged motion to adjourn, or a main motion dealing only with establishing the continued meeting. No additional notice of the continued meeting is required unless provided for in the bylaws.

The interval between the current meeting and the continued meeting is, in effect, similar to a recess, and the continued meeting is actually a part of the original meeting. For additional information, see "Continued Meetings" in Chapter 12.

Adjournment and Dissolution

If a motion to adjourn is made when there is no provision for a further meeting of the assembly, the motion is, in fact, a motion to dissolve the assembly (but not of the organization, unless the assembly is a mass meeting) that must be treated as a main motion and is not in order as a privileged motion to adjourn.[1] The presiding officer should call the attention of the assembly to the fact that there is no provision for another meeting and that the assembly might, in effect, be dissolved by adoption of the motion to adjourn. A final adjournment that has the effect of dissolving the assembly or closing a convention is termed *adjournment sine die,* or adjournment without day.

Voting on Adjournment

After the vote on the motion to adjourn, the meeting is not ended until the presiding officer announces the vote and declares adjournment. Before the presiding officer declares the meeting adjourned, brief announcements may be made. The decision on whether to adjourn, however, is made by the assembly, not the presiding officer. The presiding officer cannot arbitrarily declare adjournment.

A formal vote need not always be taken, however. The presiding officer, sensing that it is time to adjourn, may ask, "Is there any further business to come before the meeting?" If, after a pause, there has been no response, the assembly has, in effect, voted by general consent to adjourn, and the presiding officer may simply say, "There being no objection, the meeting is adjourned."

Frequently there is confusion in phrasing motions to adjourn. The presiding officer should find out which type of adjournment the proposer of the motion intends and then rephrase the motion, if necessary, to make it clear. For example, a member may say, "I move that we adjourn until next Thursday at 7:30 p.m." If the next regular meeting is scheduled for that date and hour, the member is merely calling attention to the time of the next regular meeting. The presiding officer should restate the motion as, "It has been moved and seconded that we adjourn." In announcing the result, the presiding officer may add, "We are now adjourning until our next regular meeting, which is at 7:30 p.m. next Thursday in Jones Hall." It is good practice for the presiding officer, in declaring any meeting adjourned, to state the time and place of the next meeting.

Adjournment at a Previously Set Time

When a definite hour for adjournment has been set by the adoption of a program, by rule, or by a previous motion, it is the duty of the presiding officer, when the hour of adjournment arrives, to interrupt a speaker or the consideration of business and to state that the time set to adjourn has arrived. A member may then propose a motion to set another time for adjournment.

Business Interrupted by Adjournment

Business that is interrupted by adjournment is affected as follows:

1. Business that is interrupted by adjournment of a meeting comes up as the first item under unfinished business at the next meeting.
2. Business that is interrupted by the final adjournment of a convention is dropped.

Effect of Adoption of the Motion to Adjourn

The adoption of the motion to adjourn has two effects:

1. Terminates a meeting or convention with the announcement of adjournment by the presiding officer
2. Adjourns (recesses) a meeting or convention immediately upon the announcement by the presiding officer and continues the meeting or convention at a later set date and time

Basic Rules Governing the Motion to Adjourn

The rules governing the motion to adjourn include the following:

1. Cannot interrupt a speaker
2. Requires a second
3. Debate restricted to a brief discussion on the time or need for adjournment
4. Can be amended to establish a continued meeting or change the time or place of a proposed continued meeting
5. Requires a majority vote
6. Takes precedence over all other motions when privileged
7. Applies to no other motion
8. Can have no motion applied to it except the motions to amend, to withdraw, to limit debate, and to close debate
9. Can be renewed after change in the parliamentary situation

Chapter 11

INCIDENTAL MOTIONS

Incidental motions are motions that deal with how the assembly conducts its business more than with the substance of the business itself.

Motion to Appeal

The purpose of a motion to appeal is to enable a member who believes that the presiding officer is mistaken in a ruling to challenge the ruling and have the assembly decide, by vote, whether the presiding officer's ruling should be reversed or upheld. For example:

MEMBER: (immediately after the presiding officer has announced the ruling, and without waiting for recognition): I appeal the decision of the presiding officer. (Seconded by another member.)

PRESIDER: The decision of the chair (*or* presiding officer) has been appealed.

The presiding officer then states the reasons for the ruling, and the member may state the reasons for the appeal. After discussion, a vote is taken, not on the appeal, but on sustaining the presiding officer's decision. "Those in favor of sustaining the decision of the presiding officer, say aye. Those opposed to the decision of the presiding officer, say no. The decision of the presiding officer is (or is not) sustained."

When an Appeal May Be Made

Any decision of the presiding officer involving judgment is subject to appeal. The presiding officer's statement of a fact, such as announcing the result of a vote count, or simply answering a question or providing information, such as a parliamentary inquiry or factual inquiry, cannot be appealed. In addition, rulings of the presiding officer related to an unambiguous provision of the bylaws or of the parliamentary authority are not subject to appeal.

An appeal is permissible immediately after the presiding officer's ruling has been rendered. If any other business has been taken up after the ruling, an appeal is not in order. However, if another member has obtained the floor, that member may be interrupted by a member wishing to move an appeal.

On a ruling by the presiding officer when no main motion is pending, the ruling can be appealed. If moved under these circumstances, the motion to appeal retains the same governing rules as the incidental motion.

Stating the Question on an Appeal

The presiding officer must always state the question on an appeal in the following form: "Those in favor of sustaining the decision of the presiding officer ..." The question on the appeal is stated in a neutral, unbiased, manner, and the appeal must focus on the decision or ruling. For example, if a motion has been ruled out of order, the presiding officer could explain that the reason for the ruling is that the motion conflicts with the bylaws. The presiding officer should not state the question as, "Those in favor of sustaining the bylaws ..." or, "Those supporting the presiding officer ..."

Statement of the Reasons for Appeal

After the appeal has been stated by the presiding officer, the presiding officer states the reasons for the ruling. In doing so, the presiding officer is not required to leave the chair. Usually the person who made the appeal would then state their reasons for making the appeal. Since an appeal is debatable, any member may debate for or against the ruling.

The member making an appeal may withdraw the appeal after hearing the presiding officer's explanation or after further debate. The presiding officer may change the ruling if the member's rationale for the appeal or the debate on the appeal is convincing. In this case the appeal is dropped. If the presiding officer does not change the ruling as a result of the debate or the appeal is not withdrawn, the members will vote, after debate, on the appeal.

Vote on an Appeal

The presiding officer's initial ruling stands as the decision of the assembly, unless a majority vote reverses the ruling through a motion to appeal the decision. The vote is always on sustaining the decision of the presiding officer as shown above in the example. Therefore, to sustain the presiding officer's ruling requires either a tie vote or a majority vote. If the vote on the appeal fails to attain a tie or majority vote, the decision of the presiding officer is reversed.

Effect of a Motion to Appeal

If the decision of the presiding officer is sustained, the decision becomes the decision of the assembly. If the decision of the presiding officer is not sustained, the decision is reversed.

Basic Rules Governing the Motion to Appeal

The rules governing the motion to appeal include:

1. Can interrupt a speaker because it must be proposed immediately after the chair's ruling and before other business has intervened
2. Requires a second
3. Is debatable
4. Cannot be amended
5. Requires a majority vote or a tie vote to sustain the decision of the presiding officer
6. Takes precedence as an incidental motion and must be decided immediately
7. Applies to rulings of the presiding officer
8. Can have applied to it the motions to close debate, to limit debate, and to withdraw
9. Cannot be renewed

Motion to Suspend the Rules

The motion to suspend the rules permits an assembly to take some action or permits an action to be taken that otherwise would be prevented by a procedural rule. For example:

MEMBER: I move to suspend the rule allowing only two hours for a meeting so we can finish the agenda tonight. (Seconded by another member.)

PRESIDER: It has been moved and seconded to suspend the rule allowing only two hours for a meeting so that we can finish the agenda tonight. Those in favor of suspending the rule, please rise. Be seated. Those opposed to suspending the rule, please rise. Be seated. There is a two-thirds affirmative vote. The motion is adopted, and the rule allowing only two hours for a meeting is suspended. (If the vote is counted, the presider also states both the affirmative vote and the negative vote.) We will proceed with the motion now pending.

It is not necessary to state the rule to be suspended. The motion offered is to suspend the rules to permit an action, or to suspend the rules and take an action, where the procedural rules would not otherwise allow this to be done. As with any motion, if suspension of the rules is likely to confuse some members of the assembly, the presiding officer should take extra precautions to explain the motion and its effect if adopted or not adopted, so that members understand the impact of the motion.

Which Rules Can Be Suspended?

Only rules of procedure can be suspended. When an organization desires to accomplish a specific purpose or to take a specific action and is prevented from doing so by its rules of procedure, it may vote to suspend the rules that interfere with the accomplishment of the specific purpose or the particular action required.

Sometimes it is sufficient to suspend the rules to permit consideration of another motion that might not be in order. In this case it would be permissible to combine the motion to suspend the rules with the adoption of that other motion. For example, "I move to suspend the rules and approve the recommendations of the treasurer in the distributed written report." Adoption of such a motion by a two-thirds vote would permit the recommendations to be considered and would also adopt the recommendations without debate.

Which Rules Cannot Be Suspended?

Suspension of the rules cannot deny a member or members any fundamental right whether inherent in parliamentary law or defined by the rules of the organization. For example, an assembly cannot suspend:

1. A rule stated in a statute, charter, or the organization's constitution or bylaws unless a specific provision in these documents of authority provides for suspension of the rule

2. Rules governing notice of meeting, notice of motion, quorum requirements, special meeting agendas, vote requirements, and voting methods (such as the requirement for a ballot vote)

Restrictions and Time Limits on Suspension of Rules

The motion to suspend rules may be made when no motion is pending, or it may be made when a motion is pending if the suspension is for a purpose connected to that motion.

Rules may be suspended only for a specific purpose and only for the limited time necessary to accomplish the proposed action. Any suspension for a longer period would require an amendment of the rules, not a suspension. For this reason, the object of the suspension must be specified in the motion to suspend the rules, and only action that is specifically mentioned in the motion to suspend the rule can be taken under the suspension.

A rule becomes effective again as soon as the purpose for which it was suspended has been accomplished.

Suspend the rules can be moved when no business is pending. When this is done, the basic rules governing the motion as an incidental motion still apply. When moved with no business pending, the motion must clearly specify when the effect of the suspension expires, but it can be no later than the conclusion of the meeting.

The "Gordian Knot" Motion

The "Gordian Knot" motion is a form of a motion to suspend the rules. The motion permits the assembly, by a two-third vote in the affirmative, to return to a place in the meeting that was less confusing, usually the last main motion stated by the presiding officer, but not yet disposed of. If there are other motions in addition to the main motion pending, these motions are dropped when the motion to cut the Gordian Knot (suspend the rules to start afresh) is adopted by a two-thirds vote. This is a useful motion when the parliamentary situation in a meeting has become so confused that the presiding officer or the members have difficulty in knowing how best to proceed. In such cases, debate can become bitter and counterproductive, focusing on procedure rather than on substance.

The wording a member may use is, "Mr. President, the parliamentary situation has become very confusing. I think it would be best to cancel the pending motions and start over with the maker of the original motion submitting a new motion. I move to suspend the rules to allow this action."

Such a motion can usually be adopted by general consent because members on both sides of the question are likely to be equally frustrated and will welcome a way out. If, however, a member objects to making the decision to suspend the rules by general consent, a formal motion to suspend the rules can be used and adopted by a two-thirds vote.

This type of motion should rarely be needed, but even groups that are sophisticated in the use of parliamentary procedure can become confused and need a way out of such meeting situations. Even an assembly that can implement the rules to accomplish its intent may find this a more direct way to do so. The motion to suspend the rules serves this purpose.

Another procedural option to starting over is for the mover of the main motion to request that the main motion be withdrawn, or another member may ask the mover of the main motion to withdraw the motion. If the main motion is withdrawn, any member may introduce a new motion that might better meet the needs of the assembly.

Effect of Adoption of the Motion to Suspend Rules

The motion to suspend the rules allows an assembly to take a specific action, within the meeting, that would otherwise be improper under its procedural rules.

Basic Rules Governing the Motion to Suspend Rules

The rules governing the motion to suspend the rules include:

1. Cannot interrupt a speaker
2. Requires a second
3. Is not debatable
4. Cannot be amended
5. Requires a two-thirds vote
6. Takes precedence as an incidental motion and must be decided immediately
7. Applies only to procedural rules and not to another motion
8. Can have no motion applied to it except a motion to withdraw
9. Can be renewed after a change in the parliamentary situation

Consider Informally

Considering something informally permits a pending motion to be discussed with the rules of debate relaxed. Considering something informally also permits a discussion to occur without a pending motion. For example:

MEMBER: I move that this motion be considered informally.

or

MEMBER: I move that the subject of (indicated) be considered informally.

Effect of Adoption of the Motion to Consider Informally

If a motion is pending, considering it informally allows the assembly to debate the motion with the rules of debate relaxed. Adopted limits on debate are no longer observed. Decorum, courtesy, and fairness in debate must still be observed.

If no motion is pending, informal consideration allows the assembly to discuss a topic without it being introduced by a motion.

Informal consideration remains in effect until a new (for example, subsidiary) motion is made or until the assembly decides to vote. If no motion is pending, it remains in effect until a motion is made to take action or to conclude informal consideration. For more information on the motion to consider informally, see Chapter 16.

Basic Rules Governing the Motion to Consider Informally

The motion to consider informally is governed by the following rules:

1. Cannot interrupt a speaker
2. Requires a second
3. Is not debatable
4. Cannot be amended
5. Requires a majority vote
6. Takes precedence as an incidental motion and must be decided immediately
7. Applies to main motions
8. Can have no motion applied to it except a motion to withdraw
9. Can be renewed after a change in the parliamentary situation

Point of Order

A point of order calls the attention of the assembly and of the presiding officer to a violation or potential violation of the rules, an omission, a mistake, or an error in procedure. Its purpose is to secure a ruling from the presiding officer or the assembly on the question raised. For example:

MEMBER: (recognition not required): I rise to a point of order.

or

MEMBER: (recognition not required): Point of order!

PRESIDER: State your point of order.

or

PRESIDER: State your point.

MEMBER: The motion to amend the main motion is not in order at this time because the motion to postpone, which is higher ranking, is pending.

PRESIDER: Your point of order is well taken. The proposed motion to amend the main motion is not in order at this time.

or

PRESIDER: Your point of order is not well taken. The assembly granted permission to the mover of the motion to postpone to withdraw his motion. The member who was speaking on the proposed amendment may continue.

Duty of the Presiding Officer to Enforce Rules

When a member violates a rule, whether intentionally or not, the presiding officer has a duty to call attention to the violation and either require the member to conform to the rule or declare the member's action not in order. The presiding officer is responsible for enforcing the procedural rules during the meeting.[1]

It is the right of any member to raise a point of order if one of the following happens:

- If the presiding officer fails to enforce a rule of the assembly or of parliamentary procedure, does not notice an error made by a member, makes an error, or something has been done or attempted to be done in violation of the bylaws, it is the right of any member to call attention to the violation by raising a point of order.
- The presiding officer does not notice an error made by a member.

- An error is made by the presiding officer.
- Something has been done or attempted to be done in violation of the bylaws.

Raising a point of order is a demand by a single member that the presiding officer give a ruling or decision on the point raised. The presiding officer has a duty to rule on the point raised or to refer it to the assembly for a decision.

When a Point of Order May Be Raised

A point of order must be raised immediately after the mistake, error, or omission occurs. It cannot be brought up later in the meeting, or in another meeting, unless the error involves a violation of law or a serious violation of the principles of parliamentary procedure or of the bylaws.

Since it is important that a mistake be corrected immediately, a point of order may interrupt, even though a speaker has the floor and has begun speaking. The member making a point of order may interrupt a speaker by saying, "I rise to a point of order," or more succinctly, "Point of order." These words let the presiding officer know that the member is entitled to immediate recognition, even though someone else may have the floor or may be seeking the floor.

It is not necessary for members to raise points of order when the violation of the rules is minor or of little or no consequence. For example, if a member's speech has exceeded the limit on debate but the member is clearly concluding the speech, this does not justify a point of order. If a motion is being debated by someone other than the proposer (thus affirming that more than one member wishes to consider the matter) and there was not a second to the motion, this does not justify a point of order.

Ruling on Points of Order

When a member has made a point of order, the presiding officer may clarify the point being raised or consult with the parliamentarian or knowledgeable staff members before ruling on the matter. When ruling on the point, the presiding officer states that the point is "well taken," agreeing with the point raised, or "not well taken," disagreeing with the point raised. The presiding officer may state the reasons for the ruling.

A point of order decided by the presiding officer may be appealed. (See "Motion to Appeal" at the beginning of this chapter.)

While the presiding officer would normally rule on a point of order, if the presiding officer is unsure of how to rule because the matter on which the point is raised is obscure, is related to the bylaws, or may set an important precedent, the ruling may be referred to the assembly to decide by vote. For example, "The member has raised the point of order that the motion just proposed is not in order because it conflicts with the purposes stated in our bylaws. The presiding officer is in doubt and will refer it to the assembly for decision. The question is, Is the proposed motion (stating the motion) in order? Is there any discussion? Those who believe that the motion is in order, say aye. Those who believe that it is not in order, say no. The decision is in the affirmative; the proposed motion therefore is in order."

A point of order referred to the assembly is open to discussion by the members. A decision of the assembly on a point of order cannot be appealed.

Effect of Demand for Point of Order

A point of order interrupts business until the presiding officer rules that the point of order is well taken and orders the mistake or omission corrected or rules that the point of order is not well taken. Business then resumes at the point at which it was interrupted unless an appeal is made on the ruling, in which case the business stays in abeyance until the appeal is decided.

Basic Rules Governing the Point of Order

The rules for a point of order include:

1. Can interrupt a speaker because a violation of the rules should be corrected immediately
2. Requires no second
3. Is not debatable unless the presiding officer refers it to the assembly for discussion and decision
4. Cannot be amended
5. Requires no vote as it is decided by the presiding officer, unless the presiding officer refers it to the assembly for discussion and decision by majority vote
6. Takes precedence as an incidental motion and must be decided immediately

7. Applies to any procedural mistake, violation, or omission
8. Can have no motion applied to it except the motion to withdraw
9. Cannot be renewed

Inquiries

There are two kinds of inquiries. The first is a *parliamentary inquiry*, which enables a member to ask the presiding officer a question relating to procedure in connection with a pending motion or with a motion the member may wish to bring before the assembly immediately. The second is a *factual inquiry*, which is a request for substantive information or facts about the pending motion or for information on the meaning or effect of the pending question from the presiding officer or a speaker. The following is an example of a parliamentary inquiry:

MEMBER: (recognition and second not required): I rise to a parliamentary inquiry.

or

PRESIDER: State your parliamentary inquiry.

MEMBER: Is a motion to refer to committee in order now?

PRESIDER: Yes, a motion to refer is in order.

Here is an example of a factual inquiry:

MEMBER: (recognition not required): I rise to a factual inquiry.

or

I rise to request information.

or

MEMBER: Point of information.

PRESIDER: State your inquiry.

or

PRESIDER: What information do you need?

or

PRESIDER: What is your question?

MEMBER: Was this proposed dues increase reviewed by the finance committee, and what is the committee's conclusion?

PRESIDER: Yes, the finance committee reviewed the proposed increase and agrees that an increase is needed.

Another kind of a factual inquiry is permission to ask a question of the speaker. For example:

MEMBER: (recognition not required): I rise to a factual inquiry.

or

MEMBER: I rise to request information.

PRESIDER: State your inquiry.

MEMBER: May I ask the speaker a question?

PRESIDER: Is the speaker willing to answer a question?

SPEAKER: Yes.

or

SPEAKER: I will answer questions after completing my remarks.

or

SPEAKER: I do not wish to be interrupted by questions.

The Right of Members to Inquire

Any member has the right to inquire at any time during the processing of a motion, provided a vote has not begun on the motion. The inquiry must be directly connected with a pending motion and can be related to procedural matters or substantive matters regarding the merits of the motion, such as the meaning or effect of the pending motion. Inquiries are requests or questions and are not strictly motions. It is a right of members to raise inquiries.

When an Inquiry Interrupts

An inquiry may interrupt a speaker only if it requires an immediate answer. A member should not interrupt a speaker with an inquiry if it can reasonably wait until the speaker has finished speaking. In order that the presiding officer may know that a member is rising to an inquiry and has the right to the floor while presenting it, the member should clearly state that he or she is rising to a parliamentary inquiry or a factual inquiry instead of merely waiting for recognition.

If a speaker is interrupted by a parliamentary inquiry and the presiding officer decides that the question does not require an immediate answer, the presiding officer explains that the inquiry will be answered as soon as the speaker has finished, and the speaker should be directed to continue.

The presiding officer should never allow a parliamentary inquiry or a factual inquiry to be used as a method of annoying a speaker who has the floor and should refuse recognition to any member who is using inquiries to harass or delay.

Inquiry Addressed to the Presiding Officer

A parliamentary inquiry is always addressed to the presiding officer and is answered by the presiding officer. The presiding officer may consult with the parliamentarian, if there is one, but normally does not ask the parliamentarian to respond directly to the questioner.

If the request is for factual information related to the meaning or effect of a motion, the presiding officer may answer the question (taking care to exhibit no bias on the matter under consideration) or may recognize an officer or staff member, the proposer of the motion, or another member as appropriate, to provide the requested information. A request for nonprocedural information cannot always be granted, as the desired information may not be known by anyone at the meeting and may not be readily obtained.

The presiding officer should answer inquiries on parliamentary procedure that are pertinent to the pending business. However, the presiding officer need not answer (and should refrain from answering) general questions on parliamentary procedure that are not directly related to the business before the assembly.

Effect of Request for Inquiry

A request for an inquiry requires the presiding officer to answer the inquiry, or requests permission to ask the speaker a question. The presiding officer may rule that the inquiry is not in order or that it may not interrupt a speaker. Until the inquiry is answered, no additional business is conducted.

Effect of Interruption

If an inquiry is directed to a member who is speaking, the speaker may agree to be interrupted for questions or may refuse to permit such interruptions. If speeches are being timed because of limitation on debate, the time taken by the question is not deducted from the speaker's time, nor is the speaker's response to the question deducted from his or her time. However, the presiding officer must take care to ensure that both questions and answers are as brief as possible and that neither the question nor the answer evolves into presentation of information that should be properly offered as debate.

Inquiries should be addressed to the speaker in the third person, through the presiding officer: "Does the speaker know the proposed motion's financial impact on the club?" rather than, "How much do you think this proposal would cost the club?" The presiding officer may overlook a very brief exchange when a member interrupts a speaker without first obtaining recognition, but should call to order a member who does not have the floor and who continues the interruption or begins arguing with the speaker.

Interrupting a speaker for a question is not a right; it is a privilege that may be granted by the speaker. It should be exercised only to obtain information, not to engage in argument, and certainly not to obtain the floor preferentially in order to provide information, which the nonspeaking member should do only after being properly recognized to debate.

Basic Rules Governing Inquiries

The rules governing inquiries include the following:

1. Can interrupt a speaker only if it requires an immediate answer
2. Requires no second because it is a request
3. Is not debatable
4. Cannot be amended
5. Requires no vote because it is a request and is decided by the presiding officer
6. Takes precedence as an incidental motion and must be decided immediately
7. Applies to any motion
8. Can have no motion applied to it except the motion to withdraw
9. Cannot be renewed on the same matter

Request to Withdraw a Motion

A request to withdraw a motion enables a member who has proposed a motion to remove it or request it be removed from consideration by the assembly. Following is an example of what happens *before* the motion has been stated to the assembly by the presiding officer:

MEMBER: (recognition not required): I withdraw my motion.

PRESIDER: The motion has been withdrawn.

Following is what happens *after* the motion has been stated to the assembly by the presiding officer:

MEMBER: (recognition not required): I wish to withdraw my motion.

PRESIDER: The member asks to withdraw his motion. Is there any objection to the withdrawal of the motion? There being no objection, the motion is withdrawn.

or (if a member objects)

PRESIDER: Those in favor of allowing Mrs. A to withdraw her motion, say aye. Those opposed, say no. The motion is adopted, and Mrs. A's motion is withdrawn.

Right of the Proposer to Withdraw a Motion

Any motion can be withdrawn. Before a motion has been stated by the presiding officer, its proposer may modify it or withdraw it without the assembly's permission, and any member or the presiding officer may request that the maker withdraw it. Usually such a request is made because some more urgent business needs consideration, or because the motion was based on erroneous or incomplete information. At this point the proposer may withdraw the motion, modify the motion, or decline to make any change.

Permission to Withdraw a Motion

After a motion has been stated to the assembly by the presiding officer, it becomes the property of that body, and the proposer may withdraw it only with the permission of the assembly, which may be granted through a majority vote or by general consent. If a member objects to the general consent, the proposer or some other member may move that the proposer "be allowed to withdraw the motion." This motion is not debatable and requires a majority vote.

Only the mover of a motion has the right to request that it be withdrawn; the consent of the seconder is not necessary. A motion can be withdrawn if there is no objection, or with permission from the assembly, up to the moment the final vote on it is taken, even though other higher-ranked motions affecting the motion may be pending or debate has been limited or closed. When a motion is withdrawn, all motions adhering to it are also withdrawn.

Recording Withdrawn Motions

A motion that is withdrawn after it has been stated by the presiding officer is recorded in the minutes with a statement that it was withdrawn. No mention is made in the minutes of a motion that is withdrawn before it has been stated to the assembly by the presiding officer.

Effect of Request to Withdraw a Motion

A request to withdraw a motion removes the motion from consideration by the assembly.

Basic Rules Governing the Request to Withdraw a Motion

The rules for the request to withdraw a motion include:

1. Can interrupt a speaker
2. Requires no second because it is a request
3. Is not debatable
4. Cannot be amended
5. Requires no vote before the motion is stated by the presiding officer, in which case the request is granted; after the motion is stated by the presiding officer, it requires the approval of the assembly by general consent or a majority vote
6. Takes precedence as an incidental motion and must be decided immediately
7. Applies to all motions
8. Can have no motion applied to it
9. Can be renewed after a change in the parliamentary situation

Division of a Question

A main motion may be composed of two or more parts that may stand independently. The purpose of division of a question is to divide a main motion containing more than one part into individual motions that may be considered and voted on separately.

For example, assume that the following motion has been introduced: "I move that the club donate $5,000 to the Children's Shelter and that funds donated to any charity this year be drawn from the reserve account."

MEMBER: I request that the motion be divided into two motions— that the club donates $5,000 to the Children's Shelter and that funds donated to any charity this year be drawn from the reserve account.

PRESIDER: (no second required; motion is divided on demand if it contains more than one distinct and independent proposal): A member has requested that the motion be divided into two separate motions. The motion will be divided. The motion now before the assembly is: "That the club donates $5,000 to the Children's Shelter." Is there any discussion?

Motions Divided by the Presiding Officer

When a motion contains two or more distinct proposals, any member has the right to request that it be divided into separate motions. If the presiding officer agrees that the motion contains more than one independent proposal, it is considered as two or more separate motions since members may favor one part of the motion but be opposed to another and therefore could not vote properly if the two parts remained as one. In addition, each part must be suitable for adoption, even if one or more other parts are defeated.

For example, a motion, "That the organization promote the use of the Internet's social media in our public relations efforts, and that the association hire an assistant to the executive director" is clearly divisible.

On the other hand, a motion "That the association purchase fifteen laptop computers and give one of the computers to each member of the board of directors" cannot be divided because if the motion to "purchase fifteen laptop computers" is defeated, it would be absurd to vote on the motion to "give one of the computers to each member of the board of directors." The presiding officer must deny a request to divide such a motion and explain the reason for the denial.

Motions Divided by the Assembly

If the presiding officer rules that the motion is not divisible and denies the request, a member has the right to disagree by appealing the decision of the chair. The presiding officer should explain why the motion is not divisible. During further debate on the appeal, the member may explain precisely how it may be divided.

A motion may contain several proposals that are worded in such a way that they cannot be divided easily or without extensive rewriting. In this case, the motion to divide the question should clearly indicate the wording of each of the individual proposals. In important cases, where clarity is required by the assembly, the assembly can refer the original motion to a committee to divide the motion and carefully rewrite its parts so that each can stand alone and be discussed and voted on separately.

Consideration by Paragraph

Parts of a motion may be considered separately when the motion is not easily divisible or when dividing the question may result in ambiguities. In such cases the motion may be considered paragraph by paragraph or section by section. The various paragraphs are not independent and are not treated as separate motions, but each paragraph is discussed and amended separately, after which the entire motion is open to discussion and further amendment, if appropriate, and is then finally voted upon as a whole.

If after consideration by paragraph has been completed, the final vote defeats the entire motion, none of the amendments that have been adopted when considering the matter by paragraph are in effect.

Consideration by paragraph is helpful when the assembly is dealing with a lengthy or complicated proposal. It permits the assembly to focus on each paragraph or section of a proposal, perfecting it through amendments before moving on to the next paragraph or section. For example, a committee may report a motion with a number of changes, and consideration of each paragraph (or section) separately can aid in focusing the discussion on specific points. After every paragraph has been discussed (and amended, if necessary), the full motion is opened to further discussion and amendment and finally voted upon as a whole. A proposed bylaws revision is often considered in this manner.

Only the motion to amend can be applied to the separate paragraphs. Other subsidiary motions cannot be applied to separate paragraphs, which could be done if the question were divided.

Consideration by paragraph can be suggested by the presiding officer or any member. It is often approved by general consent.

A motion can be made for consideration by paragraph, and the decision is made by majority vote. Such a motion requires a second and is not debatable. During consideration of the motion by paragraph, a member may move that the motion "be considered as a whole." This requires a second, is not debatable, requires a majority vote, and if adopted, the process of considering each paragraph separately is halted and the motion is fully open to debate, amendments, and other subsidiary motions.

When Division of Question May Be Proposed

A request to divide a question is most effective if is proposed immediately after the introduction of the motion that it seeks to divide. However, since it is an incidental motion, it may be proposed at any time before the vote has begun.

Alternative Proposals for Dividing a Question

A motion to divide should state clearly how the question is to be divided. Any member may propose a different division. Such proposed divisions are alternative proposals, not amendments, and should be voted on in the order in which they are proposed. The proposal to divide receiving the highest majority vote is chosen.

Effect of Request for Division of a Question

A request for division of a question divides a main motion containing two or more independent proposals and enables the assembly to debate and act on each proposal separately.

Basic Rules Governing a Request for Division of a Question or for Consideration by Paragraph

The rules governing a request for division of a question or for consideration by paragraph include the following:

1. Cannot interrupt a speaker
2. Requires no second if granted by the presiding officer as a request, but if offered as a motion, requires a second

3. Is not debatable
4. Cannot be amended
5. Requires no vote if granted by the presiding officer as a request, but requires a majority vote if offered as a motion
6. Takes precedence as an incidental motion and must be decided immediately
7. Applies to main motions only
8. Can have no motion applied to it except a motion to withdraw
9. Can be renewed after a change in the parliamentary situation

Call for Division of Assembly

Division of assembly is called to verify an indecisive voice vote or an indecisive show of hands vote by requiring members to rise and, if necessary, to be counted. For example:

MEMBER: (immediately after the vote has been taken or announced; recognition not required): Division!

or

MEMBER: I call for a division of the assembly.

or

MEMBER: I ask for a standing vote.

PRESIDER: (second is not required): A division of the assembly has been called for. Those in favor of the motion that (stating the pending motion), please rise. The secretary (or a teller) will please count. Be seated. Those opposed, please rise. Be seated. There is an affirmative vote in the majority, and the motion is adopted.

When Division May Be Demanded

A call for division is a demand that an indecisive vote, which has been taken by voice or a show of hands, be verified by a standing vote and, if necessary to determine the result, that the vote be counted.

Any member, without waiting for recognition, may call for a division as soon as a question has been put to a vote and even before the vote is announced. This right continues even after the vote has been announced and another speaker has claimed the floor, but the right must be exercised promptly before the speaker has begun to speak.

If a member is not satisfied with the presiding officer's declaration of the outcome of a vote taken by division, the member may demand a count of the division. In response, the presiding officer must proceed with a repeat of the division with a count if there is any doubt as to the outcome of the uncounted division. If there is no doubt of the outcome, the presiding officer should inform the member that there is no need for a count of the division. The presiding officer should then ask if the member wishes to put the question of taking a vote by counted division to the assembly. If the member moves that the division be counted, and it is seconded, the decision will rest with the assembly. The motion to take a counted division requires a majority vote.

Any member who feels a vote has not been correctly announced or reported has the right to insist on verification, but a member cannot use this privilege to obstruct business by calling for division on an obviously decisive vote.

Verification of a Vote by the Presiding Officer

The responsibility of announcing a vote correctly rests with the presiding officer.[2] When in doubt, the presiding officer should take the initiative in calling for a standing vote or, in a small assembly, a show of hands. If still in doubt, the presiding officer should take the initiative in ordering a counted vote.

Effect of Call for Division of Assembly

A call for division of assembly requires that the presiding officer take a standing vote on the motion just voted on and may count the votes if there is any doubt as to which side prevailed.

Basic Rules Governing Call for Division of Assembly

The rules governing a call for division of assembly include the following:

1. Can interrupt proceedings because it requires an immediate decision
2. Requires no second
3. Is not debatable
4. Cannot be amended

5. Requires no vote unless the presiding officer's denial of a counted division is unsatisfactory to a member
6. Takes precedence as an incidental motion and must be decided immediately
7. Applies to an indecisive voice or hand vote
8. Can have no motion applied to it
9. Cannot be renewed

Chapter 12

TYPES OF MEETINGS

A *meeting* is an official assembly of the members of an organization or board during which the members remain together in one place except when there is a recess. It covers the period from the time the group convenes until the time it adjourns.

A *convention* usually refers to a series of meetings that follow in relatively close succession. It is regarded as a single meeting with intervening recess periods, some of which may be from day to day. (Appendix A provides information on flag etiquette for conventions, as well as for other meetings, and Appendix B provides information on protocol for conventions.)

Regular Meetings

A *regular meeting* of an organization or board is one of a series of meetings for which the dates and sometimes location are established in the bylaws or set by adoption of a motion. At a regular meeting, the usual business of the organization is conducted, week to week, month to month, or otherwise periodically, as required by the nature of the organization. Since members are presumed to be familiar with the bylaws and standing rules, no additional notice of regular meetings need be given unless the bylaws or standing rules provide for further notice or unless notice of regular meetings is customary. In the event that a regular meeting is to be cancelled, postponed, or the date or time changed, the authority and process for doing so should be stated in the bylaws, even if the regular meeting dates were established by motion.

The regular time and place for meetings that have been established by rule or custom cannot legally be changed without notice to all members.

At any regular meeting, any business can be transacted that comes within the scope of the organization's purposes unless otherwise restricted by the governing documents—for example, election of officers is often restricted to the annual meeting of the members. The organization should be cautious in choosing to restrict items of business to the annual meeting because this may limit flexibility in accomplishing necessary business.

No meeting may begin before the time stated in the notice or set by custom unless all members are present and consent to the earlier time.

Special Meetings

A *special meeting* is a meeting that is not regularly scheduled and is held to transact specific business as stated in the call of the meeting. Any special meeting of an organization or a board must be called in accordance with the bylaw provisions governing special meetings or in accordance with applicable statutory requirements. The organization's documents may provide that special meetings must be called by the board or upon petition by a certain minimum number or percentage of members. The bylaws section on special meetings should state who may call a special meeting.

All members must be notified of a special meeting, and the call or notice must state the items of business that will be considered and voted on.[1] A copy of the call for the special meeting must be inserted in, or attached to, the minutes of the meeting.

Only those items of business stated in the call for a special meeting may be considered at the meeting. No new items of business may be added to the agenda. The special meeting is conducted in the same manner as any other business meeting, but it is limited to the items described in the meeting notice. The statement of business to be considered must be specific, and if action is to be taken at the meeting, this fact must be stated in the notice. If a notice states that one of the purposes of a special meeting is "to hear a report of the Land Purchase Committee," the report can be read, but no action can be taken on recommendations of the committee unless the recommendations are stated in the notice and it is clear that they are to be voted on at the meeting. General broad statements describing business to be transacted, such as "any other proper business that may come before the meeting," do not provide valid notice.

Minutes are not read or approved at the beginning of a special meeting, but any section that applies to items under consideration may be read for reference at the time of the discussion of that item.

Minutes of the special meeting are read and approved at the next regular meeting.
In large state, national, or international organizations, provisions in the bylaws for special meetings of the whole membership are often unrealistic. The governing board should be empowered to handle most emergency or urgent organizational business, and the bylaws section on special meetings should be limited to extreme situations, contain high requirements for holding the meeting, and include specific details on member notification.

Continued Meetings

When members wish to continue a regular or special meeting at a later time, a motion to adjourn the meeting and to continue it at a definite later time makes the second meeting a *continued meeting*, which is legally a continuation of the original meeting. (For more information on use of the motion to adjourn to establish a continued meeting, see Chapter 10.) The meeting is continued on the date and time and at the location set forth in the adopted motion. The interval between the two meetings is a recess that may last for days or even weeks but must not extend past the start of the next scheduled regular meeting.

A continued meeting is sometimes referred to as an *adjourned meeting*, but the term *continued meeting* is recommended because it is less confusing concerning the intent of the action taken. The continued meeting is legally a continuation of the previous meeting. The meeting is called to order and a quorum established and recorded to open the continued meeting. From that point on, the meeting follows the agenda from the original meeting, beginning exactly where the prior meeting finished. If a question was pending when the meeting adjourned, that question is still pending, as noted in the secretary's notes, when the continued meeting is called to order. An organization can transact any business at a continued meeting that it might have conducted in the original meeting, and any limitations, such as debate limits that might have been imposed at the original meeting, remain in force at a continued meeting.

Special notice is not required for a continued meeting because it is legally a resumption of the original meeting, but it is good practice to notify all members of continued meetings when possible, and organizations would be wise to adopt rules regarding notice requirements for continued meetings that would meet their needs. For more information on notices of meetings and proposals, see Chapter 13. A continued meeting may be again continued to a later date as long as the continuation is scheduled prior to the next regular scheduled meeting. A continued special meeting can transact only such business as could have been transacted at the original special meeting.

Closed Meeting

A *closed meeting* (sometimes referred to as an *executive session*) is a meeting open only to current members of the body that is meeting and is a meeting in which sensitive or confidential matters may be discussed and acted upon. A motion to go into a closed meeting is privileged, is not debatable or amendable, and is adopted by majority vote. Any discussion held or actions taken are legally considered as confidential and all information must remain within the confines of the meeting unless the meeting directs otherwise.

In a board or committee, the members of the board or committee would be the only members allowed to attend. In a membership meeting, only members may remain during the session. Guests, such as witnesses, advisors, or staff, may attend only by invitation extended by action or consent of the assembly. For example, disciplinary actions against a member of an organization should be handled in a closed meeting.

Boards and committees are normally considered to operate in a closed meeting unless the organization documents state otherwise. Boards and committees may invite members of the organization or staff to attend as observers. Personnel matters, such as discussion of salaries and evaluation of employees, are handled in a closed meeting, as are discussions of pending legal problems and other matters of a highly sensitive nature that may cause harm to the organization if not held in a closed meeting.

Some states have *sunshine laws* that restrict the use of closed meetings. These laws may apply to such organizations as corporations, charities, not-for-profit groups, municipalities, and school boards. Closed meetings cannot be used to conceal matters that members or the public have a right to know, such as financial information or any matters that may be required by law to be conducted in open meetings.

The minutes of a closed meeting are available only to members of the body holding the meeting, unless the law requires otherwise or the assembly, the board, or the committee votes to make its minutes available to others.

Telephone and Electronic Meetings

A regular meeting, a special meeting, or a continued meeting may be held by telephone or electronic means, provided that the procedural rules associated with such meetings are adhered to and that such meetings are authorized in the bylaws and in applicable law.

The use of technology allows some members to be grouped together in a specific location with other members participating at individual remote locations. Rules for recognizing members to speak, for taking a vote, and for ensuring that only members attend the meeting, should be developed for use in such meetings.

For all meetings in which members are not in the same place, some basic rules must be established. Some of these may be:

- A quorum is established through a roll call.
- Members always state their names before speaking.
- At the presiding officer's discretion, discussion takes place on a rotating basis.
- Votes are taken by roll call or by general consent.

Meetings held by videoconference are similar to meetings held by telephone, and the same rules can apply.

As is the case with postal mail or exchanges of facsimiles, in which members are unable to communicate simultaneously with all other members, Internet or e-mail discussions cannot be easily substituted for traditional meetings and are not meetings in the true sense. Nevertheless, several forms of Internet use, such as e-mail and chat rooms, are useful for rapid exchange of information and ideas. Where the law permits, and the procedures are developed within the organization's documents, decisions may be validated through electronic means.

In a meeting in which the participants do not all meet in the same physical location but communicate through various technologies, the rights of absentees must be carefully protected. These include ensuring that quorum requirements are met and sustained throughout the meeting and that reasonable notice of the meeting is given to all members. As with any meeting, minutes must be produced. Organizations may need to develop procedures by which members are able to confirm their identities in cases where visual or voice identification of each participant is not possible. The rigidity of such procedures will depend on the technology available and the level of identification that meets the needs of the organization.

Failure to Call Meetings

If officers or directors fail to call a meeting in accordance with the organization's governing documents, members may demand that a meeting be scheduled and that the membership be notified. This is especially critical if there is a significant action, such as an election, to be taken by the assembly. If the leadership fails to perform its duty to issue the call, statutes may provide that a group of members or a single member may call the meeting and designate the time and location. In such cases, the requirements of any applicable statute should be strictly complied with.

Chapter 13

NOTICE OF MEETINGS AND PROPOSALS

Meetings, conventions, and certain important proposals that will come before the members for decision require advance notice to members. The courts will not uphold the decisions of a meeting if the notice requirements for the meeting, or for any action that requires notice, have not been complied with. If there is proof that notice of a meeting is purposely or negligently withheld from any member, actions taken at that meeting are not valid.[1, 2] The only variation from this rule is that an affirmative vote of *all* of the members may waive the lack of proper notice. For more information on this rule, see "Waiver of Notice" at the end of this chapter.

Notice Protects Members

Common parliamentary law provides for the full protection of every member by rigid enforcement of notice requirements before a meeting. It does not protect absentees who have received notice but who fail to attend, or members who come late or leave early. A member who has been sent notice of a meeting or a convention or of an action that requires notice and who does not attend relinquishes the right of decision to those who are present. When proper notice has been given and a quorum is present, it cannot be contended that those members present are "not representative" or that the meeting is "not representative," since legally all members are equal.

Notice of Meetings

Notice of a meeting must be sent to the postal address of all members or, as an alternative (if approved by the membership), to the electronic address of all members. The notice must clearly indicate the date, the time, and the place of the meeting, and it should be signed by the secretary or by another authorized officer if the secretary is absent. The time and place of a meeting cannot be changed after notice has been given, except in an emergency or if a notice of the change is also sent. Notice of any meeting sent so late that a substantial number of the members cannot attend is not a valid notice, even if all other requirements have been met.

The method of notice should be specified in the governing documents of the organization to establish the organization's requirements. Provisions should include the acceptable methods for giving notice, including the timing of such notice, as it applies to the annual meeting and to regular meetings if notice is required for such meetings.

Notices sent to the membership should state the following basic information:

1. The exact date and time of calling the meeting to order
2. The exact place of the meeting
3. Any additional information that would assist the members in preparing for the meeting.

Convention notices are often issued in the form of a call to the convention. The call must give notice of the exact time and place of the convention and usually includes the method of accrediting delegates and directions for sending in resolutions, reports of officers and committees, and proposed amendments to the bylaws. The call is usually sent by letter or electronic means, or is printed in the organization's magazine. A call can be in the form of a notice or a greeting, or in any form that makes it clear that a convention is being called and when and where the convention will be held.

An *annual meeting* may refer either to the annual convention of an organization or to the meeting of a local organization that is held annually at the termination of the organizational year to elect or install officers and to hear reports. Annual meetings require notice to all members of the time and place of the meeting and of any special business to be transacted, such as election of officers. The organization's governing documents may indicate the items of business to be covered at an annual meeting. If this information is included in the organization's governing documents, specific business need not be included in the notice unless it is a variation from the expected items.

Regular meetings require whatever notice is stated in the organization's governing documents, and no notice is required if the governing documents of the organization provide for meetings to be held on specific regular dates—for example, the third Wednesday of each month. Any regular meeting of an organization may transact any business not requiring advance notice. However, if the officers responsible for giving notice know that a proposal of great importance, but one that may not require advance notice, will be brought up at a regular meeting, they should, as a matter of good faith, give notice of the proposal.

Special meetings require notice of time and place of meetings, of specific proposals to be considered and decided, and of subjects to be discussed. At the meeting, the members may amend the proposals stated in the notice but cannot consider any business that is not stated or reasonably implied in the notice. For example, the purpose stated in the notice, "To purchase a new car for the executive director," reasonably implies that the current system of renting a car for the executive director's use will be ended. Under this statement of purpose, however, the meeting could not consider the employment of a consultant. For more information on special meetings, see Chapter 12.

Continued meetings (that is, meetings that are a resumption of meetings that were adjourned to a particular hour or date) do not require notice unless this requirement is in the organization's governing documents. If either a regular or a special meeting that has been properly called votes to adjourn to a later time to continue the meeting, this is sufficient notice to those present. However, good organizational practice requires that notice of the continued meeting be sent to all members.

Board and committee meetings require that members be sent whatever notice is specified by the governing documents of the organization.

Notice of Proposed Actions

A proposal that according to the law, charter, or provision of the bylaws (that is, the organization's governing documents) requires advance notice cannot be considered at any meeting unless proper notice of the proposed action has been sent. Even with unanimous approval of the members present at a meeting, if members did not receive advance notice of a proposal, the proposal will be invalid. Amendments to the bylaws or charter, sale of property, large and unusual expenditures, election of officers, and other items of similar importance require whatever notice is specified by the bylaws or rules of the organization. The proposals to be voted on must be stated specifically.

Amendments to motions must fall within the scope of the notice given.[3] For example, if an organization's bylaws set the number of members of the board at 13 and notice was given to reduce the board to 9 members, any amendment specifying a figure between 9 and 13 would be in order, but an amendment increasing the number of members to over 13 or reducing the number of board members below 9, would be out of order. Scope of notice relates to actions that can reasonably be expected to be adopted at the meeting. Actions that are between the status quo and the proposed action for which notice was given are within scope of notice.

When an action that required advance notice has been taken, any motion having the effect of voiding or changing the original action requires the same notice. For example, if a motion to lease property belonging to an organization originally required notice for its adoption, a motion to cancel the lease requires the same notice.

Waiver of Notice

If there was a mistake in a notice or a failure to send notice to every member and yet every member is present at the meeting and no one protests a lack of notice, the members waive notice simply by their attendance and their participation in the meeting. Members may also waive notice by signing a written waiver of notice before, during, or after a meeting.

Chapter 14

ORDER OF BUSINESS AND AGENDA

An *order of business* is a blueprint for meetings. It is a defined sequence of the different sections of business covered in the order in which each will be called up during business meetings. Whereas the order of business is the sequence of business, the agenda is the listing of specific items to be considered at a given meeting, usually following the sequence as defined in the order of business.

Usual Order of Business

The purpose of the order of business is to provide a systematic plan for conducting business.

If the bylaws or standing rules do not include an order of business, parliamentary law has established the following pattern:

1. Call to order
2. Reading, correcting, approving, or disposing of minutes of previous meetings
3. Reports of officers
4. Reports of boards and standing committees
5. Reports of special committees
6. Unfinished business
7. New business
8. Announcements
9. Adjournment

When there is an invocation, an opening ceremony, preliminary remarks, a roll call, the establishment of a quorum, or approval of the agenda, these should follow the call to order and precede the other items of business.

Just prior to adjournment some organizations include an agenda item called *for the good of the order*. This is an informal agenda item in which members may make suggestions for the improvement of the organization, suggest how the meeting processes may be improved, or make general announcements. No business may be conducted and no motions may be proposed. Some organizations also include a "program," such as a guest speaker or entertainment. The more common practice is to adjourn the business meeting prior to the program or activities of a social nature or to recess for such activities and adjourn afterwards. It is incumbent on an organization to define an order of business that best meets the needs of the assembly. For example, a board of directors may have a different order of business from a general meeting of members. While most organizations use the traditional order of business shown above or a variation thereof, some organizations structure their order of business around different segments of the organization's business. Others may opt for a structure based on the organization's strategic plan.

The order of business for a special meeting consists only of the call to order, consideration of the items of business stated in the notice of the meeting, and adjournment.

The order of business of a convention should be prepared to fulfill the particular needs of the organization and its members. When a program or schedule for a business meeting has been adopted by a convention and a time has been fixed for considering certain items of business, this schedule cannot be deviated from except by general consent or by majority vote. If an item that has been set for a particular time is postponed to a later time in the same meeting, the motion to postpone is sufficient notice to all delegates present.

Agenda

An *agenda* is a list of the specific items under each division of the order of business that the members agree to consider in a meeting.

The list under "unfinished business," for example, would include any item of business that was interrupted by the adjournment of the previous meeting or any motion that was postponed to the current meeting.

An agenda is usually prepared by the president and the secretary, with the assistance of staff, and is usually sent to the members before the meeting, with additional meeting materials. Sometimes an agenda is not formally adopted and is used by the presiding officer as a guide. In other organizations, a printed agenda, which is a proposed or "draft" document, is circulated at the meeting, may be amended, and is then adopted by majority vote or by general consent. The adoption of the agenda occurs after the meeting is called to order and a quorum is established.

Call to Order

The presiding officer calls the meeting to order at the scheduled time by rapping the gavel and announcing, "The meeting will please come to order," or, "The Annual Meeting of the American Institute of Parliamentarians is called to order."

Reading of Minutes

Unless there is an invocation, an opening ceremony, a roll call, the establishment of a quorum, adoption of convention rules of order, or approval of the agenda, the first item of business is the reading, correction, and approval of the minutes of the previous meeting. If minutes have been printed and sent to each member before the meeting, they usually are not read in the meeting or convention. However, the presiding officer must call for corrections to any minutes approved by the assembly. Corrections can be handled by general consent, but, in the case of a dispute, debate is permitted, and a majority vote is required to adopt a correction. After corrections, if any, the minutes can be adopted by general consent, or if in dispute, by a majority vote. If a minutes approval committee has approved the minutes, the approval is announced and no further action is required.

Postponement of Reading the Minutes

The reading of the unapproved minutes may be postponed to a certain time or to a subsequent meeting by general consent or by majority vote, although this generally is not advisable. If the reading of the minutes of several previous meetings has been postponed to the current meeting, the agenda should list them in chronological order for approval. For more information on minutes, see Chapter 25.

Reports of Officers

The presiding officer usually calls on the treasurer to give a brief report. This may consist simply of an oral report of the cash on hand.

The report may also include additional items such as outstanding obligations, or it may include a summary of collections and expenditures since the previous meeting, with mention of any unusual items. The presiding officer inquires whether there are any questions on the report. If questions are asked, the treasurer answers them. The presiding officer then states that the report of the treasurer will be filed. No action by the assembly is required on such a report. For more information on financial reporting, see Chapter 27.

Some organizations at this point in the order of business also call for reports from the president, secretary, or other officers. The secretary's report, if any, usually relates to official correspondence.

Reports of Committees

When there is a report of the board of directors or governing board, this report comes first. The presiding officer calls on the chairman of the board or board secretary, then standing committees, and then special committees to report. Written reports of committees are filed but not voted on, except where the organization's rules require specific reports to be approved by vote.

In constructing the proposed agenda, the presiding officer should be aware of which committees, standing or special, are prepared to report. Only those prepared to report should be called upon. Committees that are not called on to report may rise and request permission to report.

If an officer or committee also presents recommendations, these are considered and voted on either immediately after the report or under new business, as the organization chooses.

Unfinished Business

The presiding officer introduces unfinished business with the statement, "Unfinished business is now in order."

Unfinished business includes only two types of items:

1. Any motion or report that was being considered and was interrupted when the previous meeting adjourned
2. Any motion or report that was postponed to the current meeting except those which have been set for a particular hour on the agenda.

The presiding officer presents an item of unfinished business to the assembly by stating, for example, "The resolution concerning the use of the new social media technology was pending at the time of adjournment of the last meeting and is now before the assembly for consideration. The secretary will read that motion." After the motion is read, the presiding officer continues, "Discussion is now in order on the motion as read by the secretary."

The fact that a subject had been discussed previously does not make it unfinished business. Items of business that were referred to a committee are not unfinished business. In addition, an item of business not covered, because of adjournment, is not unfinished business, but may be placed on the next meeting's agenda as required. With the assistance of the secretary or parliamentarian, the presiding officer should determine whether there is any unfinished business for consideration, and if there is none, should announce this and immediately proceed to new business. The presiding officer should not ask for unfinished business.

New Business

The presiding officer opens new business by declaring, "New business is now in order."

New business includes any proposal that any member may wish to present to the assembly, except items of business that must be presented under other divisions of the order of business. If an agenda was adopted and items of business were placed under new business at that time, these items are automatically taken up in the designated sequence unless the assembly orders otherwise. The opportunity to present new proposals continues until the meeting is declared adjourned.

Announcements

A meeting is expedited by having a regular place in the order of business for announcements. After making announcements, the presiding officer may call for announcements from members.

Adjournment

When a motion to adjourn has been made, seconded, and adopted, the presiding officer formally ends the meeting by declaring it adjourned.

Alternatively, after asking, "Is there any further business?" and getting no response, the presiding officer assumes general consent and says, "There being no further business, the meeting is adjourned." Unless there is no quorum present, the presiding officer cannot, without a formal vote or general consent, declare the meeting adjourned if any member wishes to bring up additional business. The decision on whether to adjourn is made by the members, not by the presiding officer.

If a motion to adjourn is adopted and announcements have not already been made, they are usually permitted by the presiding officer before the actual declaration of adjournment.

Flexibility in the Agenda

Unless the organization has a rule to the contrary, the use of an adopted agenda does not preclude other items of business from being added, deleted, or moved around on the agenda during the meeting. An agenda is flexible, and may be changed by general consent or by a majority vote. For example, if a committee chair is absent but will be present later, the presiding officer may state, "The chair of the committee on finance is absent but will arrive later. Is there any objection to taking up the report of the special committee on offshore opportunities at this time? There being no objection, the chair of the special committee will report." If any one member objects, a vote must be taken to authorize the variation from the agenda.

While an agenda for a special meeting may not be added to, the agenda items may be taken up in a different order either by general consent or by a majority vote.

Consent Agenda

Organizations having a large number of routine or noncontroversial matters to approve can save time by use of a *consent agenda*, also called a *consent calendar*. This is a part of the printed agenda listing matters that are routine or expected to be noncontroversial and on which there are likely to be no questions or discussion.

Before taking the vote, the presiding officer allows time for the members to read the consent agenda to determine whether it includes any matters they may have a question on, or which they would like to discuss or perhaps vote against. A single member has a right to remove any item from the consent agenda, in which case it is transferred to the regular agenda so that it may be considered and voted on separately. A member may ask a question to clarify a consent agenda item without removing it from the consent agenda, but if this proves to be more than a clarification, the presiding officer can insist that it be removed and placed on the regular agenda. The remaining items are then approved *en bloc* (as a whole), by majority vote, without discussion, saving the time that would be required for individual consideration and votes.

The organization can adopt a special rule to determine who shall establish the consent agenda. Also, if the presiding officer or any member senses that the assembly could dispose of a large number of items *en bloc*, such as multiple recommendations from a committee, the presiding officer or the member can propose that they be considered as a consent agenda. When this is proposed, any member may remove any item from the group of items for individual consideration, and the remainder is voted *en bloc*.

For an organization that uses a consent agenda in conventions, see Chapter 23 for an extensive description of the use of the consent agenda by convention reference committees.

Priority Agenda

A *priority agenda* allows a meeting to take up important agenda items, or business of significant consequence, early in the meeting. This is useful when there are many items of business and limited time for their consideration. The items of business in the priority agenda are taken up after the consent agenda is disposed of.

The organization can adopt a standing or special rule to determine who decides the business items to be placed on a priority agenda. It could be, for example, the president of the organization alone, the officers, the executive committee, a reference committee, or a special committee. The assembly has final say on the priority items and can amend the priority agenda by majority vote or by general consent.

Chapter 15

QUORUM

A *quorum* is the minimum number or minimal proportion of the members of an organization that must be present at a meeting in order to transact business legally. If a quorum is not present, the presiding officer may call the meeting to order to establish that a meeting was held, but the organization may not transact business. However, agenda items that do not require official action may be dealt with, such as hearing reports, hearing speeches by guests, having a program, or other non-business activities . Urgent or emergency business can be conducted at the discretion of those in attendance, but if the business is not subsequently ratified at a meeting with a quorum present, all actions taken are the responsibility of the individuals in attendance, not the organization. The minutes will document that a meeting occurred, noting the absence of a quorum, and should briefly describe the activities that were conducted.

Quorum Requirements

The bylaws of an organization should state, as a minimum, the number or proportion of members that constitutes the quorum at board meetings and meetings of members. In the absence of such a bylaw clause or applicable statutory provision, under parliamentary law: (1) in the case of membership organizations with a verifiable roll of members, the quorum is fixed at a majority of the voting members[1]; and (2) in the case of organizations with an indefinite number of members, such as some churches or neighborhood groups that do not charge dues, the voting members who attend a meeting, however few in number, constitute a quorum.[2]

At members' meetings, this quorum requirement is often too high, and most groups have a more realistic provision. The number required for a quorum should be small enough to ensure that a quorum will usually be present but large enough to protect the organization against decisions being made by a small minority of the members. A mass meeting (organizing meeting) or an organization without a definite membership considers the members present, no matter what their number, as a quorum.

In organizations with a fluctuating membership, it may be wise to select a *proportion* of the membership as a quorum so the quorum will vary as the membership varies. Many organizations provide, for example, that one-eighth or one-tenth of the members constitutes a quorum. However, using a proportion of the membership as quorum may cause disputes when the membership number is not easily known at any particular time. When a fixed number is required for a quorum, a reduction or increase in the number of members of the organization does not alter the number constituting a quorum. Organizations that are incorporated should review the applicable corporate law in the jurisdiction of incorporation, as many jurisdictions' nonprofit corporation law includes a minimum quorum provision.

In conventions where the business of the organization is transacted by delegates who are expected to be present at all business meetings, the required quorum should be higher—for example, a majority of the delegates registered at the convention.

In some organizations, a quorum is defined as a proportion of members present and a proportion of constituencies present. For example, a quorum can be defined as 200 members present, representing at least 25 member clubs. This type of quorum is called a *qualified quorum*. It is useful when an organization requires a balance of representation from constituencies (or geographic regions) and members.

In boards and committees, the quorum is a majority of the members then in office unless set at a different level in the organization's rules or by statute. Neither a board nor a committee can set its own quorum unless expressly granted this authority by the membership.

Computing a Quorum

A quorum always refers to the number of members *present*, not to the number *voting*. If a quorum is present, a vote is valid even though fewer members than the number specified as present participated in the vote.

In computing a quorum, only members in good standing are counted. The meaning of the phrase "in good standing" varies with different organizations according to their bylaws. (See Chapter 29, the section "Member in Good Standing," for more information on the concept of in good standing). However, a member in good standing, or more frequently a member of the board, may be disqualified from voting on a particular question because of that member's personal interest in or benefit from it. Organizations should look to applicable law in their jurisdiction to ensure compliance with the quorum requirements and specifically where a member has declared a personal interest in a question currently before the body. In organizations adopting this book as their parliamentary authority, a member with a personal interest may not vote or debate on the matter, but if present, is counted toward the quorum unless the bylaws of the organization or applicable law requires otherwise. The presiding officer, if a member, is counted in computing a quorum.

If a quorum is present, a majority of those voting, which is often a small proportion of the total membership, has the right to make decisions for the organization. This fact suggests that rigorous and exacting requirements for notifying all members of meetings should be observed so that all members will have an opportunity to attend and vote.

Raising a Question on Quorum

It is the duty of the presiding officer to notify the assembly any time it becomes apparent that a quorum is not present. If the presiding officer fails to do so, any member who doubts that a quorum is present at a particular time during a meeting has the right to rise to a point of order and request that the members be counted (called a *quorum count*). A member may also ask the presiding officer whether a quorum is present. This question is in order at any time.

The presence of a quorum is determined by counting the members present or by calling the roll. The presence or absence of a quorum at any particular time can be established by entering the number present in the minutes. When a quorum is obviously present, the question of the presence of a quorum cannot be raised repeatedly for the purpose of delay.

Presumption of a Quorum

The question as to the presence of a quorum at the time of a vote on a particular motion must be raised at the time the vote is taken, if it is to be raised at all. It cannot be raised later. Unless the minutes document that a quorum was not present at the time of voting on a motion, it is presumed that since the minutes show that a quorum was present when the meeting began, a quorum continued to be present until recess or adjournment. It is not permissible at some later time to question the validity of an action on the grounds that there was not a quorum present at the time the vote was taken.[3] Some organizations, by custom, will call the roll after a substantial break in the proceedings and always after an overnight recess.

Chapter 16

DEBATE

The purpose of deliberative bodies is to secure the collective judgment of the group on proposals submitted to it for decision. This purpose is best served by free exchange of ideas through discussion and debate before the deliberative body makes a final decision on the pending question.

The Right of Debate

The right of every member to participate in the discussion of any matter of business that comes before the assembly is one of the fundamental principles of parliamentary law. Every member may speak for or against a motion; the maker of the motion, while the need is unusual, may speak against the motion he or she moved.

Debate is regulated by parliamentary rules in order to assure every member a reasonable and equal opportunity to speak. Knowledge of the rules governing debate is essential to every member.

Extent of Debate on Motions

Motions are classified into three groups according to the extent of debate that is permitted on them. The groups are:

1. Motions that are fully debatable
2. Motions that are debatable with restrictions
3. Motions that are not debatable

Motions that are *fully debatable* are those that may require unlimited discussion in order for the group to reach a decision. These motions are: main motions, to amend a previous action, to rescind, to ratify, to amend (unless applied to an undebatable motion), to adopt in-lieu-of, and to appeal.

There are eight motions that are *debatable with restrictions:* the privileged motions to adjourn and to recess; the subsidiary motions to limit debate, to postpone to a certain time, to refer to a committee, and to amend a motion for which debate is restricted; and the specific main motions to recall a motion or subject from a committee (or board) and to reconsider. Debate on these motions is restricted to a brief time and to specific points. The restrictions can be viewed as an application of the rule that debate must be germane, since the restrictions require debate to be limited to the merits of the proposal and to the characteristics of the particular motion.

All other motions are *not debatable* and must be put to a vote immediately. To permit debate on a motion to close debate, for example, would defeat the purpose of the motion.

Obtaining the Floor for Debate

As soon as a debatable motion has been stated to the assembly by the presiding officer, any member has the right to discuss it after obtaining the floor. A member waits until no one has the floor, then rises, addresses the presiding officer, and waits for recognition. The floor is obtained in this manner whether the purpose is to present a motion or to participate in discussion. In a large meeting or convention, special rules may be adopted describing the method to be used to obtain the floor. (A limited number of undebatable motions allow a member priority to the floor, but these motions deal with emergency actions or actions that must be taken prior to the final decision of the assembly.)

A member who has been recognized is entitled to be heard so long as the rules of debate are observed.

Recognition of Members During Debate

When no member has the floor, usually the first person who rises and asks for recognition is entitled to be recognized. When several members seek recognition at the same time, the following rules help the presiding officer decide which member should be recognized first:

1. The person who has proposed a motion or the committee member who has presented a report should be allowed the first opportunity to explain the motion or report, and is usually

given the opportunity to speak again when it appears that all others who wish to do so have spoken.

2. A member who has not spoken on the immediately pending motion has prior claim over one who has already spoken on the motion. Similarly, a member who seldom speaks should be given preference over one who claims the attention of the assembly frequently.

3. The presiding officer should alternate between proponents and opponents of a motion whenever possible. When there are opposing opinions, the presiding officer may inquire of a member seeking recognition which viewpoint the member will represent, or may ask if there are members wishing to speak to the position opposite that of the member who has just spoken. Thus the presiding officer is able to divide the opportunities to speak equitably.

Speaking More Than Once

It is important that the debate be balanced. No member, or small group of members, should be permitted to monopolize the discussion. In particular, a group of members should not be permitted to dominate debate to the extent that only one side of the issue is presented, and even more so if that group then attempts to close debate before opposing opinions are heard. In the interest of balanced participation, good decision making, and the protection of the rights of the minority, the presiding officer should ensure that such strategies are not allowed.

If members wish to speak, they should be recognized in preference to the member who has already spoken on a question. However, if no other members seek recognition, a member who has already spoken may be recognized again.

Sometimes a few members who are interested in and informed on the subject being discussed will speak several times on that particular question. This is permissible, provided that members who have not already spoken are not seeking recognition.

What Is Not Debate?

A brief comment or remark by the proposer of a motion before stating it is generally permissible. Similarly, a very brief explanatory remark or a question is sometimes permitted on an undebatable motion. An inquiry, or a brief suggestion or explanation, is not debate.

When debate has been limited and a member responds to a question asked through the presiding officer, the reply is not debate, and the time is not subtracted from the time allotted to the speaker. However, the presiding officer must ensure that both the question and answer are as brief as possible and that neither evolves into debate.

Before voting on a question, every member is entitled to know precisely what the question is and what its effects will be, and is entitled to ask for a reasonable explanation or to raise an inquiry. Such an inquiry is not considered debate. A member has the right to have a motion restated before voting or at any time when there is uncertainty about its meaning or wording. Such a request is not debate.

Relevancy in Debate

All discussion must be relevant or *germane* to the motion before the assembly. A member who is given the floor may use that privilege only for the purpose of discussing the pending question or making a permissible motion. Discussion that departs from the subject is out of order. Illustrations or stories may be used in discussing a point so long as they are relevant to the motion under discussion.

Discussion is always restricted as much as possible to the immediately pending motion. When a motion is under discussion and a motion of higher rank is made, discussion is confined to the motion of higher rank until it is decided or until a higher ranking motion is proposed. Occasionally, brief mention of lower-ranking motions may be appropriate while debating the immediately pending motion; for example, with an amendment immediately pending, its impact on the general intent of the main motion may be considered germane, or with a motion to refer immediately pending, a brief statement of a preference for adoption of a pending amendment to the main motion is permissible. Another example is the occasion when the urgency of adoption of the main motion might sometimes be germane to the need for referral.

If a speaker departs from the subject, the presiding officer should interrupt and request that the speaker's remarks be limited to the pending motion. If the presiding officer fails to do this, any member may rise to a point of order and call the attention of the presiding officer to the speaker's digression. The presiding officer should then direct the speaker to limit discussion to the motion before the assembly.

Dilatory Tactics

Dilatory tactics—that is, delaying the proposal or the vote on a subject by making unnecessary motions, asking pointless questions, or talking around and not on the question—are always out of order. As soon as it is evident that a member or group of members is using dilatory tactics, the presiding officer should point out that such conduct is not in order. If members persist, the presiding officer should refuse to recognize them or should rule the dilatory tactics to be out of order.

Members' Conduct During Debate

Debate must be impersonal. All discussion is addressed to or through the presiding officer and must never be directed to any individual. The motion, not the advocate, is the subject of debate. A motion—its nature or consequences—may be attacked vigorously. It is never permissible to attack the motives, character, or personality of a member either directly or by innuendo or implication. It is the duty of the presiding officer to quickly stop any member who engages in personal attacks, discusses the motives of another member, or speaks or acts in a discourteous manner. Debate must address the merits of a motion, not people.

Out of respect for the time of other members, arguments and opinions should be stated as concisely as possible. A speech is made not for the pleasure of the speaker or for the entertainment of others, but to assist the assembly in arriving at a decision on the question under consideration.

A member is more likely to be effective in debate when demonstrating courtesy toward the presiding officer and other members. Anyone who uses improper language or acts in a disorderly manner should be called to order promptly by the presiding officer. When a point of order is raised concerning a speaker's conduct, the speaker must be seated until the point of order is decided by the presiding officer.

A member who fails or refuses to speak in an orderly and courteous manner may be denied the right to the floor and, if necessary, may be expelled from the meeting by order of the presiding officer or by a vote of the assembly.

Members who do not have the floor should listen attentively and respectfully to the remarks of the speaker. Good decision making is more likely to take place if members judge the speaker's remarks on their merits, and not on the perceived merits of the speaker.

Presiding Officer's Duties during Debate

The presiding officer has the responsibility of controlling and expediting debate. A member who has been given the floor has a right to the undivided attention of the assembly. It is the duty of the presiding officer to protect the speaker in this right by suppressing disorder, by eliminating whispering and walking about, and by preventing annoyance, heckling, or unnecessary interruptions. The presiding officer should insist that every member be attentive to the business before the assembly. The assembly owes respectful attention to the presiding officer and to each speaker.

It is also the presiding officer's duty to keep the subject clearly before the members, to rule out any irrelevant discussion, and to restate the motion whenever necessary. The presiding officer must make sure that the assembly is aware of the immediately pending motion at all times.

If there are aspects of the motion that are being overlooked, the presiding officer may ask questions that will stimulate discussion of those points. The presiding officer must remain impartial when providing guidance and comments, but should seek to draw out all facts that will contribute to a clear understanding of the motion and its effects, thus leading to a better-informed decision by the assembly. The presiding officer must refrain from participating personally in debate.

It is sometimes appropriate for the presiding officer to call on someone else, in accordance with any provisions in the bylaws, to preside while the presiding officer vacates the chair to participate in debate. In such a case, the presiding officer should not resume the chair until the pending main motion is disposed of .[1] Considerable care should be exercised to ensure that the presiding officer does not exhibit any bias on the pending business while actually presiding.

Time Limits on Debate

Parliamentary law fixes no limit on the length of time or number of speeches during debate. Each organization has the right to establish limits on debate if the members wish to do so. Debate can ordinarily be kept within reasonable time limits by the presiding officer's insistence that all discussion be confined strictly to the subject. However, especially in meetings with large memberships and extensive agendas, assemblies may find it necessary to adopt limits on the duration or number of speeches that members may make on any pending motion. Such restrictions often increase the opportunities for more members to participate in debate and the likelihood of timely completion of the assembly's business.

If debate has been limited, time allocated to one member cannot be transferred to another member. In legislative bodies, members may yield portions of debate time to other members, but this is not permitted in ordinary organizations.

Cutting Off Debate

It is unwise to make a practice of cutting off or preventing debate on most debatable questions. This is applicable whether debate is closed or limited by recognized motions or by arbitrarily bringing questions to vote without adequate opportunity for discussion. Members cannot be expected to maintain interest in an organization if they are frequently denied the right to participate in its deliberations, and assemblies cannot be expected to make good decisions if voting occurs before there is adequate opportunity to learn the facts that bear on the pending motion and to hear the opinions of others.

Bringing a Question to Vote

When it appears that all the members who wish to speak have done so, the presiding officer inquires, "Is there any further discussion?" If there is no further discussion, the presiding officer should take the vote on the pending question. For more information on the motion to close debate and vote immediately, see Chapter 9. The presiding officer should never end discussion arbitrarily. It should be ended only by the assembly, whether by general consent (that is, by silence when the presiding officer asks for further discussion), by a vote on the motion to close debate, or by a previously adopted limitation on debate.

The presiding officer does, however, have a responsibility to assist the assembly in disposing of its business efficiently. If all debate has been on one side of an issue and the presiding officer has called for debate on the other side with no response, it may be appropriate to ask the assembly, "Are you ready to vote?" Members still seeking the floor, seeing no opposition to their position, may be willing to proceed directly to a vote, or a member may move to close debate and vote immediately.

If the presiding officer starts to put the question to a vote prematurely, this does not cut off the right of a member to speak. A member, if reasonably prompt in claiming the floor, can assert the right to speak at any time before the vote is taken. After the presiding officer has begun to take the vote, no further debate is permitted.

Informal Consideration

There are times when it is wise to set aside the formal rules governing discussion and have relaxed rules of debate. These objectives may be accomplished by a motion to consider a particular motion, subject, or problem informally. Informal consideration permits freedom in the length and number of speeches, allows possible amendments and motions to be discussed together, and gives broader latitude in debate. For more information on the incidental motion to consider informally, see Chapter 11.

There are two basic types of events that may require informal consideration (consideration without the strict rules of debate of the organization). One is when an idea or concept is presented that is not ready to be stated as a motion. The other is when the pending motion requires more informal deliberations.

There are times when it is desirable to have discussion of a problem *precede* the proposal of a motion so that some agreement may be reached on the type and wording of the motion that is needed. Sometimes an assembly wishes to consider a problem that is not sufficiently understood or formulated for a member to propose a clear and adequate motion covering it. There may not be time to refer the problem to a committee. Informal discussion often brings understanding and agreement and makes it evident how the motion should be worded. Rather than offer a poorly framed motion, which will consume time and effort to perfect by amendment, it is better to consider the problem informally and then formulate a good motion.

For example, a member might say, "We realize that some action must be taken to raise more funds for this organization. I move that we consider informally the problem of fund raising." If this motion is adopted, the presiding officer opens the problem to informal discussion. When the problem is clarified and there appears to be a solution or a consensus, a member should offer a motion embodying the idea. This motion automatically terminates the informal discussion, and the motion is considered and voted on under the regular rules of debate. On the other hand, if no agreement on the problem is reached, informal discussion may be terminated by a motion to end the informal discussion.

If a motion is already being considered by the assembly, the motion to consider the pending motion informally is an incidental motion. If it is adopted, the pending motion is considered informally until the members decide to take a vote on it. This vote or the presentation of another permissible motion (such as an amendment, referral, or postponement) terminates the informal discussion. The remaining consideration of the motion is conducted under the assembly's usual rules of debate.

Chapter 17

VOTES REQUIRED FOR VALID ACTIONS

Assemblies express their will on proposals by voting. The proper method to determine the outcome of a vote must be understood in order to determine whether or not proposals have been properly approved and thus become valid actions of the assembly. This chapter presents details of determining the outcome of a vote.

Significance of a Majority Vote

One of the fundamental concepts in a democracy is that the ultimate authority lies in a majority of the citizens of the democracy. Likewise in an organization, the ultimate authority lies in a majority of the members when they meet to take action through majority votes. This fundamental principle of voting allows members to democratically and legitimately operate their organization. A majority vote is required to take an action. A *majority vote* in this book, unless otherwise qualified, is defined as a majority of the legal votes cast by members present and voting. Thomas Jefferson said, "Until a majority has spoken, nothing has changed." To permit less than a majority to decide for any group would subject the many to the rule of the few, and this would be contrary to the most basic democratic principle. Democratic peoples universally accept decision by majority vote.

If a majority agrees, that is an agreement by the body since all members by the act of joining the organization have agreed that the majority should govern. For more discussion on the relationship between members and the organization, see Chapter 29.

As a general principle of good governance, an organization should not authorize less than a majority to decide anything. Likewise, more than a majority, sometimes called a *supermajority*, should also not be required for most decisions. However, some organizations do adopt a rule that permits a mere plurality—for example, one vote more than any other candidate receives—to elect an officer or director. Others go to the other extreme of requiring a high vote, sometimes as high as an 80 percent vote, on certain proposals. The requirement of an 80 percent vote to adopt a measure allows one-fifth of the members to control the decision on that measure. Sometimes such policies may be justified, but they should be used with great caution since under either of these rules the minority, not the majority, controls.

Any requirements permitting decisions by *less* than a majority vote (for example, by plurality as in an election) or requiring *more* than a majority vote (for example, a two-thirds vote on a substantive proposal) are not valid unless they are included in a statute, the charter, or the bylaws. An exception is made for procedural rules in the parliamentary authority or standing or special rules of order, where, for example, the decision to close debate may require more than a majority vote. These procedural exceptions are in place to protect the rights of the minority.

Requiring More Than a Majority Vote

Sometimes members mistakenly assume that the higher the vote required for taking an action, the more democratic the process is and that it provides for greater protection of members' rights. The opposite is true. Whenever a vote of more than a majority is required to take an action, control is taken from the majority and given to a minority. For example, when a two-thirds vote is required, the minority needs to be only more than one-third of the votes cast to defeat the proposal. Thus a minority is permitted to overrule the will not only of the majority, but of almost two-thirds of the members. If a two-thirds vote is required to pass a proposal and 65 members vote for the proposal and 33 members vote against it, the 33 members have won; the 65 have been defeated. This is minority rule, not majority rule.

The higher the vote required, the smaller the minority to which control passes. The requirement of a unanimous vote means that one member can overrule the will of all other members.

Recognizing that a decision by a majority vote is an integral and vital element of democracy was clearly stated by Thomas Jefferson in a letter to Baron von Humboldt in 1817:

> The first principle of republicanism is that the *lex majoris partis* is the fundamental law of every society of individuals of equal rights; to consider the will of the society enounced by the

majority of a single vote, as sacred as if unanimous, is the first of all lessons in importance, yet the last which is thoroughly learnt. This law once disregarded, there is no other but that of force, which ends necessarily in military despotism.

One exception to the principle of requiring only a majority vote is when a vote has an adverse impact on the rights of the members. For example, members have the right of full and free discussion. This right can be restricted but only by a two-thirds vote, such as required by the motions to limit debate or to close debate. Another exception is when there is an immediate need to suspend the rules of order to do something that could not be done under the current rules. While the urgency may be real, common parliamentary law requires a two-thirds vote to suspend the rules in order to avoid abuse of such a powerful rule by a slim majority. Another exception is when the rights of absentees are involved. For example, most organizations stipulate in their bylaws that the bylaws can be amended only by a two-thirds vote (and in most cases, advance notice is also required). Bylaws of some nonprofit corporations (and some corporation codes) require a two-thirds vote to buy or sell real estate or to mortgage property owned by the organization.

As a general rule, it is unwise to require more than a majority vote to commit the organization to a course of action because of the power it gives to a minority to override the majority's wishes.

Requiring Less Than a Majority Vote

The effect of deciding proposals or electing candidates by less than a majority vote is similar to requiring a higher vote than a majority. It takes away the power of decision making from the majority and gives it to a minority.

Electing a candidate or deciding a proposal by plurality vote (more votes than any other candidate or alternative proposal) means that officers may be chosen by a minority and that they therefore do not have the support that is behind a candidate chosen by a majority. If there are a large number of candidates for an office, the candidate elected may be chosen by only a small fraction of the members of the organization. Therefore, no candidate may be elected to office and no proposal may be decided except by a majority vote, unless the bylaws provide otherwise.

Importance of Defining the Vote Required

Every organization should state in its bylaws the vote required for election of candidates and also the vote required for important decisions. Whenever the basis on which a vote must be computed is not defined in statute, charter, or bylaws, it is a majority of the legal votes cast by members present and voting.

The term *majority vote* sometimes causes controversy when the basis for computing the majority is not stated clearly. Hundreds of cases have wound up in the courts because of the resulting confusion. For this reason, whenever such terms as *majority, two-thirds, three-fourths,* and *unanimous vote* are used in bylaws or in standing rules, it is advisable to qualify them by stating clearly the basis on which the vote is to be computed.

Different Meanings of Majority Vote

A majority vote, or any other vote, may be qualified or defined in many ways. For example, consider an organization consisting of 100 memberships (limited to 100 members) that currently has 80 members in good standing, with a quorum requirement of one-eighth of all the memberships, which is 13. If there are 75 members present at a meeting and only 10 members vote, a majority vote could be variously computed as follows:

A majority of all the membership positions	51
A majority of the members in good standing	41
A majority of the members present	38
A majority of a quorum	7
A majority of the legal votes cast	6

A *majority vote of all the membership positions* is often required to take an action in organizations having a fixed number of members. When this rule is applied to a board of education that has eight membership positions, a majority is five. If there are two vacancies, reducing the actual number of members to six, the required vote is still five because a majority of the eight membership positions of the board is necessary to adopt a proposal.

A *majority vote of all the members in good standing* means a vote of more than half of all the members both present and absent. Such a vote is often required in organizations in which the members serve in a representative capacity, such as a house of delegates or an executive board. (For a definition of *good standing,* see "Member in Good Standing" in Chapter 29.)

A *majority vote of the members present* is sometimes required to take an action. Under this rule, the failure of some members to vote does not reduce the number of affirmative votes required. If there are 75 members present, an affirmative vote of 38 is necessary to act, regardless of the number of members voting. In large assemblies a vote based on a majority of the members present can cause problems if votes are generally close and an ongoing tally of those arriving or leaving the assembly is not maintained.

A *majority vote of the quorum*, or a majority of the number of members who are authorized to act for the organization, is the minimum number that some organizations require to make a decision for all the members. It means a majority of those present and voting, assuming a quorum is present, with the further stipulation that the affirmative vote must include a majority of the number required for a quorum. For example, suppose a board consists of nine members and the quorum is five, with a majority of the quorum being three. There are five members present at a meeting and two vote for a proposal, one votes against it, and two abstain from voting. Because the passage of a motion requires at least three affirmative votes, the motion would fail—even though it has a two-thirds vote of those "present and voting" at a legally constituted meeting. In essence, in this example, those abstaining have been counted in the negative, whereas in normal majority voting their abstentions would be ignored in computing the result.

A *majority of the legal votes cast* is the requirement that most commonly approves a motion or elects a candidate. When the term "majority" is not qualified and no type of majority is specified, the law holds that a majority of the legal votes cast is required. This decision has been agreed on to resolve some of the confusion that resulted when the basis for counting a majority was not defined. Unless it is qualified in some way, a majority vote means a majority of the legal votes cast by members present and voting. Unless stated otherwise, this is the meaning of a majority vote when used in this book. For a discussion of what constitutes a legal ballot, see Chapter 19.

In the case of an election by mail, if the law, charter, or bylaws do not specify the requirement to elect a candidate to office, the requirement is a majority of the legal votes cast, regardless of the number of votes received.

The legal theory behind which the decisions of an organization may be made by a majority of those present and voting, a quorum being present, is that all members have the right to attend meetings and to vote. The members who fail to attend or to vote are presumed to have waived exercising their rights and to have consented to allow the will of the organization to be expressed by those present and voting. The result of a vote is based on the number of members present *and* voting. An abstention is not considered a vote and is therefore not counted in determining the result. A member who abstains has in fact relinquished his or her vote.

It is possible for a majority to consist of only one vote. A member may propose a motion that is of little interest to other members, and when the presiding officer calls for a vote, the proposer votes aye and no one votes no. The question is adopted because it received a majority of the legal votes cast. A single affirmative vote, when there are no other votes cast, has been held by the courts to approve a motion because that vote is the majority of the legal votes cast.

Abstentions

A member has the right to abstain from voting on any motion, and *must* abstain from voting if the member has a financial interest or conflict of interest in the outcome of the vote. When a member must abstain from voting because of a conflict of interest and the majority of legal votes cast is not the requirement to adopt a proposal or elect a person to office, the organization must make clear in its bylaws the vote that is required to adopt a proposal.

Plurality Vote

A plurality vote means more votes than the number received by any other candidate or alternative proposition. There is no requirement in plurality voting that a candidate or any proposition receive a majority vote. Thus, it may be less than a majority, and often is, when there are more than two choices. A plurality vote does not elect a candidate or adopt a motion except when the bylaws provide for a decision by plurality vote. For example, the result of a vote might be as shown below:

Candidate	Number of votes
Candidate A	100
Candidate B	90
Candidate C	80

The total number of votes is 270. The first candidate has a plurality, but no candidate has received a majority vote (136). If election to office is by plurality vote, Candidate A is elected. But if the election requires a majority vote to elect, no candidate is elected, and another ballot must be taken.

While election by plurality is simple and fast, it is usually not advisable. In the above example, for instance, Candidate A might represent an extreme viewpoint, whereas Candidates B and C both represent moderate viewpoints, and perhaps a majority of the members would consider either of them preferable to Candidate A. Nevertheless, with plurality voting, the wishes of the majority in such a case would be thwarted, and Candidate A would be elected with 37 percent of the vote. In subsequent votes, as would be necessary with a majority requirement to elect, one of the moderate candidates might pick up enough votes from the other to win; or, as often happens, the weaker candidate, recognizing a hopeless situation, might withdraw. In either case, the interests of the majority are served.

For the foregoing reason, when a majority is required to elect, repeated voting is required unless the bylaws or rules of the organization have designated some method other than repeated voting. One such method is to omit the candidate receiving the lowest number of votes on the second ballot. If that fails to produce a majority, the process of eliminating the lowest candidate is repeated again. Another method is the "runoff" system, with the second ballot being limited to the two candidates who received the most votes on the first ballot. Before an election takes place, the organization should establish a clear rule stating what will be done when no candidate obtains a majority. This will avoid the assembly determining the rules at the last minute in the middle of an election or important vote.

Unanimous Vote

A unanimous vote on a proposal is a vote in which all the legal votes cast are on the same side, whether affirmative or negative.

A unanimous vote for a candidate for a particular office is a vote in which one candidate receives all the legal votes cast for that office.

The essence of a unanimous vote is that all those who vote cast their votes on the same side of a proposal or for one candidate. A proposal is adopted unanimously if one vote is cast for it and no vote is cast against it, or is defeated unanimously if no vote is cast for it and one vote is cast against it.

If the term "unanimous vote" is qualified in some way, the qualification determines the meaning of that particular unanimous vote. For example, the unanimous vote of "all the members of the board" means that all the members of the board must be present and that all of them must vote on the same side of a proposal. A unanimous vote of all the "members present" means that all the members who are present must vote and that all of them must vote on the same side of a proposal.

A requirement that an action be taken only by unanimous vote is an example of decision by minority—in this case a minority of one—and is a violation of the democratic principle of decision by majority. It gives the minority "an absolute, permanent, all-inclusive power of veto." In 1693, the court of the King's Bench ruled that "the major number must bind the lesser, or else differences could never be determined."[1] The requirement of a unanimous vote is seldom necessary or wise.

Tie Vote

A tie vote on a *motion* means that the same number of members has voted in the affirmative as in the negative. Since a majority vote, or more than half of the legal votes cast, is required to adopt a motion, an equal or tie vote means that the motion is defeated. It is a common misconception that a tie vote on a motion is a deadlock vote that must be resolved, but in fact, a tie vote is simply not a majority vote, and the motion is defeated.

A tie vote that constitutes a *deadlock* that must be resolved can occur only when two or more candidates, or two or more alternative propositions, are being voted on at the same time and two or more of them receive the same number of votes. Then no candidate has been elected and no proposal has been adopted. Such a tie vote results in a deadlock, and the vote must be retaken until the tie vote is resolved by additional voting or is resolved by some other method the assembly may choose.

Vote of the Presiding Officer

No officer relinquishes the rights of membership by accepting office, except that the presiding officer of an assembly should not propose motions or generally participate in debate. The presiding officer, if a member of the assembly, does have the right to cast a vote. However, in an assembly the presiding officer customarily exercises that right only when the vote is by ballot or when his or her vote will make a difference in the result. This preserves the presiding officer's duty of impartiality and objectivity. The presiding officer cannot be required to cast a vote.

In case of a tie vote, the presiding officer, if a member of the assembly, may vote with either side, thereby establishing a majority, provided that the presiding officer has not already voted. Or the presiding officer may choose not to vote, in which case, lacking a majority, the motion is defeated.

If a motion is about to be adopted by a single vote, the presiding officer may choose to vote against it, thereby *creating* a tie, in which case, lacking a majority, the motion is lost.

Although a tie vote is not an issue in matters requiring a two-thirds vote for decision, there are situations in which the presiding officer, not having voted, may wish to do so to change the outcome of the vote.

When voting is by ballot, the presiding officer (if a member of the organization) casts a ballot at the same time as other members. But in such cases, if a tie results, the presiding officer cannot break the tie by voting a second time unless the bylaws provide that this may be done in case of a deadlock tie vote. Such a provision in the bylaws is often based on a misunderstanding that a tie vote cannot decide a proposal, and that the tie must therefore be resolved. This assumption is not correct, and if this is the only basis for such a provision, it may be unwise to give the presiding officer a vote in excess of that of any other member.

Computation of a Two-Thirds Vote

In calculating whether a two-thirds vote has been attained or not, the presiding officer should first double the negative vote. Second, if the affirmative vote is equal to or higher than the negative vote doubled, the proposal has obtained the necessary two-thirds vote and is adopted.

For example, if the vote is 87 in favor and 44 opposed, the motion fails, because twice 44 is 88, and the affirmative vote is one short of that number.

Computing a Majority for Separate Questions

When more than one question is voted on at the same time or is on the same ballot, the number of votes cast, on each question, is counted separately. A majority of the legal votes cast relating to each particular question is required to approve that question.

In an election, when candidates for more than one office are voted on at the same time, a majority of the legal votes cast for each particular office is required to elect a candidate to that office.

Computing a Majority When Electing a Group

Frequently candidates for several positions or offices of *equal* rank, such as members of a board, committee, or group of delegates, are voted on at the same time. With offices of equal rank and no differentiation between the offices, the majority vote required to elect is computed differently.

When several equal positions are voted on simultaneously, the majority vote is based on the total number of ballots cast, not the number of votes cast for each position. The ballots cast must contain at least one legal vote for the group of equal offices.

When several offices of equal rank are being voted on simultaneously and require a majority vote, there are two requirements for election, as follows:

1. The nominee must receive a majority vote based on the total number of ballots cast for all of the equal offices.
2. Among those nominees receiving such a majority vote, those receiving the highest vote are declared elected.

A candidate who receives a majority vote but who fails to rank high enough to place within the number of offices to be filled is not elected. Similarly, a candidate who ranks among the highest candidates but does not receive a majority vote is not elected. For example, if five board members are to be elected at the same time and there are seven nominees for these five positions, with 95 members voting, the vote might result as follows:

Nominee	Number of Votes
A	80
B	79
C	75
D	75
E	69
F	52
G	43

Six members received the necessary majority vote (48), but only the top five are elected. The two nominees who tied for third and fourth place are both elected. Therefore, there is no need to break this tie vote. However, had there been a tie between the fifth and sixth places, it would have been necessary to vote again to determine who was elected.

If only three of the nominees had received a majority vote, only those three would have been elected; it would then be necessary to take another vote to fill the two remaining vacancies. Unless the assembly adopts a motion to the contrary, all nominees except the three already elected remain candidates on the second ballot, whether it is needed to resolve a tie or to complete an election in which insufficient candidates were elected.

Double Majority

Some organizations consist of individual members and caucuses (often a geographic region). For large expenditures or important decisions that significantly affect the organization, a double majority vote may be required to adopt a proposal. A *double majority* means that a majority of the individual members and a majority of the caucuses must vote in favor of the proposal for it to be adopted. This type of voting is seen as fair when the caucuses are of different voting strength. For example, a national organization may have a constituent unit with 50 members, while another has 9 members. This is 59 members and 59 votes at the member level. At the caucus level there are only two votes. If the larger constituency favors a proposal while the smaller does not, the vote at the membership level could be 50 for and 9 against. However, at the caucus level, the vote would be 1 for and 1 against. A double majority vote requirement may balance the voting strength between the constituent units and, in addition, may ensure group decisions to be acceptable to a broader base of support.

Such votes, if carefully designed, can be taken with one ballot. With electronic voting the process is much simpler.

Voting Separately for Equal Positions

Some organizations favor differentiating between equal positions by numbering each position and nominating candidates separately for each position. For example, candidates A, B, and C might be nominated as candidates for Board Vacancy No. 1, and candidates D and E for Board Vacancy No. 2. In this case, a majority of the legal votes cast for each particular position would elect a candidate. This practice may result in the defeat of a popular candidate and the election of an unpopular one. In the example given, candidates A, B, and C might be much more popular than the other candidates, but two of them are sure to be defeated, while with candidate D or E, despite relative unpopularity, one is sure to be elected.

Sometimes the reason for differentiating is that one of the terms is, for example, for two years and the other one is for one year. A common way of handling this situation is for the two candidates receiving the highest vote to be declared elected, with the allocation of terms to be determined by lot, or with the successful candidate or candidates receiving the highest vote obtaining the longest term or terms and the successful candidate or candidates with the next highest vote receiving the next longest term or terms. If the method is not specified in the bylaws or in the standing rules, a motion clarifying the procedure should be made prior to the election.

When Members Cannot Vote

Membership in an organization carries with it the fundamental right to vote on proposals. However, there are certain situations in which a member has no right to vote.

As a general principle, a member having a direct personal or financial interest in a matter should not vote on it. (Stockholders are an exception to this.) For example, if a motion is made to award a contract to a member, the member cannot legally vote on it. (See "Conflicts of Interest" in Chapter 21.) Courts have recognized an exception to this rule when the organization is authorized to fix the compensation of its members; otherwise, it would be impossible to vote to fix the compensation.

A member may vote on a question involving the whole organization when others are equally affected by the vote, even though the member has a direct personal or financial interest. For example, every member has the right to vote on a motion that determines convention expenses to be paid to delegates by the organization.

When charges have been made against a member, that member cannot vote on the charges. However, if other members are also named in the charges, all members can vote on the charges. This rule prevents a small proportion of members from gaining control of an organization by filing charges against the majority of the members.

Chapter 18

METHODS OF VOTING

A member of any democratic body has the fundamental right to participate in electing officers and in deciding issues. In an assembly, a vote is a formal expression of the will of the assembly.

While it is the right of each member to vote on every question, in ordinary assemblies the members cannot be compelled to vote.

The proposer of a motion has the same right as any other member to speak for or against the motion, or to vote for or against it. The person who proposed a motion may have changed his or her opinion during the course of discussion, or the motion itself may have been changed by amendment.

Voting in Meetings

When not prescribed in the bylaws, the method of voting on a motion or candidate is usually determined by the presiding officer. At any time before the vote is taken, the assembly may also determine the method of voting by majority vote. The usual methods of voting are:

1. General consent
2. Voice vote
3. Standing vote or show of hands
4. Roll call
5. Ballot

As a practical matter it is best that visitors and nonvoting members be seated separately from the voting members to ensure that only voting members vote. Some organizations define such seating arrangements through a standing or special rule of order.

Voting by General Consent

Routine or noncontroversial questions are often decided by *general consent*—without taking a formal vote. When members are in general agreement, this method (sometimes called *unanimous consent*) saves time and expedites business.

For example, if a member moves, "That the calling of the roll be dispensed with," the presiding officer may respond, "It has been moved and seconded that the calling of the roll be dispensed with. Is there any objection to dispensing with the calling of the roll?" If any member says, "I object," a vote must be taken on the motion.

The presiding officer may propose action by general consent without any motion, or may proceed by assuming general consent. For example, if a member asks to make an announcement at an unusual time, the presiding officer may say, "If there is no objection, the member will be allowed to make an announcement now." Even when the presiding officer has announced that an action has been taken by general consent, if any member immediately objects, the question must be stated and voted on. If no one objects promptly, the motion is adopted by general consent, and the presiding officer moves on to other business.

Voice Vote

Voting by voice is the most commonly used method of voting. The presiding officer determines the result of the vote by the volume of voices. When there is doubt as to how the majority voted, the presiding officer should call for the vote again, asking for a standing vote (a division of the assembly) or a show of hands. These kinds of votes can be counted.

Any member who believes that a vote is indecisive or that the presiding officer has not announced it correctly may interrupt, if necessary, and call for a division of the assembly to verify the vote. This right continues even after the vote has been announced and another speaker has claimed the floor, but the right must be exercised before the speaker has begun to speak.

In taking a vote by any method, the presiding officer must always call for the affirmative vote first and announce it first.

The negative vote must always be called for, even if the affirmative vote appears to be overwhelming or unanimous. The only exception is a courtesy vote. For example, the presiding officer should call for only the affirmative vote on a motion thanking a speaker for participating.

Standing Vote

A standing vote (also called a rising vote) may be used by the presiding officer to verify an indecisive vote or in response to a call from a member for a division of the assembly. The vote on a motion requiring a definite number or proportion of votes, such as two-thirds, is usually taken initially by standing so that a count may be made if necessary.

When the standing vote is close, the members should be counted; they *must* be counted if a count is demanded by a member and if there is any doubt as to the result of the vote. The presiding officer usually asks the secretary to count the vote. However, in a convention or a large meeting, the presiding officer appoints several tellers, including a head teller, to assist. Each teller counts a particular section of voters, and the head teller reports the numbers of votes for and against to the assembly or sometimes only to the presiding officer. The presiding officer then repeats the totals and announces the result: "The vote is 99 affirmative, 101 negative. The motion is defeated."

In very large assemblies, one way of ensuring accuracy in counting a standing vote is a *serpentine* count. Members in favor stand. Then, beginning with the first row, each person counts off and sits down, with the count running back and forth along the rows in serpentine fashion. When all who voted in the affirmative are seated, the same is done with the negative vote. This minimizes the risk of any error in the count, increases the confidence in the result of the vote, and is conducted quickly when the assembly is accustomed to this method.

When visitors or others who are not entitled to vote are seated with voting members, voting methods should be used that ensure that only voting members participate in voting. Such methods include requiring the use of a voting card, electronic keypad, or taking a roll call vote.

Show of Hands

In boards, committees, and small assemblies, the chair will usually ask for a show of hands rather than a standing vote. And even in large assemblies a show of hands may be used at the discretion of the chair, because it is usually quicker and simpler. In a large assembly, however, when a vote needs to be counted, a standing vote usually ensures greater accuracy.

Many organizations issue voting cards to voting members of the assembly. The voting cards are rectangular and often colored; the members when voting use the voting cards by raising them in a show of hands vote to accentuate their vote. This makes it easier for the presiding officer to determine the result of the vote.

Roll Call Vote

A recorded vote is often advantageous when members vote as representatives of others—for example, delegates, proxies, or members of governmental boards or commissions. A roll call vote is sometimes called *voting by yeas and nays* or *a recorded vote*. A vote by roll call may be required by the bylaws or may be ordered by the assembly following a motion from a member. A majority vote is required to order a roll call.

When a roll call is taken, the presiding officer states the question as follows: "The motion is ... Those in favor of the motion will vote aye (*or* yea) as their names are called; those opposed will vote no (*or* nay). The secretary will call the roll."

The names are called in alphabetical order, or in the numerical order of districts, or in some other appropriate order. The name of the presiding officer is usually called last. A member who does not wish to vote may remain silent or answer "present" or "abstaining." Just as a member who remains silent, responding with "present" or "abstaining" will not affect the outcome of the vote and will not affect the number of votes required to adopt, but unlike the silent member, these responses will document the presence of the member, which may be important to show the presence of a quorum. The secretary should always have lists of names ready for use in calling the roll and should repeat each member's vote to ensure that it is recorded correctly. The minutes should record how each member voted in a roll call vote.

Another form of roll call vote is a signed ballot. In this method of voting a member is provided with a ballot with the stated question or proposal typed on it. The member then votes by printing his or her name (or constituency, if required) on the ballot, signing the ballot, and indicating the preferred choice. The ballots are then collected.

For each ballot, the secretary reads, or records, the name of the voter and how that member voted on the proposal. The count is tallied, and the presiding officer announces the result. How each member voted is entered in, or attached to, the minutes, as well as the final result as announced by the presiding officer. The recording of the vote in the minutes is identical to a roll call vote. The advantage of this form of roll call is that no member knows how another member has voted at the time of voting.

Ballot Vote

Voting by ballot is the only method that enables members to express their decisions without revealing their opinions or preferences. (The use of a voting machine, or any other method in which the person expressing a choice cannot be identified with the choice expressed, is considered a form of voting by ballot.) Secrecy is implicit in a ballot vote, and an election requiring a ballot vote may be invalidated by the courts if it is shown that by any means (such as numbering of ballots in a way that would identify the voter) it would be possible to determine how an individual voted.[1]

A ballot vote is usually required in contested elections and frequently in voting on important proposals. If a ballot vote on a particular proposal is not required by the bylaws, it may be ordered by a motion, which is adopted by a majority vote. If a vote by ballot is required by the bylaws, a motion to dispense with the ballot vote, or to suspend the provision requiring such a vote, is not in order unless this procedure is provided for in the bylaws.

The presiding officer should give careful instructions about how the members should prepare their ballots and should ask before the voting begins whether anyone is without a ballot.

When voting by ballot (or voting by electronic means, including Internet voting), the organization needs to ensure that only those entitled to vote actually vote; that members vote only once; if secrecy is a requirement for the vote, that the secrecy of the vote is maintained; that members can change their votes prior to the votes being cast (to correct errors on their ballots or screens); and that members are given clear written instructions, and if necessary, some training on how to vote for their preferences, especially when the vote is by electronic means or by Internet.

Voting by Mail

In organizations whose members are scattered over a wide area or who work during different hours of the day, provision is sometimes made for members to vote on important questions by mail. Voting by mail cannot be used unless it is authorized in the bylaws.

Voting by mail has certain disadvantages. When voting by mail, the members do not have the opportunity to discuss or listen to debate on proposals or to amend proposals. In elections, there is no opportunity to nominate candidates from the floor.

Voting by mail by some members who cannot attend a meeting cannot be combined successfully with voting at a meeting or convention by those who attend. Since proposals and amendments to bylaws can be discussed and amended at a meeting or convention, those voting by mail and those voting at a convention might each be voting on quite different proposals or amendments. Similarly, when candidates are being elected, members voting by mail would have no chance to nominate additional candidates from the floor, to consider candidates nominated from the floor, or to vote for another candidate if their candidate withdraws or is eliminated from the ballot.

An organization should choose between voting on proposals or amendments to the bylaws by mail and the right to discuss, amend, and vote on them at a meeting or convention. It should similarly choose between voting for candidates by mail and the right to nominate additional candidates from the floor.

Any method of voting by mail may be followed so long as it ensures that voters fully understand the issues to be decided and the instructions for returning their votes. Unless the bylaws provide for a particular plan, a ballot containing proposed measures, amendments to bylaws, or a list of candidates is mailed to each member by the secretary together with voting directions from the election committee. When mailing out the ballot, some organizations enclose information concerning the qualifications of candidates and arguments for and against each proposal to be voted on.

The ballot must be marked and returned to the secretary within a specified time. The usual way to preserve secrecy in a mail vote is to provide each member with a blank envelope which has no mark of identification on it. The marked ballot is placed inside the unmarked envelope, which is then sealed. The unmarked sealed envelope, in turn, is enclosed in another envelope which the member signs and seals, so that the member's name may be checked against the list of members eligible to vote. The blank inner envelope is delivered, still sealed, to the tellers or election committee.

Internet Voting

The twenty-first century has seen a new development in elections—casting of ballots electronically on the Internet. Most of the considerations involved in voting by mail apply also to voting online. The first use of Internet voting in a legally binding public election was in March 2000 when the Arizona Democratic Party used the Internet in its presidential primary. Prior to that, however, a number of associations used the Internet to elect officers or to vote on resolutions or bylaw amendments, and the number of groups using electronic voting is increasing rapidly.[2]

Because many members may not have access to the Internet or may choose not to use it, online voting is usually combined with mail balloting. In addition, because it requires special expertise, most organizations using it obtain the services of an elections administration company experienced in the field. To ensure authentication and complete security, a voter's personal identification number (PIN) is used, together with a ballot control number randomly assigned by the company. When voting by mail, the voter enters the two numbers on the outer envelope. When voting electronically, the numbers are entered after the voter logs on to the secure encryption-enabled website. (This sophisticated data transfer procedure should not be confused with a simple e-mail transaction.) The vendor's computer technology is able to restrict the voter to casting only one electronic ballot and can identify and invalidate any duplicate ballots cast on paper.

The advantage of electronic voting is that many thousands of ballots can be tabulated in several minutes. For large organizations, which otherwise would have to print, mail, and process returned paper ballots, the saving in production costs, as well as in time and labor, can be significant. The contract with firms handling electronic elections normally stipulates that all information connected with the balloting be kept confidential.

Acting by Proxy

A *proxy* is a written authorization empowering another person to act, in a meeting, for the member who signs the proxy. This means that a particular member or person is authorized to act on behalf of an absent member in a meeting or convention, which includes voting in place of the absent member. The term *proxy* may mean either the statement authorizing another to act in place of the member signing it, or it may refer to the person who attends the meeting in place of the absent member. To avoid confusion, the member giving the proxy statement is often called the proxy giver, while the person who will actually act for the proxy giver is called the proxy holder. Unless restricted by the bylaws or standing rules, the proxy holder need not be a member. The proxy holder may cast votes to the same extent that the absent members represented could if they were in attendance. In addition to voting, unless otherwise restricted by the proxy, the proxy holder may act in all ways for the absent member, including speaking in debates and making motions.

In business corporations, where ownership interests are typically widely dispersed and obtaining a wide representation of the shareholders at meetings is important because of their investment interest, voting by proxy is a common occurrence.

In nonprofit corporations, voting by proxy is authorized in most jurisdictions. In some jurisdictions, the applicable corporate statute allows proxies unless prohibited in the charter or bylaws, while in others, the charter or bylaws of the organization must specifically authorize the use of proxies. In a voluntary (unincorporated) association, proxies would not be allowed unless specifically authorized in the bylaws. While statutes and bylaws may permit members (proxy givers) to give their authorization to another to act for them in a meeting, the organization, if not disallowed by statute, can restrict the number of proxies that a proxy holder may carry and vote, and may restrict who a proxy holder may be. The most common restriction is that the proxy holder must be a member. Any such restriction must be clearly stipulated in the bylaws.

Directors or board members in most jurisdictions cannot vote by proxy in their board meetings because this would mean the delegation of a discretionary legislative duty, which cannot be delegated. In addition, directors are bound by their fiduciary duties, duty of care and loyalty to the organization, and their requirement to act in good faith when carrying out their duties as director. Transferring these duties to another through a proxy would be contrary to their responsibilities in the organization.

A proxy may be in almost any form as long as its meaning is clear. (See Appendix C for a sample proxy form.) It may be limited to one meeting, one motion, one issue, one person, or a specific time, or it may be unlimited (often called a *general proxy*). Many nonprofit corporation statutes set a maximum effective period for proxies. A proxy holder may be given full discretion to vote on all matters during a meeting or can be instructed to vote in the affirmative, the negative, or to abstain on a specific proposal, or to vote for specific candidates running for office. Generally, proxies in nonprofit organizations are revocable by the proxy giver, although it may be helpful to provide explicitly on the proxy statement that it is revocable. A proxy procedure requiring advance registration of proxies should include provisions addressing how to revoke a proxy after it has been registered.

Even though a proxy may give specific instructions on how a proxy holder may vote on a resolution that will come before the meeting, the resolution may have amendments applied to it. If the organization uses this book as its parliamentary authority, the proxy holder is given discretion to vote on such amendments or other such subsidiary motions unless the proxy statement or the bylaws say otherwise. This discretion flows from the authority of the proxy holder to vote on the resolution or main motion.

Some nonprofit corporation statutes allow proxies to be used to establish a quorum and therefore establish a legal meeting. If an organization allows proxies, the bylaws should specify whether they count toward establishing a quorum. Some organizations choose to have two quorum requirements, both of which must be satisfied to conduct business: (1) a minimum number of members need to be present in person, and (2) a somewhat higher number that includes members present in person and by proxy.[3]

The organization must carefully set up procedures to receive proxies, ensuring that they are valid. The process in which the authenticity of each proxy is validated is crucial to the integrity of the overall proxy process. Only after a proxy has been verified can the proxy holder receive a voting card and ballots—if votes are to be taken by ballot. The proxy holder will receive as many voting cards and ballots as are warranted by the proxies held.

Most organizations, by rule, disallow proxies to be used that are simply made out to an unnamed holder of the proxy. This inappropriate use of the proxy process can be mitigated if the organization adopts a proxy procedure requiring all proxies to be registered with the organization a few days before the meeting.

If used, all proxies must conform strictly to the provisions of the statutes, charters, bylaws, and rules of the organizations, including restrictions on the number of proxies a proxy holder can carry.

Preferential Voting

Sometimes an organization does not wish to conduct repeated ballots if an election is not won by majority vote on the first ballot. Rather than permit the winner to be determined by plurality on the first ballot, the election can be conducted by a preferential ballot.

There are many preferential voting systems. The preferential voting system described below is the default for those organizations that use this book. In such an election, members mark their ballots to indicate their first, second, third, and subsequent choices among the candidates. Tellers count the ballots and report the results based on first-choice votes only, and if no candidate receives a majority of the votes on this basis, the candidate with the fewest first-choice votes is dropped, and the ballots that voted for that person are recounted, based on second-choice votes. These votes are added to the original totals. If no candidate has a majority after this (or any subsequent) count, the process is repeated, dropping the lowest candidate and distributing that candidate's first-choice votes among the remaining candidates until one has received a majority.

This is a single-ballot method of conducting the election as it would occur if repeated ballots were taken, and if the lowest candidate were dropped after each ballot on which no candidate received a majority. It is useful when a mail ballot is necessary, or when a meeting will end before counting is completed and the members cannot be reconvened for additional balloting.

This method of voting sometimes produces unusual results under certain circumstances and should be used only when necessary.

Preferential voting can be used not only to select among many candidates in an election, but also to select among many choices in deciding any other matter. When conducting preferential voting, the method of dealing with any ties that may occur should be determined in advance of the voting. In fact, the question of how to resolve ties should be determined in advance before voting occurs by any method, unless the assembly wants to revote until the election is complete.

When using preferential voting, the presiding officer and the tellers committee should be instructed on methods of explaining to members how to cast their votes, how the tellers will count votes and allocate them to the candidates, and what is to happen when the last place candidate is dropped and how that person's votes are redistributed. When the number of voters is large, it would be wise to use computer technology to ensure an accurate result.

Borda Count Voting

The *Borda Count* method of voting is not a majority voting system; it is based on a points system. For example, if there are four candidates running for office, members rank each candidate on the ballot in accordance with their preference—one, two, three, or four. The member's first-choice candidate will receive four points, the second-choice candidate three points, third-choice candidate two points, and the fourth-choice candidate one point. The tellers committee will tally all the points for each candidate. The candidate with the most points is elected.

Members must vote for all candidates, or the ballot is spoiled. A member may, of course, leave the ballot blank. Write-in candidates are not permitted. In the event of a tie, the vote would be taken again.

The Borda Count was championed by J. C. Borda, a French scientist of the eighteenth century, who devised the method to overcome anomalies in elections and, in particular, elections held by plurality. In modern times, it has been shown by mathematical analysis that the Borda Count achieves fairness in elections when more than two candidates are running.

Changing a Vote

When a vote is taken by voice, a show of hands, standing, or roll call, members may change their votes up to the time that the result of the vote is announced. After a vote by roll call has been announced, a member may change a vote only with proof that an error was made in recording it. When voting is by ballot, a member may not change the ballot after it has been placed in the ballot box.

Announcing the Result of a Vote

It is the duty of the presiding officer to announce the result of the vote according to the facts. However, an incorrect or untrue announcement of the vote cannot make the vote as cast by the majority illegal. In case of a disputed vote, the courts will examine the facts to determine whether the vote was correct as announced.

All Votes Binding During a Meeting

A few organizations follow the improper practice of taking an informal test, or straw vote, in meetings, which they interpret to be a vote that is not binding. Such a vote is sometimes used to influence members to reach a consensus. A unity of opinion, if it is reached without coercion, is desirable; but informal votes cannot properly be taken during a meeting.

No body, board, or committee can, during its meeting, properly take a vote that is not binding. If an assembly wishes to vote to recess to determine the probable vote of the members, it may do so; but under the law, all votes taken during a meeting are binding.

Chapter 19

NOMINATIONS AND ELECTIONS

The process of nominating and electing officers is vital to every organization because the abilities and talents of the leaders largely determine the achievements of the group. Parliamentary law permits wide latitude of choice in each step of the nominating and electing process. There is no one perfect method, but there are certain procedures that have proven to be better than others for electing good leaders.

Bylaw Provisions on Nominations and Elections

The bylaw provisions on nominations should include the offices to be filled, the eligibility and qualifications of candidates, the person or group who may nominate, the method and time of nominating, and the term of office. If a nominating committee is to be used, provisions for selecting its members and determining their qualifications, instructions, duties, and reporting should also be included. The bylaw provisions on elections should include the time, place, and method of voting; the notice required; a statement of who is eligible to vote; the vote required to elect; the method of conducting the election; and the time when the new officers take office. Some bylaws include a provision for special elections if needed to fill vacancies.

Some organizations have certain procedural requirements, such as advance announcement of candidacy, certification of eligibility, statement of willingness to serve, submission of conflict of interest statements, or other requirements, including compliance with deadlines. Consideration should be given to how some restrictions might limit the organization's choices and thereby prevent the election of a member who might be the best-qualified candidate.

Care should be taken to provide sufficient flexibility in the overall nomination and election processes to allow the organization to address unanticipated circumstances. Often a provision authorizing the board or a standing committee to resolve such issues is sufficient.

Nominations from the Floor

A *nomination* is the formal presentation to an assembly of the name of a member as a candidate for a particular office. If the bylaws do not provide the method for nominating officers, any member may propose a motion determining how nominations are to be made.

Unless the bylaws provide otherwise, nominations from the floor are always permitted even if the initial nominations are made by a nominating committee.[1] To open nominations, the presiding officer may ask, "Are there nominations (or further nominations) for the office of president?" Any member may then rise and say, for example, "I nominate Jonathan Swift."

It is customary in some organizations to permit a nominator to give reasons for supporting the nominee. Nominations do not require seconds, but some organizations permit other members to give endorsing statements, which are called "seconding speeches." If the report of a nominating committee states the qualifications and abilities of its nominees, a member who nominates from the floor may also state the qualifications and abilities of the candidate.

Relying solely on nominations from the floor is often not the most satisfactory method for securing the best candidates. The lack of time for considering qualifications, the tendency of nominees to decline nominations from the floor, and the resulting confusion often prevent the organization from securing the best leaders. A nominating committee, so long as it is fairly chosen and is representative of the membership, will usually select good candidates, but nominations from the floor should always be provided for as a safeguard.

Closing Nominations

The presiding officer should repeat the request for further nominations and should pause to allow ample opportunity for members to present nominees. When there appear to be no further nominations for a particular office, the presiding officer may declare nominations for that office closed. A motion to close nominations is not required but, if made, is unamendable and undebatable and requires a two-thirds vote for adoption. The presiding officer should not recognize a motion to close nominations or declare them closed if any member is rising for the purpose of making a nomination.

If nominations have been closed, they may be reopened by a motion to this effect, until voting has begun. The motion to reopen nominations is unamendable, undebatable, and requires a majority vote for adoption.

Voting for Candidates Not Nominated

A member need not be nominated for an office, either from the floor or by a committee, when the vote for election is taken by ballot or by roll call. Unless the bylaws require a nomination, members may vote for anyone who is eligible, regardless of whether the person has been nominated, by writing in the name of their choice on the ballot or voting for that person during roll call. Any member receiving the necessary number of votes is elected, whether nominated or not.[2] The member does, of course, have the right to decline the office.[3]

Nominating Committee

A nominating committee is one of the most important committees of an organization because it can help secure the best officers. Nomination of candidates by a committee has advantages. A committee has the time to study the current leadership needs of the organization and to select candidates to meet these needs. The committee can interview prospective nominees; investigate their experience, qualifications, and abilities; persuade them to become candidates; and secure their consent to serve if elected. The committee is also able to apportion representation equitably among different groups and different geographical areas.

Selecting a Nominating Committee

A nominating committee should be a representative committee. Some organizations provide, for example, that if the nominating committee consists of five members, three of the members are elected by the membership, and the chair and the fifth member are appointed by the governing board. The members chosen by the board are usually current or recent members of the board who, by reason of their service, have a broad and up-to-date knowledge of the needs of the organization and of the leadership abilities of its members. The members of the committee elected by the membership usually reflect the viewpoint of the general membership.

When possible, the committee should represent the demographics of the whole organization. Any plan in which experienced leaders choose some of the members of the nominating committee and the membership chooses the other members is usually effective in securing a committee that is both representative and knowledgeable.

The president, president-elect, and immediate past president should not appoint any members of the nominating committee, serve on the committee, give the committee instructions, or take any part in its deliberations. This requirement protects both the officer and the committee from accusations of favoritism or self-perpetuation.

When a nominating committee is used, it is essential that the members be chosen wisely and democratically and that both the committee and the membership be protected by permitting nominations from the floor.

Duties of a Nominating Committee

A carefully chosen nominating committee should be permitted to use its judgment in selecting the candidates who will give the best service to the organization. It should choose the candidates on the basis of what is good for all the members and not with the view that office is a reward to be given to a deserving member. The committee may invite suggestions but should not be limited by them.

A few organizations use the nominating committee merely as a data gathering group to which names from various areas or local groups are sent and the results tabulated. This type of committee does little more than compile a list of nominees.

On the other hand, many organizations believe that the best leaders are secured by delegating to the nominating committee the duty of finding and nominating the best candidates. The duties usually assigned to such a nominating committee are:

1. To select nominees whose experience and qualities meet the needs of the organization
2. To contact prospective nominees and obtain their consent to serve if elected
3. To prepare and submit a report, which may include the reasons for the selection of the nominees

Qualifications of Nominees

Qualifications for each office should be stated in the bylaws or other document of authority as designated in the bylaws, such as a policy established by the board or by the members. No member who lacks the qualifications specified in the bylaws or document of authority can be a candidate for, or be elected to, an office. The nomination of an unqualified member must be ruled out of order.

Nomination to More Than One Office

No member can hold two incompatible offices. In their bylaws, some organizations combine two offices, thus, in effect, declaring them compatible. For example, the offices of secretary and treasurer are sometimes combined as secretary-treasurer. Membership on the governing board is usually compatible with other offices, such as president or secretary, and officers in local units might also be elected as delegates to the assembly of the parent organization. The fact that bylaws usually provide that the officers serve on the board is a determination of compatibility. Incompatibility does not consist of the physical impossibility of performing the duties of both offices but lies in a conflict of interest between the duties of the two offices.

If it is not clear whether certain offices are incompatible, the organization should clarify the compatibility or lack thereof in its bylaws.

A member who is nominated for two incompatible offices at the same election should choose which office to run for and decline the other nomination, but is not required to do so if the member is qualified for each position. If, however, the member is elected to both positions, the member must immediately choose which office to fill and forfeit the other.

Unless the bylaws state otherwise, a member who holds an office may be a candidate for another office, without first giving up his or her current office, but if the member is elected to and accepts an incompatible office, the current office is forfeited.

Nominating Committee Members as Candidates

Members who are likely to become candidates should not serve on a nominating committee, but members of the committee can become candidates. A member of a nominating committee who becomes a candidate should resign from the committee immediately.

Single and Multiple Slates

If an organization chooses a representative nominating committee carefully and democratically, it may be desirable to nominate a single candidate for each office. A single slate, meaning one nominee for each office, frequently offers certain advantages provided that nominations may also be made from the floor and that election by write-in votes is not forbidden.

In some organizations the belief persists that it is more democratic to have two or more nominees for each office so that there will be a contested election. For a number of reasons, it is usually not best practice to require the nominating committee to submit more nominations than there are positions to be filled. A nomination process that requires the nominating committee to select two nominees for a position is inefficient in terms of time, energy, and possibly money. If a fully qualified candidate is selected, but the governing documents of the organization require two nominees, the committee may find itself in the position of finding a "throwaway" candidate to fill the second position. A member nominated only to fulfill the requirement may be unwilling to run in the future after having been defeated once.

If the nominating committee fails to express the will of the majority of the members in its selection of nominees, this is most readily corrected by adding nominees from the floor to provide a contested election.

Election Committee

Organizations usually appoint an election committee to conduct the election. The members of this committee should be well respected in the organization, not openly supportive of any one candidate, detail-oriented, thoroughly knowledgeable of the election rules, and if possible, selected from different constituencies or geographic regions. Members of the nominating committee should not serve on the election committee because of their involvement in the nominating process.

The committee supervises the preparation and printing of ballots, their distribution to voting members either at a meeting or convention or by mail, the collection and counting of the ballots, and the preparation of a report showing the results of the election. Those who count the ballots are typically called "tellers" in non-profit membership organizations and "inspectors of elections" in business corporations. Tellers also frequently distribute and collect the ballots. In organizations with an election committee, the tellers are usually members of the election committee or a subcommittee of the election committee.

An organization should define in its bylaws the method and procedures by which it elects its leaders. At a minimum it should prescribe the vote required to elect (usually a majority) and the method by which votes are cast (usually by ballot). However, it is incumbent upon the organization to define the method and procedure that will best meet the organization's needs. Chapter 18 lists and explains a number of voting methods. See the section below "Vote Necessary to Elect," which pertains to the situation in which the bylaws are silent on the rules for electing leaders. If the rules are silent on a tellers committee, the presiding officer has the authority to appoint a tellers committee. Alternately, if the bylaws are silent on election methods and procedure, the assembly, by motion, may define the method and procedure of conducting an election.

Counting Ballots

The election committee is generally responsible for seeing that ballots are counted accurately. One effective method of counting ballots is for one member to read the votes for all offices from each ballot while another member stands near enough to check the correctness of the reading. The votes are recorded by two other members whose tabulation is also checked to ensure accuracy. If a ballot has several offices to be voted upon, the recording of the votes may be divided between two or more teams of recorders and checkers, each recording only the votes for one or two offices. While counting the votes, there should be silence except for the reading of the names. If there is a possible error, some member says, "Stop," and the vote is verified before proceeding.

In large organizations, where hundreds of votes must be counted, electronic keypads or voting machines are often used. If counted by hand, the paper ballots are divided among many teams of readers, recorders, and checkers and counted in the same way by each team. Votes are usually tallied in groups of five. Many organizations have developed effective ballot-counting methods which meet their own needs. Any method is appropriate if it is accurate and efficient.

Announced candidates or their designees have a right to attend and observe the vote count.

Security and Privacy of Balloting

It is of critical importance to implement procedures and safeguards that ensure ballot security and a correct report of the vote count. Ballot security measures include: only an eligible member is able to obtain a ballot and cast a vote, no one may cast another member's ballot without authorization of proxies, and no one may vote more than once.

Because the intent of voting by ballot is secrecy, procedures should be in place to protect the privacy of members in casting their votes and to ensure that no one can identify a member's ballot. In fact, the term "secret ballot" is often used to emphasize this principle, although any ballot is presumed to be secret unless other provisions are made.

Determining the Legality of Ballots

The legality of ballots is governed by the following rules:

1. A mistake in voting for a candidate for one office does not invalidate the vote for candidates for other offices on the same ballot.
2. A technical error, such as a misspelling or using a cross instead of a check mark, does not invalidate a ballot if the *intent* of the voter is clear.
3. A torn or defaced ballot is valid if the *intent* of the voter is clear.
4. Votes for ineligible persons are considered illegal ballots.
5. Blank ballots are ignored; they are not counted and do not affect the number necessary to elect a candidate or adopt a proposal.
6. If several nominees for equal offices (for example, members of a governing board) are voted for in a group, a ballot containing fewer votes than the number of positions to be filled is valid. But a ballot containing votes for more than the number of positions to be filled is illegal.

If the results of the count by the committee appear to be incorrect, a recount must be taken. For example, if more ballots have been cast than there are members entitled to vote and the result of the election could have been affected by the extra ballots, or if there has been any substantial violation of the right of members to vote in secret, the vote must be retaken. If there are minor errors that could not change the result of the election, a vote need not be retaken.[4]

Report of Election Committee or Tellers

Table 19.1 shows the essential requirements of a report of an election committee or tellers committee.

Table 19.1   Report of election committee

REPORT OF ELECTION COMMITTEE
April 7, 20—
CARTER COUNTY LITERARY SOCIETY

Qualified voters	205
Legal ballots cast	201
President	
Legal votes cast for president	197
Illegal votes (cast for ineligible person)	2
Number of votes necessary to elect	99
Candidate A received	130
Candidate B received (write-in votes)	67
Secretary	
Legal votes cast for secretary	201
Number necessary to elect	101
Candidate D received	198
Candidate E received (write-in votes)	3
Board of Trustees (three to be elected)	
Legal ballots cast for trustees	197
Number necessary to elect	99
Candidate F received	190
Candidate G received	181
Candidate H received	153
Candidate I received (write-in votes)	6

Signatures of Committee

In this election committee or tellers' report, three elections are reported on the one form. See Appendix D, Tellers' Report—Election, for a typical tellers' report for the election of a single office. The report must account for all ballots cast, both legal and illegal. Blank ballots need not be reported. If any ballots or votes are rejected as illegal, the number must be reported and the reasons for rejection must be given. The number of votes received by each candidate and the number of write-in votes for any member, qualified or unqualified, must be included in the report and must be read.

The chair of the election committee reads the report to the assembly without stating who is elected and hands it to the presiding officer. The presiding officer reads to the assembly only the names of those who are elected and declares them elected.

The report is signed by all members of the election committee. Tally sheets are signed by those who marked them. All ballots, tally sheets, and records are delivered to the secretary of the organization, who keeps them sealed until directed by the governing board or the assembly to destroy them.

Vote Necessary to Elect

The vote necessary to elect should be fixed in the bylaws. Unless otherwise stated, the following rules govern:

1. A candidate who receives a majority of the legal votes cast for a single office is elected.
2. A candidate who receives a plurality of the legal votes cast, but not a majority, is not elected unless there is a provision in the bylaws for election by plurality.
3. When election to an office requires a majority vote but no candidate receives a majority vote, the requirement for a majority vote cannot be waived, but the assembly may adopt motions to enable it to complete the election within a reasonable time.[5]

For more information on adopting rules for conducting an election, see "Supplementing Procedural Rules by Motion" in Chapter 26.

Alternatives to a Ballot Vote Election

When the bylaws require a ballot vote for election, then the election must be conducted by ballot vote unless the bylaws also provide exceptions. Such a useful exception would be when there is a single nominee for an office or the number of candidates for a specific office is equal to or less than the number of positions to be filled. For example, the bylaw exception might be as simple as allowing the presiding officer to request that the single nominated candidate (or the candidates for equal positions) be elected by general consent or acclamation. If there is an objection, the election must proceed by ballot. If there is no objection to the general consent request, the single nominee is elected, and the election is complete.

If the bylaws are silent on requiring a ballot vote or another alternative voting method for conducting the election, the assembly can decide how to conduct the election. If this book is the parliamentary authority and there is only one nominee or there are fewer nominees than positions open for an office (or the number of nominees is equal to the number of open positions), the presiding officer may conduct the election by general consent, or acclamation, unless a single member objects. In the event an objection is made to the general consent request, the assembly can determine the method of carrying out the election. The method of election chosen may be a show of hands, standing vote, roll call, ballot vote, or any other method the assembly decides on.

Some organizations use electronic keypad voting at their meetings. This method of voting is a form of ballot voting. The system being used should preserve the secrecy of the ballot vote. If such a keypad system cannot provide a mechanism for write-in votes, the use of the system should be formally authorized by the assembly, and such authorization is presumed to include a prohibition of write-in votes.

Motion to Make a Vote Unanimous

A unanimous vote means that all the legal votes cast were cast on one side and that there were no votes cast on the other side. One common error is to suppose that a vote that is not unanimous can be made unanimous by adopting a motion to that effect by majority vote. Sometimes the candidate receiving the second highest number of votes, or one of that candidate's supporters, proposes a motion to make the vote unanimous for the elected candidate. This is only a complimentary gesture, and no vote should be taken to make the vote unanimous. This gesture does not change the legal vote.

When Elections Become Effective

An election becomes effective immediately if the candidate is present and does not decline. Election of a candidate who is absent becomes effective as soon as the person is notified and agrees to serve. Unless some other time is specified in the bylaws, a person assumes office when declared elected, and no formal installation is necessary. Often, the bylaws provide that the new officers should take office at a specific time—for example, at the end of the meeting at which the election takes place.

The ceremony of installing officers does not determine the time at which they assume office unless the bylaws contain a provision that the new officers take office at the time of their installation.

Challenging a Vote

A member who chooses to challenge the right of another member or members to vote, or the validity of a proxy, should do so by presenting the challenge to the credentials committee or to the election committee. This should be done before the voting has begun or at least before the challenged vote is cast. If the right of a member to vote is challenged, the credentials committee or the election committee holds a hearing and decides the matter subject to an appeal to the assembly. If there is no credentials or election committee, the challenge is decided by the assembly. Additional information on credentials committees is provided in Chapter 23.

Challenging an Election

An election may be challenged only during the time that it is taking place or within a reasonably brief time thereafter. Unless an organization provides special procedures for challenging an election, elections may not be challenged after the adjournment of the election meeting or convention, unless the election challenge is based on fraudulent activity. Once brought forward, election challenges should be resolved, if at all possible, at the same meeting or convention as the election. If resolution of the challenge is not possible, the assembly should authorize the board or some other body to resolve the matter shortly after the meeting.

In a case where an election may have been based on election fraud or criminality and such activity is discovered after the meeting has adjourned, it should be promptly reported, and appropriate action should be taken. Such a challenge cannot be raised, however, after the term of office of the individual challenged has expired.

In situations where elections take place electronically, by Internet, or by mail ballot, or where the announcement of the election results takes place after the adjournment of the meeting or convention, the bylaws should specify who resolves an election challenge and within what time limits the challenge may be made. If the bylaws are silent, this book specifies a time limit of 48 hours to register an election challenge after the results have been announced or officially posted to the membership; and, that the challenge is to be resolved by the governing board of the organization. The governing board may delegate its authority to resolve the challenge.

The grounds for challenging an election are usually that persons who are ineligible have voted, that procedures required for carrying out a fair election were not observed, that procedures or actions during the election were unauthorized or illegal, that there was gross negligence in conducting the election, or that the election requirements in the bylaws were not correctly interpreted or followed, and that these violations could have changed the result of the election.

If a bylaw provision or the assembly authorizes a voting system, its reported outcome is presumed to be accurate and may not be challenged solely on the basis of the system or technology that was used. For example, if a keypad voting system reports fewer total votes cast than the number of members eligible to vote, in the absence of clear evidence that some members cast votes that were not counted, the reported votes are presumed to be complete and correct.

When an election is challenged, an investigation is usually made by the board of directors or by a committee selected by the board, or by the election committee. The board or committee reports its recommendation to the meeting or convention for final decision. If the meeting or convention is no longer in session, the governing board decides the matter and takes whatever action seems best. In the event that a declared winner of a board position is challenged, that person is not permitted to be seated on the board or vote on matters until the challenge is decided. The board must report its action to the members.

When an election is challenged while it is in progress, it continues unless a decision is reached to stop the election and declare it void. If it is challenged after it is completed, the officers chosen as a result of the election take office and remain in office until a decision on the challenge is reached. If illegal votes cast or illegal practices engaged in could not have changed the results of the election, the fact that there were illegal votes or practices does not void the election.

It is good practice always to be prepared to conduct a paper ballot vote in case there are technical problems with electronic voting systems that can't be resolved in a timely manner, or in case a challenge to such a system results in the assembly ordering a ballot vote.

It is recommended that the organization adopt its own procedures and rules for challenges of elections, for resolution of such challenges, and for addressing its particular voting procedures, customs, and associated (real or potential) election problems. Such procedures should carefully balance the fair treatment of all parties involved and the need for a correct election outcome against the need to resolve any disputes with finality and as promptly as possible.

Chapter 20

OFFICERS

The officers of an organization are members who are usually given important responsibilities, duties, and powers because of their elected positions. Without officers to carry out these responsibilities and duties, much of an organization's work might go undone. Without officers, the ability of the organization to make necessary decisions and to function fully between meetings might be significantly hampered.

The President

The *president,* the head of an organization regardless of the title, usually has three roles—leader, administrator, and presiding officer. Each role calls for different abilities.

The President as Leader

There are certain fundamental qualities that most good leaders have in common. One is the *ability to plan*—to sense what the members want and to help them crystallize their ideas. Another is the *ability to unite*—to rally members behind a plan and behind their leader. Perhaps the most important is the *courage to win*—to overcome all obstacles.

A good leader works with the members and keeps them happy while they are working. Such a leader has power *with* people, not *over* them. Carrying out their will is a project in human collaboration, which the president leads.

An organization is not merely a group of people working toward some common aim. It is also a powerful medium through which members can realize their individual hopes. A competent leader forges ahead toward the collective goal, but is not blind to individual aims. A good leader does not sacrifice individual human relationships and hopes.

A leader skilled in handling people recognizes that sentiment and tradition are important influences, both in welding people together and in dividing them. This human understanding is one of the most important elements of good leadership.

The President as Administrator

The following are important duties usually performed by the president as an administrator:

1. Acts as chief administrative officer and legal head of the organization
2. Exercises supervision over the organization and all its activities and senior employees
3. Represents and speaks for the organization
4. Presides at business meetings
5. Appoints committees as directed by the bylaws or the assembly
6. Signs letters or documents necessary to carry out the will of the organization
7. Presides at meetings of the governing board

The President as Presiding Officer

As presiding officer, the president is the leader and representative of the entire assembly. Respect for this position is respect for the organization. The president must maintain firm control of meetings, yet always act primarily as the "servant leader" of the organization.

Just as a judge exercises wide discretion in a courtroom, the presiding officer should exercise wide discretion in a meeting. Instead of being limited to mechanical responses, the president must meet each situation with flexibility of judgment, common sense, and fairness to all members—always acting impartially and in good faith. For example, if a member moves to adjourn and the presiding officer knows that there is important business that should be attended to, this should be explained to the member, who may then withdraw the motion. If the member refuses, the presiding officer should explain the business that needs attention before the vote on adjournment is taken.

The presiding officer may be able to relax procedure from its most formal level, depending on the group's size and the complexity and controversial nature of the issues involved. A degree of informality can often facilitate the conduct of business, but the presiding officer must be prepared to return to greater formality at the first suggestion of difficulty and should lean toward greater formality at all times with larger assemblies.

The presiding officer may be flexible in assisting members as they exercise their rights and privileges during discussion. It is appropriate for the presiding officer to state facts of which members may not be aware, provided that this is done in an unbiased manner.

The president should encourage discussion and should see that all sides of a controversial question are examined by asking if members wish to present a different viewpoint and by alternating the discussion opportunities between those in favor of and those opposed to the question.

The president should make sure that members understand all proposals and what the effects will be if they are or are not adopted. The president must make certain that members understand and must restrict discussion to the pending question.

A presiding officer should prevent improper conduct and should warn obstructionists who are using dilatory tactics. The presiding officer should deny recognition to those who persist in such behavior. He or she should expose parliamentary trickery, prevent railroading, and promptly rule out discussion of personalities.

A presiding officer must be firm and decisive, yet not dictatorial; courteous and patient, yet alert to ensure progress.

Presiding is an art that cannot be learned entirely from a book. A skillful presiding officer knows how to discourage tactfully a member who talks too much or too often and how to encourage a shy member who speaks only when driven by strong convictions. When an assembly grows impatient, a good presiding officer knows how to shorten discussion and how to make business move along. This person also senses when members are confused and when the business should move more slowly.

One factor that will distinguish a presiding officer is having a very good working knowledge of parliamentary procedure and how to apply it with authority.

Associate Justice Felix Frankfurter described the ideal presiding officer when he wrote (of Chief Justice Charles Evans Hughes):

> He presided with great courtesy and with a quiet authority … with great but gentle firmness. You couldn't but catch his own mood of courtesy.

He never checked free debate, but the atmosphere which he created, the moral authority which he exerted, inhibited irrelevance, repetition, and fruitless discussion. He was a master of timing: he knew when discussion should be deferred and when brought to an issue. He also showed uncommon resourcefulness in drawing elements of agreement out of differences, and thereby narrowing, if not always escaping, conflicts.[1]

When the President Presides

The president, or in the absence of the president the officer next in rank, should preside at all meetings at which business may be transacted. If no officers are present at a meeting, a member calls the meeting to order and presides until a temporary presiding officer is elected. At social or program meetings, the program chair or another member may preside; but at business meetings the president, if present, presides and cannot delegate this duty without permission from the assembly.

If the president wishes to participate in a debate on a controversial question, the chair should be turned over temporarily to the president-elect, if there is one, or the vice president or some other ranking officer who has not expressed an opinion on the question. Or, if the other officers also prefer to participate in the discussion, the chair may be turned over to some other impartial member. If there is controversy over the person so designated, the matter is settled by majority vote, with the person named by the president being considered one of the nominees for the temporary chairmanship.

The presiding officer does not leave the chair merely to present important facts that need to be presented. However, if a motion is directed at the president personally, the president-elect, if there is one, or the vice president, is asked to take the chair until action on the motion has been completed. This is true whether the motion affects the president favorably—such as, to award a life membership—or adversely—a vote of censure.

Although there is a general principle that a person does not give up any basic rights of membership by becoming an officer, the presiding officer of an assembly should not propose or second a motion or nominate a candidate while presiding at a business meeting of members. However, the president does preside during an election even when he or she is a candidate for office.

The President-Elect

Some organizations elect a future president as much as a year before the term of office begins, and in the interim period they assign specific duties to the president-elect to increase that person's familiarity with the workings of the organization. The president-elect is in training for the office of president and automatically becomes the president when the president's term of office expires.

The president-elect assumes the duties of the president when that officer is absent or is incapacitated, unless the bylaws provide something different. The president-elect also presides when it is necessary for the president to leave the chair temporarily.

When acting in the place of the president at a meeting, the president-elect has all the powers, duties, responsibilities, and privileges that the president may exercise at a meeting.

The Vice President

When there is no president-elect, the vice president assumes the duties of the president in case of the absence or incapacity of the president and becomes president on the death, resignation, or permanent incapacity of the president unless the bylaws provide something different.

When acting in the place of the president at a meeting, the vice president has all the powers, duties, responsibilities, and privileges that the president may exercise at a meeting.[2]

The vice president has only a few responsibilities established by parliamentary law, but is often assigned other duties through the bylaws. Vice presidents frequently direct departments of work or study; head important committees, such as the finance or strategic planning committee; serve on the governing board; and perform other assigned duties.

When there are ranking vice presidents, the first vice president presides in the absence of the president and becomes president if that office is vacated, unless the bylaws provide otherwise. If the vice president becomes president or otherwise vacates his or her office, the remaining vice presidents move up in rank, and the vacancy in the lowest ranking office of vice president is filled by the body assigned to fill vacancies in office unless otherwise directed in the bylaws of the organization.[3]

The Secretary

The president and the secretary are recognized by law as the legal representatives of the organization. The secretary has extensive duties, serving as the chief recording and corresponding officer and the custodian of the records of the organization.[4] In some organizations, employees perform these functions, and the bylaws may permit the organization to designate an employee to be the secretary. Most membership organizations, however, elect a member as secretary, who is responsible for ensuring that the secretarial duties are performed properly, either by performing them personally or by directing the appropriate staff in those duties. The secretary works closely with the president.

The chief duties of a secretary are to:

1. Take careful and accurate notes of the proceedings of the meetings as a basis for preparing the minutes
2. Prepare and certify the correctness of the minutes and enter them in the official minutes book or other means of storage
3. Read or submit the proposed minutes to the organization for correction and approval
4. Enter corrections approved by the members into the minutes
5. Record the approved minutes as the official minutes of the organization, include the date of their approval, and sign them to attest to their validity
6. Provide the presiding officer or the assembly with the exact wording of a pending motion or of one previously acted on
7. Prepare a list of members and call the roll when directed by the presiding officer
8. Read all papers, documents, or communications as directed by the presiding officer
9. Bring to each meeting the minutes book; a copy of the bylaws, rules, and policies; a list of the members; a list of standing and special committees; and a copy of the parliamentary authority adopted by the organization
10. Search the minutes for information requested by officers or members
11. Assist the presiding officer before each meeting in preparing a detailed agenda
12. Preserve all records, reports, and official documents of the organization except those specifically assigned to the custody of others

13. Prepare and send required notices of meetings and proposals
14. Provide the chair of each special committee with a list of the committee members, a copy of the motion referred to the committee or the motion referring a subject to the committee, instructions, and other documents that may be useful
15. Provide the chair of each standing committee with a copy of all proposals referred to it, instructions, and other materials that may be useful
16. Sign official documents to attest to their authenticity
17. Carry on the official correspondence of the organization as directed, except correspondence assigned to other officers
18. Perform any additional duties required by applicable statutes

In addition to these duties, the secretary performs many other tasks, such as calling attention to actions in the minutes that have not been carried out and keeping a report book or file of all reports submitted, a correspondence file, and a book of adopted policies and procedures. The secretary is responsible for calling attention to deadlines and the dates on which certain actions must be taken.

In the event that the secretary resigns, is unable to act, or willfully neglects to carry out the secretarial duties, the senior officer then in office, may send out any necessary notices as de facto secretary.

The elected secretary does not forfeit any rights of membership by reason of holding office and may propose motions and discuss and vote on all measures.

For more information on minutes, see Chapter 25.

The Corresponding Secretary

In some organizations, the secretarial duties are divided between a secretary, sometimes called a recording secretary, and a corresponding secretary. The corresponding secretary conducts the official correspondence for the organization as directed by the president or board, answers official letters, and maintains a correspondence file. The corresponding secretary also communicates with outside organizations that have relationships with the organization.

With the advent of correspondence and communications carried on by electronic means, including e-mail, websites, and social media, the corresponding secretary can be assigned to monitor the electronic media and respond to members and nonmembers as appropriate.

The Treasurer

The treasurer is responsible for the collection, safekeeping, and expenditure of all funds of the organization and for keeping accurate financial records. The treasurer should be a person of unquestioned integrity and should have knowledge of how to keep, or supervise the keeping of, financial accounts. In many jurisdictions, the treasurer of a corporation may have additional duties prescribed by statute.

In organizations that delegate to employees the work of collecting, disbursing, and accounting for funds, the treasurer, whether an elected member or an appointed employee, is ultimately responsible for the performance of these duties and for the accuracy of the treasurer's reports.

The treasurer collects and disburses funds only as directed by law, the bylaws, the membership, the board of directors, or other authority provided for in the bylaws. The treasurer does not have the power to borrow money or issue funds or checks except as authorized to do so by the assembly or the bylaws. The treasurer usually helps prepare the budget and serves on the finance committee.

The treasurer should report briefly on the finances of the organization at each membership and board meeting, answer any questions on financial matters, and submit a full report to the membership annually. For more information on the report of the treasurer, see Chapter 27.

The Parliamentarian

There are two types of parliamentarians. One is an employed consultant who has had training and professional experience in parliamentary law and who is not a member of the organization. Nearly all professional parliamentarians are accredited by either the American Institute of Parliamentarians or the National Association of Parliamentarians, or both. For more information on the role of the parliamentarian, see Chapter 30.

Professional parliamentarians not only can be of substantial assistance during the course of a meeting by advising how rules and procedures can be utilized properly to facilitate good decisions, but also by providing valuable services outside of a meeting setting. Examples of a professional parliamentarian's services include: the planning of business meetings; reviewing, drafting, and organizing documents of authority; and training and assisting officers, board members, and meeting staff for optimal service in their respective roles.

The other type of parliamentarian is the member parliamentarian elected by the members or appointed from the membership by the presiding officer. The choice of a member parliamentarian should be based primarily on the member's knowledge of parliamentary procedure. The member parliamentarian should be a source of information on parliamentary procedure, but, like all parliamentarians, has no authority to make rulings and should act only as an advisor to the presiding officer.

Organizations should consult a professional parliamentarian whenever complex procedural issues are anticipated, but they will usually find the services of such a professional of value on a routine basis as well.

The Sergeant at Arms

The sergeant at arms, under the direction of the presiding officer, helps to maintain order and decorum at meetings. The sergeant at arms acts as doorkeeper, directs the ushers, and is responsible for the comfort and convenience of the assembly. In a small organization, these duties may be performed by one person, but in a large one, there may be a staff of assistant sergeants at arms.

Honorary Officers

Some organizations provide in their bylaws for honorary officers and members. Honorary titles are created as a compliment to those on whom they are conferred. Honorary titles generally carry with them the right to attend meetings and to speak. However, they do not confer the right to propose motions, vote, or preside. The bylaws of the organization should set forth specific authority for honorary officers or members. Holding an honorary office does not prevent a person who is a member from exercising any rights or from holding a regular office.

Powers of Officers

The actual powers and duties of officers are stated in the bylaws and sometimes in statutes and charters. In addition, officers have the implied power to do whatever is necessary to carry out the functions and duties of their office. For example, a president who has the duty of appointing a committee has the implied power to fill a vacancy on the committee or to remove and replace a committee member who fails to perform prescribed duties. However, when an officer's powers and duties are listed in the organization's governing documents, the officer has no additional powers or duties except those that arise directly from those listed.

Delegation of Authority by Officers and Boards

Both officers and members should understand their responsibilities in delegating to other members or employees the powers, duties, and responsibilities assigned to them by the law or the bylaws of the organization.

The basic principle of the delegation of powers, duties, and responsibilities is that the members, officers, boards, or committees delegating authority retain full responsibility for the performance or exercise of the powers, duties, and responsibilities that they have delegated.[5] They also are responsible for negligence and its consequences in the exercise of the delegated authority.

There are two general types of powers, duties, and responsibilities—legislative and administrative. *Legislative* powers and duties, which are defined as adopting rules and policies intended to have a long-term effect on the organization, and are provided for by statute or bylaws, either expressly or by implication, cannot be delegated, except in profit-making corporations where most duties are delegated to the board. For example, if the bylaws provide that an organization elects its officers by a ballot vote of the delegates at the annual convention, the assembly of delegates cannot delegate this duty to its board of directors.

Administrative powers and duties are of two kinds—discretionary and ministerial. *Discretionary* powers and duties are those that depend on a special trust in the officer, board, or committee member and involve personal reliance on that person's wisdom, integrity, and discretion. An example of a discretionary duty is the appointment of committees by the president or the certification of minutes by the secretary.

Discretionary powers and duties assigned to a particular officer or board by statute, charter, or bylaws can never be delegated. For example, a board of directors of a nonprofit corporation cannot delegate its power to borrow money. The board of directors can authorize a committee or an employee to investigate and recommend the best rates and sources for borrowing money, but the final decision must be made by the board.

Ministerial powers or duties are those that require simply carrying out specifically described duties that do not call for the use of discretion but involve only the faithful performance of a mechanical or clerical function. Ministerial powers and duties can be delegated freely to members or employees. For example, a secretary has the ministerial duty of sending out notices of a meeting and can delegate this duty to other members or employees.

A committee may delegate some of its powers and duties to a subcommittee, but the committee remains responsible for all actions of its subcommittees.

Powers and duties should be delegated carefully and with the knowledge that the responsibility for supervising their exercise and execution remains with those doing the delegating.

Terms of Office

The bylaws should define the terms of office of all officers, directors, and committees. Bylaws sometimes limit the number of consecutive terms that a member may hold an office, and in some cases the total number of terms permitted to be served. This provision is intended to prevent domination of the organization by a few members. However, a limitation on terms is viewed as a limitation on the right of members to elect whom they please. The deciding principle should be the overall good of the organization.

Many organizations favor a short term of office, which brings officers up for review by election frequently. If the members are alert and interested, it is often unnecessary to limit the number of terms to which a member may be elected. One term may be too long for a poor officer, and three terms may be too short for a good officer.

When there is a provision in the bylaws restricting the number of terms to which a member may be elected to a particular office, a member who fills a vacancy in that office for a partial term is not barred from being elected to a full term or terms, unless the bylaws provide otherwise.

When eligibility to hold a certain office includes a requirement that a member must have served a term in another office, serving for half or more of a term to fill a vacancy fulfills the requirement unless the bylaws provide otherwise.

Officers are not always elected with the regularity or at the precise time prescribed by law or the bylaws. The ordinary rule in such cases is that the incumbents continue to hold office until their successors are elected or appointed.

It is generally not a good practice to limit the total number of years a member can serve on a board without regard to which positions are held. The restriction can cause unwelcome and unforeseeable problems as members move through the officer positions and use up their limited time on the board.

Vacancies

The bylaws should include rules governing vacancies. A vacancy in an office, on a board, or on a committee usually occurs because of the death, resignation, or departure of the member from the locality, and in these instances, there is no question that a vacancy exists.

There is sometimes uncertainty when a vacancy occurs because it may be discovered that an officer is ineligible after he or she has been elected. Uncertainly may also occur when there has been an abandonment of the office, an implied resignation, or prolonged neglect or inability to act. If there is a question as to whether an office is vacant, the board or the members should declare the office vacant to clear the record before a member is chosen to fill the vacancy.

Declaring a vacancy is not a means of removing an officer. An office cannot be declared vacant when there is an eligible incumbent willing and able to perform the duties of the office.

A vacancy is filled by the same authority that selected the officer, director, or committee member unless the bylaws provide otherwise. A special election is sometimes called to enable the members to fill a vacancy.

Some bylaws provide that the officer who is next in rank automatically moves up to fill a vacancy. Other bylaws require the board of directors to fill vacancies not otherwise provided for. If this duty is delegated to the directors or to any other group except the membership, unless the bylaws provide otherwise, the member chosen to fill the vacancy serves only until the next election at which time the vacancy can be filled by the membership.

Vacancies in elective offices must not be ignored or concealed. Members should be informed promptly of a vacancy, and the vacancy should be filled as soon as possible. If the board of directors or the president knows that there is, or is about to be, a vacancy, this knowledge cannot properly be withheld until after a meeting, convention, or election at which the members could have elected someone to fill the vacancy; to do so would permit the president or board to fill the vacancy by appointment.

Neither officers nor members should try to outwit the provisions of the bylaws by maneuvering to fill vacancies in elective offices by appointment. No member should accept an elective office with the intention of resigning in order to create a vacancy and thereby permit the appointment of another member to the office.

Discipline and Removal of Officers

An organization has an inherent right to remove an officer, director, or elected committee member from that position for valid cause.[6] If it has adopted this book as its parliamentary authority, it also has the right to suspend an officer or director from office. The bylaws should provide for procedures for removal or suspension. These procedures are quite different from those for the disciplining or expulsion of a member from an organization. In the absence of an established procedure, the disciplinary body may adopt its own procedures.[7]

Officers, directors, or committee members can be removed from office by the same authority that elected or appointed them. The power to select carries with it the power to remove. An elected officer or director can be removed by vote of the members. An appointed officer or committee member can be removed by the authority that made the appointment.

The common *valid* causes for removal from office are:

1. Continued, gross, or willful neglect of the duties of the office, which, in part, include duties of care, loyalty, and diligence, in addition to fiduciary duty
2. Actions that intentionally violate the bylaws
3. Failure to comply with the proper direction given by the assembly or the board
4. Failure or refusal to disclose necessary information on matters of organization business
5. Unauthorized expenditures, signing of checks, or misuse of organization funds
6. Unwarranted attacks on any officer, member of the board of directors, or the board as a whole on an ongoing basis
7. Misrepresentation of the organization and its officers to outside persons
8. Conviction for a felony

Examples of conduct that are *not valid* grounds for removal from office are:

1. Poor performance as an officer due to lack of ability
2. Negligence that is not gross or willful
3. A tendency to create friction and disagreement
4. Mere unsuitability to hold office

The procedures for suspending or removing officers, directors, and elected committee members must provide adequate notice to the accused, a fair hearing, the right to counsel, and a reasonable opportunity to present a defense, including the right to present and to cross-examine witnesses. An organization may want to provide in its bylaws that an officer may be temporarily suspended by the board during the course of investigation if there is reasonable cause to believe that the officer has engaged in a legal or financial impropriety. If the bylaws or statute are silent, the normal vote for removing an officer, director, or elected committee member is the same by which the position was filled, usually a majority vote. Any proposed suspension motion (including a motion to suspend temporarily, pending investigation) should be complete, including mention of (1) what duties and authority, if any, the suspended officer will have during the course of the suspension; (2) what requirements are necessary to terminate the suspension (for example, mere passage of a specific period of time, passage of time and good behavior, passage of time and request for reinstatement, or occurrence of an event); and (3) appointment of a temporary officer, if necessary to carry out duties essential to the functioning of the organization during the suspension.

An officer who complains of improper removal, or a member who believes that he or she has been disciplined improperly, must exhaust the procedures for relief afforded by the organization before appealing to the courts.[8] If proper procedures are followed, the courts will seldom interfere with the removal of an officer for valid cause.

Chapter 21

COMMITTEES AND BOARDS

Committees and boards are subdivisions of the membership charged with the day-to-day working of the organization. The board is often composed of the officers and may include some committee chairs. Committees may be established for a fixed term or for a specific duty.

Importance of Committees

Committees are important because they perform the bulk of the work of organizations. Members share in the work and responsibilities of their organizations through committee service. Recommendations from committees often become the final decisions of organizations. Most well-run business meetings spend considerable time on committee reports and recommendations. Usually the conclusions of committees are accepted as the conclusions of the organization.

Committees are valuable and should never become burial grounds for issues that members want to avoid; nor should committees be used to reward members or friends or to placate troublemakers. Committees render valuable service and can be excellent training grounds for future leaders of an organization.

No committee should be established unless it is needed. When placed on a committee that has no real work to be done, members will quickly lose interest in the organization and its goals.

In some states, it is necessary to comply with applicable law that may provide restrictions or rules regarding the composition and operation of an organization's committees.

Advantages of Committees

Following are some of the advantages that enable a committee to work more efficiently than the larger parent organization:

1. Greater freedom of discussion is possible.

2. More time is available for each subject assigned to the committee.
3. Informal procedure is used in committee meetings.
4. Better use can be made of experts and consultants.
5. Delicate and troublesome questions may be considered privately.
6. Hearings may be held giving members an opportunity to express their opinions.

Standing Committees

A standing committee is a committee that has a fixed term of office and does the work within its particular field that is assigned to it by the bylaws or referred to it by the organization, or the governing board. The term of service for members of standing committees is usually the same as the terms for the officers. Standing committees are ready to do the work that may be referred to them at any time and handle assignments that are expected to be carried out regularly. A membership committee, which investigates and passes on applications for membership, is an example of a standing committee.

An organization may provide for and fix the duties of as many standing committees as it finds useful. The name, number of members, quorum, method of selecting members, duties, term of office, and requirements for reports of each standing committee are often included in the bylaws. The bylaws may provide that the board or the membership create standing committees.

Special Committees

A special committee performs a specific task assigned by the organization. Even if it is called by another name, such as an ad hoc committee, a task force, a commission, or anything else, and unless otherwise designated by the organization, groups of members that are performing a specific task assigned by the organization are, in practice, special committees and are subject to the same rules as special committees.

A special committee ceases to exist when its final report is issued. If the organization votes to delegate additional work to a special committee, it continues until the new assignment is completed and another report is submitted. A committee created to arrange a social gathering is an example of a special committee.

Special committees are created and appointed as directed by the assembly or the organization's bylaws. Special committees report to the authority that established and appointed them. For more information on the delegation of power and authority by officers, boards, and committees, see Chapter 20.

Special Committees for Deliberation

Committees may be classified, according to the nature of their assignments, into committees primarily for deliberation and committees primarily for action. It is vital that a committee appointed for deliberation and investigation, or one that performs discretionary duties, be representative of all important elements and groups within the organization. The report of a representative committee will reflect the opinions of the whole organization and, as a result, the committee's recommendations will have a good chance of being approved. A nominating committee and a committee to determine the location for a new building are examples of committees that should be representative of the whole organization.

Special Committees for Action

A committee for action carries out a particular task that has already been decided on. Such a committee does not function well unless it is composed of members who favor the job to be done. A committee established to raise an endowment fund is an example.

Selection of the Committee Chair

A committee chair should be chosen for the person's ability to plan and direct the work of the committee and to function well with its members. On a deliberative committee, this may not be the person with the most expertise but rather the one with the best facilitation skills. On an action committee, it would be the person best able to lead the implementation of the action. Unlike the presiding officer of an assembly, the chair of a committee takes an active part in its discussion and deliberations and has all the rights of the other members, including the right to present motions and vote.

If no committee chair is elected or appointed, one may be selected by the committee from its own membership. If no chair is designated, the member first named calls the committee together and presides during the election of a chair. There is no parliamentary rule requiring that the member who proposes the creation of a committee be appointed as chair or a member of it, although there is no rule barring such appointment.

Selection of the Committee Members

Members of standing committees are appointed as directed in the bylaws, usually by the president with the approval of the governing board or assembly. The advice and suggestions of members enable the president to utilize effectively the talents of a large number of members.

It is often advisable to consult a prospective committee chair regarding the selection of the other committee members and an incumbent committee chair regarding the appointment of a successor.

Ex Officio Members of Committees

The bylaws of some organizations provide that because of the office held, the president or other officers or holders of a position outside of the organization are automatically members of certain boards or committees. Such members are termed *ex officio* members. An ex officio member is not elected or appointed to a committee, but becomes a member when elected or appointed to a particular office. When an ex officio member ceases to hold office, that person's membership on the committee terminates, and the new holder of the office assumes the ex officio membership. For example, the president is often an ex officio member of all committees except the nominating committee, and the treasurer is usually an ex officio member of the finance committee and is excluded from the audit committee.

Unless the organization's governing documents provide otherwise, an ex officio member has all the rights, responsibilities, and duties of other members of the committee, including the right to vote. The ex officio member is a full-fledged working member of a committee and is counted in determining the quorum. Anyone who is not expected to be a regular working member of the committee should be designated as an advisory or consultant member instead of being given ex officio status. An advisory or consultant member has the right to attend meetings and participate in debate, but is not counted in determining the quorum and does not have the right to propose motions or vote.

Powers, Rights, and Duties of Committees

The powers, rights, and duties of each standing committee and of important special committees that are appointed periodically should be provided for in the bylaws. The powers, rights, and duties of other special committees should be provided for in the motions that create them or in the instructions given to them. Since no committee has inherent powers, rights, or duties, these must be delegated to it by the authority that established the committee. Even an executive committee or board of directors has no powers and no duties except those delegated to it by the bylaws or by vote of the membership.[1] For more information on the delegation of powers and duties to boards and committees, see Chapter 20.

Unless otherwise provided in the bylaws or in a resolution establishing a committee, all committees are responsible to and work under the direction and control of the authority that created or established them. Standing committees are ultimately responsible to and under the control of the voting body, and they report to the governing board when it is acting for the voting body in the intervals between meetings. Standing committees are responsible to the board only if this is stated in the bylaws.

Special committees appointed by the membership, the governing board, or the president are responsible to the authority that established the special committee.

Any subject or duty that has been assigned to a special committee may be withdrawn at any time and assigned to another committee or considered by the body as a whole. Any proposal or assignment of work to a standing committee may be withdrawn by the governing body unless the subject or motion is assigned exclusively to the committee by the bylaws. Any special committee may be dissolved by the authority that created it.[2]

The members of a committee may be replaced by the appointing or electing authority. A member of a committee who is unable or fails to participate in committee activities should be removed and notified of the removal by the president or by the body that appointed the committee, and another member should be chosen to fill the vacancy.

A committee cannot represent the organization to any outside person or organization except when it is clearly authorized to do so. Unless there is specific authorization given to a committee to collect, hold, or disburse funds, all funds should be collected, held, and disbursed through the regular financial channels of the organization.

A committee has the right to appoint subcommittees of its own members to which it may delegate authority and which are directly responsible to the committee. Subcommittees report only to the committee that created them.

Working Materials for Committees

The secretary is responsible for ensuring that each committee is furnished with specific instructions on the work it is expected to do and with all helpful information that is in the possession of the organization, such as:

1. A list of the committee members, including addresses, telephone numbers, e-mail addresses, and fax numbers
2. A statement of the motions, problems, or tasks referred to the committee
3. Any instructions to the committee from the membership, governing board, or president
4. A statement of the duties, powers, and financial limitations of the committee
5. Available information that will be helpful to the committee— for example, reports of former similar committees
6. Policies, rules, or decisions of the organization relating to the committee's work
7. The nature of the report desired by the appointing power and the date the report is due

It is the duty of the secretary of the organization to ensure that these materials are provided for each committee. If the secretary of the organization does not provide such materials, it is the duty of the chair of the committee to obtain them for the committee members.

Committee Meetings Limited to Members

Since committees often consider business of a confidential nature, which should not be discussed at a meeting of the membership, the confidentiality of committee deliberations must be protected. No officer, member, employee, or outside person has the right to attend any meeting of a committee except by invitation of the committee or by direction of the appointing body.

If the committee wishes to invite a staff member, consultant, or other person to a meeting, it may vote to do so, but otherwise all meetings of a committee are limited strictly to its members. To further protect the privacy of the proceedings of a committee, its minutes are open to no one except members of the committee, unless its minutes are ordered to be produced by the entity that established the committee.

Procedure in Committee Meetings

Committees should function under procedures that are appropriate for the applicable circumstances. While committees preferably function with relaxed procedures, greater formality may be appropriate as the committee size increases, when the issues are complex or highly controversial, or when committee members have demonstrated an inability to work cooperatively. Occasionally the organization, through its rules, dictates committee procedure, but in the absence of such direction, a committee may determine its own procedures and level of formality under the guidance of the committee chair. Unless the organization directs otherwise, a quorum in a committee meeting is a majority of the committee members.

The committee chair is expected to provide leadership, including a proposal of a plan for the committee's tasks, assignment of work, and calling of committee meetings. If the chair fails to call a meeting, a majority of the committee members may do so, or the organization's president may call a meeting of the committee.

To ensure that committee meeting time is used most effectively, it is common for committee members or small groups of committee members to do preparatory work in advance of meetings, to discuss issues by e-mail in order to identify areas of tentative agreement and disagreement, and to do the necessary research and data collection to facilitate final decision making.

During committee meetings, the chair has the usual responsibilities of a presiding officer. Procedure is often relaxed by permitting debate without limits on the number or length of speeches (if such limits would otherwise apply), permitting members to remain seated when speaking, allowing discussions to occur prior to introduction of formal motions, permitting motions without seconds, and allowing the chair to participate fully in the committee deliberations, including debate and voting. Regardless of the informality, decorum must be maintained, and the chair should attempt to ensure balanced participation by all committee members and to discourage domination of meetings by individuals or small groups. While some aspects of problem solving may allow discussions to be somewhat tangential to the subject under consideration prior to the introduction of a motion, once a motion is under consideration, debate should be germane to the motion.

Decisions are often made by general consent (without objection), but when this is done, care should be taken that the exact wording of actions is recorded and reflects exactly what everyone agreed to; if this is not the case, amendments and majority vote may be required to adopt an action.

If appropriate, and if permitted by the organization's bylaws and by statute, committees may meet by conference call or similar electronic meeting methodology. Such a meeting is as proper as a physical meeting of the members, provided the other requirements for conducting a meeting have been met (in particular, notice and quorum). For guidance in conducting meetings by telephone and other electronic means, see Chapter 12.

Committee minutes are often recorded for internal use by the committee. If minutes are to be kept, the chair should designate a member to serve as the committee secretary for this purpose. Committee minutes do not constitute the committee report, which should be a separate written document, properly approved by the committee. For more information on committee minutes, see Chapter 25.

Committee Hearings

A committee hearing is a meeting at which a committee listens to the viewpoints of members, and sometimes of experts, on the subject assigned to it. During the hearing, the committee members may ask questions to elicit information or merely listen to the comments offered. In either case, the committee members do not enter into debate with the members or show bias on the subject matter of the hearing. At the end of the hearing, the committee, with only its members present, deliberates and agrees on the conclusions and recommendations that it will present to the membership. The committee report and recommendations will provide guidance for members making the final decision.

Most committee hearings are open to all members of the organization. However, hearings for the purpose of considering matters of discipline, finance, or other subjects that should not be decided publicly (and that might be harmful to the organization or to a member) are open only to members of the committee assigned to conduct the hearing. For a discussion of reference committee hearings held in a convention, see Chapter 24.

The Governing Board

Few organizations have time in their meetings for the members to plan, discuss, and decide all the matters necessary to carry on the work of the organization. Consequently, the members typically provide in the bylaws that a smaller elected group, acting as the representatives of all the members, shall carry on the work of the organization during the intervals between meetings of the membership. The group is called the board of directors, executive board, board of trustees, or some other name meaning the governing board.

A governing board of a voluntary organization is generally composed of the elected officers of the organization and of directors (trustees) elected by the membership. Usually the president and secretary of the parent body are the chair and secretary of the governing board. All members of the governing board are sometimes referred to as officers, but the term *officers,* as used in this book, does not include the members elected or appointed to the board without additional duties assigned.

The elected officers may have the authority, within their areas of responsibility granted by the membership, to commit the organization to certain actions, but directors have no individual capacity to make determinations on behalf of the organization.[3] The duties, responsibilities, and powers of the board of directors should be clearly defined in the bylaws. Such a board is usually delegated the duty and power of acting for the membership in the intervals between meetings, except that certain powers are vested exclusively in the members.

The final authority of any organization remains in its *members assembled,* except as that assembly may direct otherwise by adopting provisions in the bylaws. Unless otherwise provided in the bylaws or by law, any action of a governing board can be rescinded or modified by the membership, except when the bylaws assign exclusive authority over the matter to the board or when the matter acted on no longer remains within the control of the organization. The board also has specific duties and responsibilities assigned to it.

The board has the right to establish and appoint committees of its own members to which it may delegate authority and which are directly responsible to the board.

All members of a governing board share in a joint and collective authority, which exists and can be exercised only when the group is in session. Members of a board have no greater authority than any other member of the organization except when meeting as a board. Officers and members to whom specific duties are assigned perform the duties of their offices or assignments in addition to sharing in the group authority and duties of the board.

Business transacted at a board meeting should not be discussed, except with other directors, unless and until the information has been issued to all members or to the public by the proper authority. The minutes of a board are open only to its members because the board considers many matters that cannot be discussed outside of the board without injury to the organization or to its members. Informal procedure in board meetings is similar to that in committee meetings.

Many organizations give continuity to the board by staggering the dates of election of members to the board so that there are always experienced members on the board.

The Executive Committee of the Board

Since many boards cannot meet on short notice, it is customary to provide for a small executive committee of the governing board, usually composed of the president, designated additional officers, and perhaps additional board members.

The specific composition, powers, and duties of this committee should be provided for in the bylaws. Some organizations give the executive committee extensive power to act for the board. Others limit it to acting on emergency matters or on recurring matters that must be disposed of promptly. In most cases, with certain specific exceptions, the board can rescind the action of the executive committee just as if it had taken the action itself.

An executive committee reports to the board at its next meeting or by mail (or e-mail, if allowed by the bylaws), and the actions of the executive committee are reviewed and included in the minutes of the board.

Conflicts of Interest

A director or an officer of an organization may have business dealings with the organization, except when prohibited by the bylaws or by statutory law. The director or officer has both a legal and a moral duty, however, to disclose any interest in such a transaction and must deal fairly with and in the best interests of the organization.[4] The member who declares a conflict of interest is to avoid debating the subject matter, unless requested to provide information by the members attending the meeting, and may not vote on the matter.

Many organizations adopt policies that define conflicts of interest and that provide the details of the expected or required conduct of officers and members with such conflicts. They also prescribe the procedures that are to be followed when the policies are violated.

Tax-exempt status of an organization is another reason for caution in dealings between the organization and a member of its governing board. If a transaction is found to unduly favor a director or officer, the tax-exempt status of the organization (for example, under the U.S. Internal Revenue Code) may be jeopardized.[5]

Chapter 22

COMMITTEE REPORTS AND RECOMMENDATIONS

Committees are often assigned the duty of investigating a motion or a subject and reporting to the assembly with their findings and recommendations for action. The committee's work relieves the full assembly of the task and is usually more efficient and effective than if the assembly considered the matter.

Committee reports usually include:

1. A statement of the question, subject, or work assigned to the committee and any important instructions given to it
2. A brief explanation of how the committee carried out its work
3. A description of the work that the committee performed or, in the case of a deliberative or investigating committee, its findings and conclusions
4. The committee's recommendations, usually in the form of main motions or resolutions.

A committee report should be as brief as possible, consistent, and clear. It should provide the background necessary to assist in understanding any recommendations the committee is making for decision by the assembly. Credit may be given to anyone rendering unusual or outstanding service to the committee, but the report does not give special mention to those who perform only their expected duties.

Recommendations from the committee should be contained in a separate section in the report or attached to the report. Each recommendation should be in the form of a motion or resolution to be presented, discussed, and acted on as a separate motion by the voting body. Such motions, as with all motions, should be written clearly and should be complete, so that reference to the report is not necessary to understand the action to be taken if the motion is adopted.

Ordinarily, the assembly should take action only on these motions. If opinions and recommendations are included in a report, and the report is adopted (or approved or accepted), the opinions and recommendations, as well as the balance of the report, are binding on the organization. Such a broad commitment may be dangerous and is appropriate only in unusual circumstances, such as when the organization wishes to demonstrate its approval of the entire content of the report, perhaps to the public.

Agreement on Committee Reports

The report and the recommendations of a committee must be agreed on at a meeting of the committee. The committee members must have the opportunity to hear all the different viewpoints on the questions involved and to discuss them freely with each other. Otherwise, the report does not present the collective judgment of the committee. The approval of a committee report or recommendation by members of the committee individually and separately, without a meeting, is not valid unless such approval is specifically authorized by the body creating the committee.

When it is difficult or impossible for the members of a committee to meet, the bylaws or a motion may authorize the committee to agree on a report without a meeting. A report may be prepared by the chair and submitted by mail or electronically to the members for their suggestions and approval. Every member of the committee must have the opportunity to review the proposed report and to present objections or changes. Members who approve of the report sign the report and the recommendations, and if a majority (or such other vote requirement as may be authorized by the body instructing the committee) signs it, the report becomes the report of the committee.

In modern times, it is not unusual for committees to do a great deal of their work by electronic communication rather than in face-to-face meetings. While a teleconference meeting may substitute for an in-person meeting, exchanges of e-mails or other asynchronous communications cannot do so. (For more information on telephone and electronic meetings, see Chapter 12.) Nevertheless, such exchanges are often useful in preparation for an in-person meeting or a teleconference, at which time, much of the work having already been done prior to the meeting, noncontroversial recommendations and segments of the report may be approved rapidly. This leaves time for resolution of any remaining differences, substantially reducing meeting time. If little or no disagreement exists, a brief teleconference may properly give final approval of the report and its recommendations and remove the need for a physical meeting altogether.

When a report in its final form, along with the report's recommendations, has been considered and approved by a majority vote at a committee meeting, it is signed by the chair and may be signed by the members who agree with it, if they wish to do so. If the report is approved at a teleconference meeting, the chair should sign the report and list the members approving it. A member who agrees to a committee report with exceptions or reservations, especially regarding the report's recommendations, may indicate the portions with which he or she does not agree and sign the report, signifying approval of the remainder.

Presentation of Committee Reports

During a meeting when in the order of business it is time for committee reports, the presiding officer calls for each report in turn. Standing committees usually report first in the order in which they are listed in the bylaws. They are followed by special committees in the order of their appointment. Only those committees that are required to report, or are prepared to report, should be included on the agenda. The order of presenting reports, however, should be flexible to meet the needs of the particular meeting, and the order of presentation may be varied by majority vote or by general consent. A committee report is presented by its chair or by some member of the committee designated to report. The reporting member may introduce the report with a brief explanation if necessary. If a committee report is long, usually only a summary of it is presented orally, and written copies of the full report are made available upon request.

In conventions or annual meetings of large organizations, committee reports usually are printed in advance and distributed to members by mail, electronically, or at the convention. In such cases, the committee chair makes such explanatory statements as are needed and presents only the recommendations of the committee.

While advance preparation and distribution of committee reports are customary for conventions and annual meetings, it is a useful process for all meetings. Utilization of this process, if members recognize and accept their responsibility to prepare for the meeting, may reduce meeting time and permit members to give more leisurely and in-depth consideration to the reports. Advance distribution also provides an opportunity for members to obtain additional information before the meeting, perhaps preventing a delay in decision making that might otherwise occur.

Consideration of Committee Reports

A committee report, after being presented to an assembly, is open for comment, questions, or critical review, but the members of the committee and their motives may not be attacked.

A committee report cannot be amended except by the committee, since no one can make the committee say anything it does not wish to say. However, motions included as recommendations in the report, like all other motions, are subject to amendment and other actions that would apply to any motion. A committee report, after it is presented, may be disposed of in any of the following ways:

1. The report may be filed. This is the usual method for disposing of a committee report. It may be filed automatically or ordered filed by a motion, or the presiding officer may announce, "The report will be filed," and proceed to the next item of business. A report that is filed is not binding on the assembly but is available for reference and information and may be considered again at any time. An expression of thanks to the committee may be combined with a motion to file the report.

2. The subject and the report covering it may be referred back to the committee, or to another committee, if further study, modifications, or recommendations are needed.

3. Consideration of a committee report may be postponed to a more convenient time.

4. A report may be adopted, but only under unusual circumstances unique to the organization. When an entire report is adopted, it commits the assembly to all the findings and opinions contained in the report and to any recommendations that might be included in it, but not to any recommendations submitted separately. The word "accept" is sometimes used instead of "adopt," but the word "adopt," which cannot be misunderstood, is preferable. A motion "to receive" a committee report is meaningless, since an organization cannot refuse to

receive and hear the report of its authorized committee. Since the adoption of a committee report binds the assembly to everything in the report, organizations are wise to file reports instead of adopting them.

5. A final or annual financial report from a treasurer or finance committee is referred to the auditors by the presiding officer without a motion. No final financial report is adopted without an accompanying report from the auditors certifying its correctness.

6. If a financial report concerns proposed or future expenditures only, as in a budget, it is treated as is any other financial recommendation of a committee.

7. A motion proposed by a committee is moved by the reporting committee member (usually the committee chair), or it may be stated by the presiding officer. It does not require a second and is handled as any other main motion before the assembly, just as if it had been proposed from the floor and seconded.

Record of Committee Reports

After a committee report has been presented, the reporting member hands it to the secretary for filing in a special book or file reserved for committee reports. A committee report is not included in the body of the minutes unless the assembly votes that a brief summary be included.

Reports of standing committees are usually filed in chronological order under the name of each committee. Reports of special committees are usually filed in alphabetical order according to the subject or name of the committee.

The minutes of each meeting should state what reports were presented, by whom, and the disposition of each report. The minutes should also record the page or file number where the particular report may be found. Some organizations attach copies of final reports to the official copy of the minutes.

Each organization should adopt its own policies on retention of committee reports and other records. Legal considerations and the organization's values and resources will affect such policies. For example, any documents that may be required to be retained for future legal action must be retained in a retrievable form.[1] In modern times, electronic retention and filing of reports may substantially reduce the need for space-consuming physical files and may facilitate searching for such reports. If filed electronically, similar precautions should be followed for such reports as are followed for minutes, ensuring security and off-site backup.[2]

Minority Reports

If any members of a committee disagree with the report submitted by a majority of the committee members, they may submit a minority report signed by members who agree with it. More than one minority report may be submitted. A minority report can be presented only immediately after the majority report. A minority has the right to present and read a report, even though a motion is pending to dispose of the majority report. However, if a motion to dispose of the majority report is pending, the minority report is not voted on unless a motion is made to substitute it for the majority report. If such a motion to substitute is adopted and the report as amended by substitution is adopted, the assembly is committed to dealing with and disposing of the recommendations of the minority report, and the majority report is filed for reference. If the motion to substitute fails, the minority report is filed for reference.

Presentation of Committee Recommendations

Recommendations, which should be presented in the form of motions, may be acted on separately when they are presented with the committee report. When several recommendations are interrelated and have not been printed or sent to the members, they should all be read before members consider and vote on the individual recommendations.

After the presentation of the report, the chair of the committee reads the first recommendation of the committee and moves its adoption. As an alternative, the presiding officer may state the motion with the concurrence of the committee chair or reporting member.

The motion should be stated in a form that will allow the assembly to vote directly on the proposal itself, not on whether to agree or disagree with the recommendation of the committee. For example, if a committee recommends, "That a membership drive should be held in the spring of each year," the motion should be stated to the assembly as "I move that a membership drive be held in the spring of each year." This statement of the proposal allows the assembly to consider, to apply motions (for example, the motion to amend), and to vote directly on the actual proposal. This motion is much clearer than a motion such as, "I move that we concur with (adopt, reject, accept, approve, or agree with) the recommendation of the committee."

A well-stated motion requiring a decision directly on the proposal prevents the confusion caused by such motions as, "I move that we approve the recommendation of the finance committee rejecting the proposal of the treasurer to modify the system of keeping financial records." It is impossible to amend or affect this motion in any way that will reach the original proposal, even though the members may wish to do so. The original motion should be stated: "I move that the treasurer be authorized to modify the present system of keeping financial records." The presiding officer or the chair of the committee would then state for the information of the members that the original motion had been proposed by the treasurer and that the finance committee recommends a no vote on it.

After a motion embodying a recommendation has been stated to the assembly, it is considered and acted on as is any other main motion.

Chapter 23

CONVENTIONS AND THEIR COMMITTEES

A convention of an organization is a scheduled single meeting or a series of meetings that follow in close succession. Regardless of the number of meetings comprising the convention, the convention itself is regarded as a single meeting and should be provided for in the bylaws. Most organizations that hold their business meetings in convention format operate through a body of delegates selected in accordance with the governing documents to represent the general membership. In addition to delegates, a convention often provides an opportunity for all members from geographically diverse areas, often at the state, national, or international level, to come together. Organizations most commonly hold an annual convention, although some will meet two or more times a year, while others may meet less frequently than once a year.

During the convention, the voting members assemble to transact important business. In addition to conducting business, the convention may offer educational sessions, social gatherings, and updates in the organization's particular field, as well as opportunities to exchange ideas and experiences and to enjoy the fellowship of others who share a common interest.

While every member of an organization is ordinarily entitled to attend the convention, in larger organizations the business is commonly conducted by a smaller legislative body provided for in the bylaws, such as a house of delegates or another representative delegate assembly.

Business conducted by the assembly may include election of officers, consideration of informational reports, and action on resolutions. The assembly often carries out much of its work through standing or special committees.

Delegates and Alternates

Delegates to conventions are usually selected by the various constituent, component, and affiliate groups, chapters, or branches of the parent organization. At-large delegates (delegates without a constituency) may exist, and some or all officers (or others) may serve as delegates by virtue of the positions they hold, but delegates usually have a specific constituency of members within the organization.

It is the responsibility of delegates (or other voting members) to learn about the business to be transacted by the assembly, both before and during the convention, and to act in the best interests of the organization as a whole. The actions of the assembly determine the fundamental direction of the entire organization until the next convention, providing for its policies, programs, and use of resources. Actions of the assembly may facilitate or block the ability of the organization's leadership to move the organization forward in the immediate future.

While delegates should attempt to communicate with their constituents and to learn their opinions, values, and concerns, it is usually not wise for delegates to be instructed by their constituents to take specific actions on items of business. The delegates should be free to weigh the pros and cons and vote according to what appears to be the wisest course for the organization. The members whom the delegates represent may be unaware of the full range of arguments and information to be presented at the convention and cannot know the final wording of the proposed action, if it is amended.

Delegates also have a responsibility to report to their constituencies on the actions taken and to explain the facts and arguments that resulted in the decisions that were made.

Bodies selecting delegates are often authorized to select alternates as well. The duties of alternates may include but are not limited to: (1) serving in place of a delegate who is unable to attend all or part of the meetings, (2) learning about the operation of the organization and its convention and becoming educated in the matters of concern to the assembly, and (3) assisting in communicating the concerns of constituents to the assembly's members and communicating the business of the assembly to their constituents. In many organizations, alternates have virtually identical responsibilities as the delegates, except for the right to vote.

Convention Committees

Committees common to most conventions are the credentials committee, standing rules committee, and the program committee. Other committees described below, such as the tellers committee and bylaws or governance committee, while applicable to conventions, may also have application at the general meetings of organizations.

Adoption of the credentials committee's report establishes the voting body and is followed immediately by consideration and adoption of the reports of the standing rules committee and the program committee.

Some of an organization's standing committees may also be assigned tasks related to the work of the convention. A tellers committee may be utilized to assist with counting votes. Other members or committees may also be assigned duties to ensure the smooth operation of the convention and its meetings.

Organizations with a high volume of resolutions to consider often provide for one or more reference or resolutions committees, the ultimate role of which is to assist delegates in their decision making by summarizing facts and arguments and recommending actions that should be taken on resolutions.

Credentials Committee

The credentials committee is a standing committee of the assembly. The credentials committee examines the credentials of each member, delegate, or alternate and authorizes the issuance of the documents identifying members who may be admitted to the business sessions and who are entitled to vote. If there is a question regarding the eligibility of a member to serve as a delegate, this committee will bring the question to the seated delegates and may make recommendations for action on the eligibility of the member to serve in the assembly.

The credentials committee should maintain a continuously updated count of the members in attendance. This assists the presiding officer in determining the presence of a quorum and is essential if a roll call vote is needed.

The execution of these two duties obviously requires the cooperation of delegates in observing rules regarding "checking in" and "checking out" of the meeting room. Delegates should not be permitted to transfer their credentials, voting cards, ballot books, voting key pads, or other indicators of voting privileges to an alternate unless it is done through the credentials committee or is in accordance with the convention rules.

Some organizations may have rules authorizing individual delegates to transfer all, or some, of the privileges of assembly membership to alternates, but to do so with less involvement of the credentials committee, which may simply provide documentation to facilitate the transfer. Such rules may be useful in large assemblies, in which the more frequent but temporary substitution of alternates is desired to permit any special knowledge or expertise of alternates to be applied to the consideration of particular issues.

The credentials committee must report before any item of business can be presented to the voting body at the first meeting of the assembly. The initial report of the credentials committee must include, at a minimum, the list of the members entitled to vote. When adopted by those members on the list, this report becomes the official list of the voting members, who may then vote on any supplemental reports, as well as all other business of the assembly.

In many organizations it is also customary, if there are various classes of membership in attendance at the convention, for the credentials committee to include in its report a list of the delegates, alternates, nonvoting members, and who has voting privileges. Sometimes the report will include information on which components of the organization and geographical areas are represented and in what strength. This demographic information may be interesting and useful, but is not essential to the most important purpose of the report, which is establishing and maintaining the roster and count of voting members of the assembly.

A supplemental report is usually made daily since new delegates and members arrive and are credentialed as eligible to vote or alternates are substituted for the delegates. Supplemental reports may be requested before critical votes or elections in order to document the continued presence of a quorum and to determine the current voting strength of the assembly. It is understood that, unless otherwise provided in the bylaws or standing rules, newly registered delegates may participate immediately upon receipt of credentials from the committee and do not have to await the approval of the next supplemental report. The credentials committee stays on duty the entire time during the business meetings.

The credentials committee, the tellers committee, or an elections committee may be assigned duties related to supervision of voting and election procedures by the bylaws, standing rules, or a vote of the assembly.

Standing Rules Committee

The standing rules committee recommends to the assembly a set of convention standing rules that define the operating procedure that will be followed during the convention when it is desired to vary from, or add to, the provisions of the parliamentary authority. These standing rules are the internal policy of the assembly governing how it conducts its business and must, of course, be consistent with any convention procedures found in the bylaws or other higher-ranking documents of authority. The standing rules committee's report should be submitted immediately after the credentials committee's report. The standing rules of the assembly often are the same from convention to convention and are usually published and distributed to the voting members in advance of the convention, identifying any proposed changes from previously adopted rules. Unless otherwise provided in the bylaws or standing rules, the convention standing rules may be adopted by a majority vote and amended, repealed, or suspended by a two-thirds vote. When a standing rule is repealed, it defaults to the rule in the *American Institute of Parliamentarians Standard Code of Parliamentary Procedure*. When a rule is suspended, it is to permit a certain action to be taken that otherwise could not be taken under the rules. For more information on the motion to suspend the rules, see Chapter 11.

Some organizations will provide that their convention standing rules will remain the same from year to year, without the necessity of adopting them at each convention, until amended by a subsequent convention.

The convention standing rules ordinarily cover subjects such as:

- Seating of delegates and others
- Recognition for privileges of the floor
- Limits on debate
- Privileges of nonvoting members

Some assemblies may designate special microphones and other ways members can obtain recognition for debate and other purposes. Supplemental rules on election procedures not provided for in the bylaws may be included in the convention standing rules. If a reference committee system is used by the assembly, the details of its operations may be included in the convention standing rules if not included in the bylaws or other adopted rules of the organization.

Program Committee

The program committee of a convention is responsible for planning the schedule of meetings, activities, and special events of the convention.

This is the last of the reports required for the official organization of the convention. The proposed schedule is submitted to the convention. After approval, it becomes the agenda for the convention and establishes the nonbusiness schedule as well.

Once the agenda has been adopted, it is no longer under the control of the program committee and any subsequent changes must be made by the assembly itself, either by majority vote or general consent. However, it is often the program committee that will have information regarding necessary changes and that will therefore propose any such changes.

Tellers Committee

Many organizations have a tellers committee, which helps the presiding officer count standing votes and which usually counts ballots as well. Some organizations provide for an election committee to assist with most aspects of elections, while others may assign such duties to the tellers committee. Since the credentials committee identifies who is qualified to vote, its members may also be assigned responsibility for distribution of ballots.

The assigned committee may be responsible for preparing ballots, which may be preprinted and numbered in multicolored sets to ensure that each voting member may use a given ballot only once. To maintain ballot security and avoid confusion, the committee can designate the use of alternate colors if additional rounds of balloting are necessary.

Whichever committee is responsible, systems should be in place to ensure ballot security; that no one receives ballots unless that person is qualified to vote; that no one transfers his or her ballot(s) to another member; that no one receives a duplicate set of ballots; and that no ballot in a set is identical to any other, which might permit a member to vote more than once on a given proposal or election. Voting members are not allowed to complete their ballots before instructed to do so and are not allowed to submit their ballots after the chair has announced that the time for voting has expired.

The tellers committee issues a report for all standing and ballot votes. The tellers' report is read to the assembly and the presiding officer then announces the results, the outcome of the vote, and the effect of the vote to the assembly. See Appendix D for a sample tellers' report for elections.

Bylaws or Governance Committee

As a standing committee, the bylaws or governance committee will have duties as described in the bylaws and standing rules, which may include duties at the convention. The convention may assign additional convention-related duties to this standing committee. Such duties may include receiving and reviewing, in advance of the convention or other meeting, the wording of all proposed amendments to the bylaws and other governing documents that have been submitted for consideration by the convention. The committee may be required to review the wording of any new amendment to the bylaws or other governing documents proposed by a reference committee during the convention.

Having extensive familiarity with the entire bylaws, the members of this standing committee can provide proper wording of proposed bylaw amendments to achieve their intent without ambiguity. This committee may also prevent the occurrence of conflicting bylaw provisions resulting from amendments, assist with consistent formatting, and ensure the inclusion of additional amendments that may be needed as a consequence of adopting a proposed amendment.

The bylaws or governance committee may be empowered to: (1) approve the text of the amendment as written for submission to the assembly, (2) reword the amendment to accomplish the intent of the maker in proper form used by the organization, (3) combine several similar resolutions, with the permission of their proposers, and (4) comment on and make recommendations regarding the proposed amendments. The committee usually gives the reasons for its decisions.

The committee should not be empowered to prevent the adoption of any proposed amendment by failing to report it to the voting body. If the committee were given the power to decide which amendments should be presented to the voting body and which should be withheld, it would have the power to control amendments to the bylaws. This is a power that should be exclusive to the full assembly.

Chapter 24

REFERENCE (OR RESOLUTIONS) COMMITTEES

When an organization has a very extensive or complex agenda, it may establish reference (or resolutions) committees to assist in the timely conduct of its business and to optimize the decision-making process within the time constraints that exist. Such a system provides for the referral of all motions and reports to one or more reference committees.

These committees consider the items referred to them and provide recommendations for action by the full assembly. The following discussions assume that the reference committee system used will include open hearings, which the delegates attend to ask questions, obtain information, and offer their own opinions and testimony on the resolutions.

A reference committee system is usually provided for in the bylaws of the organization with the duties defined in the organization's convention rules. The purpose of the reference committee is typically to arrive at recommendations for action on the items of business referred to it. This is usually done by studying the resolutions and background information before the convention and then hearing testimony from the membership.

The size of the organization and its assembly, the number and complexity of resolutions, and the time available during the convention for consideration of business will determine the number, structure, and operation of the reference committees. Some organizations may find it helpful to have multiple reference committees and to assign related areas of concern to a single committee. (Budget and finances, membership, education, legal, bylaws, administrative, and legislative/governmental are examples of reference committees organized by business area.)

Reference committees divide the work of hearing, investigating, and making recommendations on proposals among a number of smaller representative groups. The voting body is able to dispose of an extensive agenda with a thorough understanding of the facts about each proposal.

Composition and Appointment

Reference committees should have at least three members and should be large enough to provide a reasonable cross section of the membership or convention delegates without becoming unwieldy. If the composition of the committees is not specifically defined in the bylaws, the bylaws should designate how they will be appointed. Appointment by the president is customary in some organizations. Those organizations that elect another officer specifically to preside at the assembly's meeting (for example, a speaker of the house of delegates) often designate that officer to appoint the members of the reference committees.

Members of a reference committee should be appointed with the assurance that they have knowledge and experience in the assigned subject matter; have no likely conflicts of interest; and will do the work of the committee, accept the work to be done in advance of the convention, attend the convention itself, and attend all the meetings of the reference committee and all of its hearings. Appointment should occur well in advance of the start of the committee's work to ensure that the composition of the committees is established when the work must begin.

An organization may provide for one or more nonvoting committee advisors to be included in a reference committee for various purposes. If available, staff members of the organization are often assigned to reference committees to provide relevant background information and facts, as well as to assist in the mechanics of each committee's operations and the writing of reports.

The advantages of using a reference committee system include:

1. The system permits the assembly to deal with a large number of business items without the full assembly having to spend the time that might be needed to hear the full debate on every item.
2. Each item of business may receive more in-depth consideration than it might receive from the full assembly.
3. Informal consideration may be permitted; the usual limits on length and number of speeches may be relaxed to allow more input from members than might occur in formal session.

4. The rules often allow members who might not otherwise have speaking opportunities (such as those who are not voting members of the assembly) to provide testimony; sometimes even those who are not members of the organization are permitted to provide testimony. This provides the assembly with a broader perspective on issues than the voting members alone might have.

Referral

Most organizations that have large conventions require that all proposals for consideration by the voting body be submitted by a certain date prior to the convention. Convention rules should provide a mechanism for the assembly to permit the introduction of late resolutions since business may arise that cannot be submitted before the designated deadline.

Depending on the bylaws, proposals in the form of motions or resolutions may be submitted by constituent (component) organizations, committees or boards of the organization, officers, delegates, and, in some organizations, by individual members. Standing and special committee reports with recommendations for action should also be referred to appropriate reference committees. Informational reports without recommendations for action may be referred to reference committees or filed without such referral, as the organization wishes.

The rules of the organization should identify how referral of resolutions to the various reference committees should be made; the most common practice is for the presiding officer to make the referrals. The referrals should be completed within a few days after the deadline for submission of resolutions.

Each delegate is usually provided with the full text of all reports and resolutions well in advance of the convention, including background material in accordance with the customs and rules of the organization; a list of which reference committee has received each resolution for consideration; and the assigned time and place for each committee's open hearings.

Hearings

The primary duties of a reference committee are to obtain and study the relevant background information on all matters referred to the committee; to hold open hearings to receive additional information, opinions, and testimony on such matters referred to the committee and requiring action by the full assembly; and to recommend the most appropriate actions to be taken by the full assembly. Hearings are most commonly open to all members of the organization, whether or not they are voting members of the assembly. Some organizations restrict testimony to voting members; others allow testimony from nonmembers (allowing this testimony is usually decided by a majority vote of the members of the reference committee).

The physical layout of the hearing room should provide for seating of the committee members at a table in the front of the room, with members who provide testimony facing the committee. Those testifying should be reminded to direct their remarks to the committee, not to other people in attendance.

Depending on the number, complexity, and contentiousness of the resolutions assigned to a reference committee and the total time assigned for the hearings, it may be necessary to place some restrictions on the amount of time available for testimony on some or all items of business, on the duration of testimony by any given person, and on the number of times any one person may testify. Such restrictions may be established by rule or may be decided at the discretion of the committee.

Usually those testifying may not testify a second time before the committee on the same issue until all those wishing to testify have had an opportunity to do so once. This restriction may sometimes be relaxed for the author of the resolution or for officers with relevant information on a specific issue. The committee chair must conduct the hearing with a careful balance of the members' right to testify and the need to complete the hearings in a timely manner.

If time constraints prevent every member who wishes to speak the opportunity to do so, consideration should be given to extending the duration of the hearing if possible. All members should have the right to be heard, and no member should be denied the right to testify.

While testimony in the reference committees is somewhat informal, decorum must be maintained. Those in attendance must be recognized to speak and must be respectful of others in their testimony. Disparaging remarks about individuals or groups should not be permitted; testimony should address the merits, or lack thereof, of the proposal itself. The committee chair should be empowered to eject from the hearing room anyone who is disruptive.

Motions are not in order during reference committee hearings. A member wishing to amend a resolution may, however, provide the reference committee with the language of the proposed amendment and urge the committee to recommend such an amendment, but the amendment is never formally introduced or considered at the hearing. In the same manner, testimony may urge the committee to recommend a referral of a resolution.

Votes, including nonbinding "straw votes," are not taken in reference committee hearings. It is not the role of those providing testimony to make decisions that would bind the reference committee in its closed-meeting deliberations. The reference committee will be making recommendations for action as described below, and the number of those in favor of and opposed to a resolution during the hearing should not be a dominant factor in the committee's decision-making process.

The members of the reference committee should take care to conduct themselves impartially. This precludes the provision of testimony by the reference committee members themselves, either while "seated" as a member of the committee, or by "stepping down" and testifying with the others in attendance. Such testimony by a reference committee member might discourage conflicting testimony and might create the perception that the committee members are not hearing testimony with an open mind, but have instead decided their position on the issue before hearing all points of view.

Reference committee members are permitted to ask questions to clarify the testimony of a member or to obtain additional information on the matter at hand. Such questions should be carefully worded to ensure that they do not reveal any bias of the committee member on the issue. Often all questions are provided to the committee chair who will ask them as appropriate.

Reference committee members who have important information on an issue or who have strong opinions on it will have the opportunity to share that information or opinion with other committee members during the committee's deliberations.

The reference committee is often authorized to combine resolutions of similar intent or composition in one group during the hearings and to arrange the resolutions assigned to it in a logical order to consolidate discussion and maximize the productivity of the hearings. In the absence of such considerations, testimony is usually heard on resolutions in sequence of the assigned resolution numbers.

The reference committee may be authorized to consider written testimony as well as that provided at the hearing. It is sometimes the case that a member who is unable to attend may provide useful information to the committee.

Development of Recommendations

After hearings have been concluded, the reference committee deliberates on its recommendations for action on each item of business that has been referred to it. The most common practice is for the committee to conduct these deliberations in a closed meeting.

Although it is helpful for the members of the reference committee to have some familiarity with developing committee recommendations and the format of a reference committee report, it is by no means essential. The committee decides what action will be recommended to the assembly. Appropriate employed staff, the parliamentarian, and officers can assist the committee in formulating the recommendations. Specific recommendations are selected to ensure the least procedural confusion while expediting final action by the assembly.

The committee recommends what it believes will be best for the organization based on the facts available and the strength of testimony provided. The persuasiveness of facts is far more important than the amount of testimony.

All items referred to the reference committee must be reported back to the full assembly for action. If an item of business is inadvertently omitted from the reference committee's written report, the presiding officer should nevertheless place that item of business before the assembly at the appropriate time.

Reference Committee Reports

Typically the reference committee develops a written report with its recommendations on each item of business referred to it.

The format of the written report may vary from organization to organization, but it should provide some orderly presentation of the recommendations for easy consideration by the full assembly. This usually will include a reprinting of the original resolution or its "resolved" clauses. Often all resolutions are presented in numerical order, but sometimes they are grouped by the nature of the recommendation of the committee. Resolutions of similar intent or content are usually grouped together.

Each organization should adopt rules governing the organization and format of reference committee reports and should provide templates to assist in the production of the reports. This will provide year-to-year consistency among the several reference committees.

However organized, the reference committee report must contain a clearly stated recommendation for action on every item of business. The recommendations may include actions similar to those available to an ordinary assembly, except that postponements are not ordinarily permitted. Recommendations may include:

1. *Approval or adoption:* The committee recommends that the resolution be adopted as submitted.
2. *Disapproval:* The committee recommends that the resolution *not* be adopted. Some organizations choose to word this recommendation as "rejection," "do not adopt," or "the reference committee recommends a no vote."
3. *Amendment and approval as amended*:
   a. One or more primary amendments to insert, strike, or strike and insert may be recommended.
   b. Amendment by substitution may be recommended.
   c. When a reference committee substitute is proposed to replace more than one of the submitted resolutions, a motion to adopt in-lieu-of the other resolutions may be recommended (see the section on adopt in-lieu-of in this chapter). Adopt in-lieu-of may also be used when two or more of the submitted resolutions are combined into a single resolution by the reference committee.
4. *Referral:* Depending on the organization and its rules and customs, referral may include details. These should include the body to which the referral should be made, instructions for studying the referred matter, and instructions on when and to what body to report. On occasion, if permitted by the bylaws and applicable law, the final referral may empower the body to which the referral is made to dispose of the referred item instead of bringing it back to the full assembly for final action. Some organizations require all referrals to be identified either as "for study and report," or "for decision" or "for action."
5. *Postponement:* Postponements are rarely used and then only if the postponement is to another scheduled meeting of the full

assembly where the membership of the assembly has not been changed by intervening elections or appointment. The motion to postpone cannot be used to postpone a motion to a later convention or to the next annual meeting. If action is to be deferred to a subsequent convention, the motion to refer is to be used.

Occasionally an informational report that would require no action (because it contains no recommendations for action or resolutions) may, as a result of testimony, seem to compel action by the assembly, in which case the reference committee may propose a motion or resolution. Sometimes one or more of the reference committees are permitted, or even expected, to originate motions or resolutions to express appreciation for service by officers, convention committees, retiring members of boards of directors, or other similar honorary matters.

Informational reports and other items presented to the assembly, but not requiring action, may be listed as filed. Such items do not require a vote of the assembly and will be filed whether or not they are included in the reference committee report. On such items, it should not be recommended that they be "approved" or "adopted" or "received."

The reference committee recommendations should result in resolutions that are worded in the affirmative and that are clear and unambiguous in their meaning. This is especially important if the originally submitted resolution does not have these features. The resolved clauses represent the action to be taken and should be complete in themselves ("stand alone") without reference to any "whereas" clauses in the resolution. Care should be taken to avoid wording that will result in uncertainty as to what action will be taken as a result of adopting the resolution. Individual members may not have skills to craft resolutions with these characteristics, and it is the reference committee's duty to perfect such resolutions to ensure that they are worded clearly.

Reference committee reports may include reasons for the committee's recommendations. This is particularly important when the recommendations are based on information that was not presented in open hearings, since members were not exposed to that information; an example might be advice from legal counsel during the committee's closed meeting. When there are not other well-functioning mechanisms for voting members to obtain such information, the explanations may include the relevant facts, arguments, and testimony that were considered so that members who did not attend the hearings may more fully understand the committee's rationale. It is always advisable, and in many organizations it is required by rule or custom, that the financial impact of adopting a resolution be included in the reference committee report.

In a closed meeting, the full committee approves all recommendations for action. The committee chair often drafts any explanatory language. When this is done, the committee should reconvene to give approval of the full final report, including the final wording of explanations. The report should then be signed by all members of the reference committee. On rare occasions, a minority report on one or more items may be necessary and is handled in the same manner as minority reports from other committees.

Consent Agenda in Conventions

In a convention, the consent agenda is usually composed of all the items on which the reference committee feels its recommendations are likely to be accepted by the assembly without objection. This conclusion by the reference committee may be based on a lack of testimony on an item or on testimony being heavily in support of the committee's recommendation. Items on which there is likely to be division of opinion or debate are usually not included on the consent agenda.

Most organizations allow any noncontroversial items to be included on a consent agenda, no matter what the reference committee's recommendation for action may be. After calling for the removal of items from the consent agenda (the removed items will then receive separate consideration), the adoption of the consent agenda enacts the recommendation of the reference committee on each remaining item, whether that recommendation be "approval" or "adoption," "defeat" or "do not adopt," "amend and adopt as amended," "referral," or "adopt reference committee motion." The en bloc adoption of a variety of parliamentary actions in a single vote is a unique feature of the consent agenda.

In its most expansive application, all items of business are placed on the consent agenda, without regard to the likelihood of removal, and only those items that are actually removed and placed on the regular agenda are given individual consideration.

In some cases, a member or component that proposed a resolution may wish to withdraw that resolution from consideration by the assembly. If there is no objection from the assembly, the resolution is withdrawn from consideration as part of the consent agenda. It will not be considered at the meeting but will be recorded in the minutes as withdrawn.

A consent agenda that is proposed with the inclusion of all items of business is most appropriate in organizations where:

1. There is a very extensive agenda.
2. Most members are willing, in the interest of time, to allow items to be disposed of as recommended, even if they disagree, because they recognize that their opposition to the recommendation is not likely to prevail if the item is removed.
3. The reference committee anticipates the will of the full assembly in most cases, providing recommendations that are acceptable to the assembly on most items of business.
4. The members fully understand and are willing to exercise their right to remove items when they believe that it is important to do so or that it will be a productive effort.
5. Members recognize that the use of a consent agenda that includes all items of business is helpful to the timely disposition of the extensive agenda.

Bylaw amendments and other actions that require a vote that is higher than a majority may be included in the consent agenda. Since the consent agenda is adopted by general consent ("without objection"), it is presumed that the assembly has acted with the necessary vote threshold. The same is true for bylaw amendments where the committee recommendation is "do not adopt."

Ordinarily, if the assembly must take action on a budget, that item should not be placed on the consent agenda. Action on other items of business may require that the budget be amended to reflect other decisions before it is adopted.

Priority Agenda

In some organizations, and particularly at conventions, if the available meeting time is less than might be desirable, a parliamentary tool called the "priority agenda" may be employed. This is a method of considering important items of business before the remainder of the agenda is considered. The priority agenda is explained in more detail in Chapter 14.

Action on Reports

The presiding officer, with the assistance of the reference committee chair, deals with business in the following order:

1. Items or resolutions to be withdrawn (and not considered by the assembly) are identified.
2. Items on the priority agenda are considered and disposed of.
3. Reference committee reports are heard, and, as each is presented, a request is made for delegates to identify items or resolutions for removal from the consent agenda and placement on the regular agenda for individual consideration and action.
4. Adoption of the remainder of the consent agenda is accomplished by general consent.
5. Items or resolutions removed from the consent agenda that are now on the regular agenda, are then considered.
6. Finally, items or resolutions that were never placed on the consent agenda are considered.

If a priority agenda is utilized, after providing an opportunity for the assembly to modify it, the presiding officer should present the items on the priority agenda for consideration by the assembly in the order designated. This takes place before any other business is considered, unless there are provisions on the regular agenda for other time-sensitive items, such as elections, to be disposed of first.

After disposition of all items on the priority agenda, reference committee reports are heard. In some organizations, the sequence in which these reports are taken up is designated, but in most, the presiding officer may determine the sequence that is felt to be most conducive to the assembly's decision-making process. Sometimes the effect of various resolutions demands that some be considered and disposed of before others are considered.

Ordinarily the presiding officer first processes the consent agenda of the reporting committee. Removal of items from the consent agenda is requested ("Are there any items to be removed from the consent agenda and placed on the regular agenda?"), and then members may be recognized by the presiding officer and identify the item to be removed. These items are considered after adoption of the consent agenda.

The remainder of the consent agenda is then adopted without debate, by general consent. The presiding officer announces that the consent agenda is adopted, but is not required to announce the outcome on the individual items in the consent agenda. When the consent agenda has been disposed of, the presiding officer then deals with any items removed from the consent agenda. After those items are disposed of, individual resolutions that were never on the consent agenda are dealt with. In each case, the reference committee's recommendation is read. Since delegates typically have the written report, it is not customary to read the entire resolution to the assembly. Custom will direct whether or not the reference committee's rationale will be read aloud. However, any member can demand that an item be read unless the organization's rules prevent such a demand or the demand is dilatory.

Unless the rules provide differently, the assembly never votes directly on the reference committee's recommendation for action unless the resolution is included in a consent agenda. Instead, the assembly votes on the original resolution or other motions proposed by the reference committee.

If the committee recommends an amendment in any form, the presiding officer may assume a motion, which is considered immediately as though introduced from the floor; likewise, a committee recommendation to refer is considered immediately as though introduced from the floor. If the motion to amend or refer is defeated, the original resolution is still before the assembly for action.

The presiding officer maintains control of the meeting while the chair of the reference committee is reporting and presenting the recommendations of the committee. It is inappropriate for the chair of the committee to usurp the role of the presiding officer by controlling debate, processing motions, or taking votes. The reference committee chair should be stationed near the podium to introduce the committee's motions, if necessary, and to explain the committee's reasoning in debate, if required.

The Adopt In-Lieu-Of Motion

In ordinary (nonconvention) assemblies, it is rare for more than one motion or resolution on a subject to be submitted in advance, and therefore only one main motion will be considered at a time. When it is desired to amend such a motion by substitution, the substitute amendment is processed as described in Chapter 9.

In a convention, on the other hand, motions and resolutions are usually required to be submitted in advance. Multiple resolutions on similar subject matter are commonly received and referred to the reference committee, which may wish to propose a single substitute that takes the best features of each of these multiple resolutions, based on testimony and other background material, and to recommend its adoption as a substitute for each and all of the "underlying" resolutions.

Since the purpose of the reference committee system is to expedite business and since there is a presumption that the reference committee usually provides a recommendation that is most likely acceptable to the assembly, a mechanism to arrive at that final action with fewer votes is appropriate.

That mechanism is the use of a motion to adopt in-lieu-of. The reference committee recommends that its motion, which is fully stated, be adopted in lieu of the other resolutions, specifically identifying those to be replaced (usually by resolution number).

If the recommendation is adopted as part of the consent agenda, the reference committee motion is adopted, and the other resolutions are not acted on directly, but are now moot.

If the recommendation is removed from the consent agenda and placed on the regular agenda, all the underlying resolutions are removed with it. In this case, the reference committee's adopt in-lieu-of motion is taken up first. The reference committee's adopt in-lieu-of motion, when pending, may be perfected by amendments, and if it is then adopted, it is enacted. With the adoption of the adopt in-lieu-of motion, the underlying resolutions are not adopted and are considered moot.

When the vote is taken on the motion to adopt in-lieu-of, an affirmative vote adopts, and that is the only vote needed. If adopt in-lieu-of fails, no options have been eliminated.

If the adopt in-lieu-of motion proposed by the reference committee is not adopted, the presiding officer announces that it is not adopted and that any member may, if he or she wishes, propose the adoption of any one of the underlying resolutions in lieu of the other remaining resolutions. Again, if the proposed adopt in-lieu-of resolution is adopted, the remaining underlying resolutions become moot. This process may be repeated until one of the resolutions is adopted in lieu of the others or until none of them are adopted.

In summary, the motion adopt in-lieu-of would be used to bring a single resolution before the assembly for its consideration in disposing of an issue for which there are multiple resolutions. By adopting that motion after usual debate and amendments, the assembly disposes of the issue with one vote instead of two or more votes without having to repeat debate. If adopt in-lieu-of fails, any member may move one of the underlying motions. For example:

REFERENCE COMMITTEE CHAIR: The chair moves to adopt Resolution A in lieu of Resolutions B, C, and D.

PRESIDER: You have before you now the motion to adopt Resolution A in lieu of Resolutions B, C, and D. Discussion is now in order on Resolution A.

After the completion of debate and any amendments, the presiding officer calls for the vote:

PRESIDER: All those in favor of adopting Resolution A in lieu of Resolutions B, C, and D, raise your voting cards. Cards down. All those opposed, raise your cards. Cards down.

The vote and disposition are then announced:

PRESIDER: There is a majority in favor, and you have adopted Resolution A in lieu of Resolutions B, C, and D.

or

PRESIDER: There was not a majority in favor; therefore, the motion to adopt Resolution A in lieu of Resolutions B, C, and D has failed. A member may now move adoption of Resolution B, C, or D. The delegate at microphone 1 is recognized.

DELEGATE: Mr. Chairman, I move to adopt Resolution D in lieu of Resolutions B and C.

Debate, amendments, and votes would continue until Resolution D is in the form the assembly prefers. The assembly would then vote on the adopt in-lieu-of resolution, disposing of it as occurred with Resolution A above, with the same consequences. The process would continue until a resolution is adopted, all are defeated or declared moot by the presiding officer, or no member approaches the microphone to move any further motions on the matter.

Reference Committee Influence

The recommendation of the reference committee is often a highly persuasive factor in determining the decision of the assembly. The great influence exercised by the committee, however, is advisory.

It is important that the assembly fully understands that it has the opportunity to consider all proposals submitted to it and to make the final decision on them. If the voting body does not agree with a recommendation of a reference committee about a resolution, the resolution may be removed from the consent agenda and disposed of in any manner the assembly finds appropriate. In fact, if the reference committee does not arrive at a recommendation that is supported by the assembly (whether through faulty judgment, simple divergence of opinion, or even by intentional disregard of testimony), the assembly always retains the power and responsibility of final decision on every item of business.

Every member must be vigilant, knowledgeable of each item of business, and prepared to lead the assembly in the decision-making process if he or she disagrees with the recommendation of the reference committee and thinks there is a reasonable probability that the assembly might concur.

Chapter 25

MINUTES

Minutes are the legal history and record of official actions of an organization. Minutes are the formal record of a deliberative assembly's proceedings, approved (as corrected, if necessary) by the assembly.[1] Minutes provide a record of reports and decisions made at a meeting on behalf of the entire membership, regardless of whether members are present at or absent from the meeting. The accuracy of minutes is essential. They are used by auditors as proof of financial actions authorized by the organization and by courts as evidence of actions taken.

Responsibility for Accurate Minutes

The secretary is responsible for recording all actions taken at business meetings, preparing proposed (draft) minutes, recording any corrections, and certifying the official minutes by signing them when they have been approved by the organization. If the minutes are prepared on a computer, an electronic signature may be used for approval of the minutes. The members of the organization or the governing board hold the final responsibility for pointing out errors and approving the minutes of the respective body.

A stenographer's verbatim record or a tape recording of the meeting is not generally used as the official record. A verbatim record or tape recording contains elements, such as debate, that should not be included in the formal minutes. These recordings may be used by the secretary as an aid in preparing the draft minutes, but they should not take the place of the minutes themselves.

The secretary is responsible for the completeness and accuracy of the proposed minutes. In the absence of the secretary, responsibilities of the office may be delegated by the election of a secretary pro tem by the assembly. The notes taken by the secretary during a meeting are not an official document but are considered to be informal notes. The secretary is the custodian of the official minutes. The minutes of a general membership meeting or a convention are open to inspection by members of the organization.[2] Except when the bylaws or rules indicate otherwise, minutes of a board or committee meeting are available only to members of the board or committee. In the case of some incorporated organizations or public bodies, the law may require that the minutes be available to members or to the public.

Minutes Format

The format of minutes should meet several specific objectives: the minutes should be easy to access and easy to review for pertinent actions. They should also contain the essential information required by the organization. The use of computers has provided the opportunity for an organization to establish a format that is easily duplicated from meeting to meeting and that meets the basic requirements in an easy-to-read format.

There are several formats that may be used, and each organization should develop the one that works best for it. The complexity of the organization's meetings may determine the format chosen. For an example of model minutes using the subject format, see Appendix E. Two types of minute templates are shown in Appendices F and G.

Minutes Preparation

The secretary should prepare the draft minutes as soon as possible after a meeting while the notes are still meaningful. A delay in preparing the minutes often results in misinterpretation of the notes taken during the meeting. An employee may prepare the minutes under the secretary's direction, but the employee may not sign them.

Closed Meeting Minutes

Minutes of a closed meeting (executive session) should be prepared by the secretary and maintained separately from the regular minutes of the organization. The minutes are prepared in the same format as regular meeting minutes and are available only to members who attended the closed meeting or who would be authorized to attend. Minutes of a closed meeting must be approved only in a closed meeting. The final actions taken during the closed meeting may be reported to the regular meeting by adoption of a motion authorizing the report. These final actions are then recorded in the minutes of the regular meeting of the organization, as well as in the minutes of the closed meeting.

Committee Meeting Minutes

Minutes kept during committee meetings are less formal than minutes of a board meeting or assembly. In committees, minutes are sometimes kept by the committee chair, but it is usually better to appoint a secretary. Committee minutes are generally brief, but in some cases they may be more detailed than those of meetings of the organization because they often serve as the basis for the committee's report. Minutes of committee hearings frequently list people who speak for or against proposals and often summarize the facts presented by each speaker.

Content of Minutes

Minutes are generally a record of all actions and proceedings but *not* a record of discussion. The opening paragraph records the date, hour, and place at which the meeting was called to order, the type of meeting (regular, special, or continued), the name of the presiding officer, and a reference to the person recording the meeting (secretary or secretary pro tem). The second paragraph should state that a quorum was present by declaration of the chair, by including the number of members present, or by listing a roll call of members. A copy of the notice or call to the meeting should be included or attached to the minutes of a special meeting. Each action of the assembly should be recorded in a separate paragraph. The minutes record all main motions or resolutions stated by the presiding officer and the way in which the assembly disposed (temporarily or permanently) of each such motion.

Some organizations do not indicate the original maker of the motion, as this is often confusing when the motion has been substantially modified and no longer is the same proposal the member originally presented. If the mover of the motion is indicated in the minutes, it is good practice to state the original motion and the motion as finally adopted.

The exact wording of a main motion should be recorded in its final form as adopted (or as adopted after amendment). When a vote is counted or taken by ballot, the number of members voting on each side is recorded. In a roll call vote, the record of each member's vote is entered in, or attached to, the minutes. Remarks of a member wishing to state a protest or a position on a motion are not recorded unless a motion permitting such action is adopted by majority vote or if such action is required by law. A motion withdrawn after being stated by the presiding officer is recorded in the minutes. If a motion is withdrawn before it is stated by the presiding officer, it is regarded as never having been made and is not recorded in the minutes.

Minutes should document any notice given that will affect a future action at a later meeting. For example, if notice of a bylaw amendment must be given prior to its consideration and such notice is given at the current meeting, the secretary should record that notice in the minutes.

Each report should be listed with the name of the member presenting the report, a brief summary of the report, and the action taken. Copies of the complete report may be attached to the official minutes. If the report is filed, the minutes should include a reference to where the report may be found. Filed attachments may be in the form of a hard copy physically placed on file with the approved minutes or electronically attached to the minutes document itself. Reports that are attached to the minutes should be available to members who have the authority to access those minutes.

Business transacted during a meeting should be stated specifically and not in generalities. Officer reports and correspondence should be identified and summarized, and any action taken on them should be recorded in the minutes.

What Minutes Should Not Contain

Minutes should not contain procedural motions that are handled during deliberation of a main motion, except when they affect future action, as when a meeting votes to adjourn with a main motion pending or a motion to refer or postpone carries a main motion forward to a subsequent meeting. For example, primary and secondary amendments are not included unless they are incorporated into the final adopted main motion. Likewise, when the motion to close debate is adopted, it is not included in the minutes.

The names of seconders are not included in the minutes unless required by the governing documents of the organization. The seconder may or may not agree with the motion but may feel that the motion should be brought before the assembly for discussion.

Minutes are a factual report and should never contain personal opinions, personal interpretations, or comments. Descriptive or judgmental phrases, such as "a heated discussion," have no place in a factual record of business and may lead to disputes and even legal consequences. Programs should be referred to by title, subject, or description and should not include any personal impressions.

Criticism of members should never be included in minutes except when action on a motion to censure or reprimand a member has been stated. Motions of thanks, gratitude, or commendation generally appear in the form of a courtesy resolution.

Correction and Approval of Minutes

Before the assembly approves the minutes, they are merely the secretary's understanding of what happened at the meeting. Minutes become the *official* record of the organization when they are approved, and the secretary certifies them as the officially approved minutes by writing the word "Approved" at the end of the document, entering the date, and signing. Some organizations that have complex minutes require that the president also sign or initial each page of the approved minutes.

At the appropriate place in the order of business, the presiding officer calls on the secretary to present the proposed minutes. It is common practice for organizations to submit the minutes as a "draft" to the membership in electronic or written form prior to the meeting. When approval of the previously distributed minutes is taken up in the order of business, the minutes are not read. The presiding officer assumes a motion for approval of the minutes and asks, "Are there any corrections to the minutes?" When corrections are suggested, they are usually approved by general consent. The presiding officer may say, "If there is no objection, the error pointed out by Mr. A will be corrected." The minutes are then adopted as presented or amended.

If there is an objection to a proposed correction, the presiding officer should take a majority vote to approve the change in the proposed minutes. The only changes that may be made to the minutes are to add or correct actions that took place during the original meeting. Additional information or actions that were taken after the close of the meeting may not be added to the pending minutes.

Minutes submitted to the members prior to the meeting at which they are approved should be clearly identified as draft minutes. Since the minutes have not been approved by the membership, they are still in the form of an unadopted motion, and the secretary may enter the approved corrections in the final document. Corrections are incorporated directly into the pending minutes of the meeting for which the corrections were made. If an error in the minutes is discovered at a later time, the error may be corrected by the assembly, regardless of the lapse of time, by a majority vote. The correction and final approval of the minutes are the duty of the assembly unless that authority has been given to a minutes approval committee.

The presentation of the proposed minutes may be postponed. However, organizations should not make a practice of postponing the reading and approval of minutes since delay makes it more difficult for members to detect errors. Until the minutes are approved by the assembly, they are not official, and they should not be approved until they are either heard or seen by the assembly or by a designated committee.

Minutes Approval Committee

If an organization does not meet often, it is important to have a committee on minutes to which all proposed minutes are referred for correction and approval. An organization that does not meet at least every three months should have a committee to approve the minutes of the meeting. Because the approval of minutes is a power normally reserved for the assembly, the authority for a minutes approval committee should be included in the organization's governing documents or granted by adoption of a motion. The committee may be given the authority only to review the minutes, in which case final approval must still be an action of the assembly, or the committee may be given complete authority to approve the final minutes and report to the assembly. In either case, the minutes may be corrected by the assembly if an error is found in the future. The approval committee may be a standing committee, a special committee appointed at the meeting, or the executive committee or governing board.

In order to carry out their responsibilities, members of the approval committee will likely find it necessary to take their own notes at the meeting in the same way that the secretary must take notes.

The secretary's draft of the minutes is sent to the appointed committee. The minutes may be sent to the committee members by electronic means and edited by using "track changes" or other word processing methods. If the members prefer to submit changes on a line-by-line basis, the secretary may use a line numbering system to make editing easier. The committee is expected to respond to the secretary with corrections in a timely manner. The secretary will then compose the final draft based on the editing from the committee and obtain the committee's approval before submitting it to the organization.

The members of the minutes committee have the final authority over the content of the document. The secretary's record of the meeting is considered to be only notes until approved by the committee or assembly. The secretary, if in disagreement with the approval committee, may file a minority report to the assembly after the report of the committee, and the assembly will determine the final copy for the official records.

Published Minutes

There are several forms of published minutes, including those printed for distribution, e-mailed to the members, and placed on a website or in the organization's official publication. Unless authorized by the organization, copies of minutes should be limited to those entitled to attend the meeting for which the minutes were created. Minutes are generally limited to the substantive action items taken at a meeting. If any discussion is included, it must cover both sides of the issue without prejudice. Minutes made available to the members prior to approval should be clearly marked as "draft" until approved.

Retention of Minutes

An exact copy of the official, approved minutes should be entered in a suitable record format and kept in a safe place. It is safest to maintain backup copies on a separate computer in another location, rather than only on the secretary's computer. Using off-site storage media is an alternative backup system. These systems will provide sources for recovering the records if the secretary's copies are compromised in any way.

Signed minutes should be maintained with the same security measures as other legal documents of the organization.[3] Electronic archiving is the standard for most organizations. Most states recognize legal documents as those that may be retrieved as hard copy. If various versions of electronic files of minutes are created as a result of corrections, the versions should be clearly identified, with the currently correct version always identified as "final" in some way and with draft versions deleted as appropriate. At regular intervals that meet an organization's requirements, a hard copy or a retrievable electronic copy of the approved minutes and all legal documents of the organization for that period should be kept in a safe location for legal and historical purposes.

Current copies of the charter, bylaws, rules, policies, and procedures of the organization should be included in the secretary's notebook for quick reference at meetings. Minutes may be bound at the end of each year or term for historical reference, and the bound volume should include bylaws and other documents that are applicable to the same time period. An index to each year's minutes by subject, date, and page is useful.

Dispensing with Reading of the Minutes

A motion to "dispense with the reading of the minutes" is confusing because the meaning is unclear. If the intent is to delay the reading until later in the meeting, the motion should be, "That the reading of the minutes be postponed to (time)." If the intent is that the minutes shall not be read aloud, but that the printed version, which has been distributed, should be approved, the motion should be "That the minutes be approved as distributed." If minutes are postponed to a later meeting, they are taken up in the order of the oldest to the current minutes and are approved individually.

The motion to "dispense with the reading of the minutes" is not in order when the intent is to avoid considering them at any time and just retain the secretary's unapproved draft as the only record of a meeting. The minutes are the official document and must be approved to provide a legal record of the meeting.

Documents published on a website, in newsletters, or in other organizational communications are often a summary of actions taken at a meeting. The intent is to keep members aware, in a simplified format, of actions taken. This format has become a standard and good practice within certain organizations. While these forms of communication may be useful, they do not replace the need for a formal set of official minutes with proper content.

Useful Tools

There are shortcuts the secretary may use for taking minutes during a meeting to provide consistency of format from meeting to meeting. There are also ways to provide the secretary with quick access to historical resources on previous actions when such access may be required during a meeting.

Minutes Template

A *minutes template* is a format of an organization's minutes that is used by the secretary to prepare an initial version of the minutes *prior to the meeting*. This allows the secretary to set up a large portion of the minutes prior to the actual meeting, and he or she has only to "fill in the blanks." For examples of minutes templates in both column and subject formats, see Appendices F and G.

Meetings have many common elements that are well known before the meeting begins. These include such items as the type of meeting, the location, the presiding officer, and presence of the secretary. These items in the first paragraph of the minutes may be formatted well in advance of the actual meeting.

The call to order, any routine opening ceremonies, and the quorum statement may also be formatted with a blank to fill in the actual time, names, or number. If a meeting does a roll call, the names of all members may be listed and then the names of members not in attendance may be deleted and not included in the final draft.

In addition, at either a regular meeting or a convention, the agenda is generally known prior to the actual meeting. Most of the activities and names of reporting members are listed on the proposed agenda. For instance, the reports of officers, standing committees, and special committees are listed on the agenda prior to the meeting. The minutes template may list this information prior to the meeting, and the actual report or item of business is added as it is presented. Any special items of business for which advance notice was given may also be incorporated into the minutes template. Often, new business items are known before the meeting begins.

Utilization of a minutes template allows the secretary to easily add the motions and items of business within the format as they come up during the actual meeting. This can save considerable time after the meeting and often will allow the first draft of the minutes to be ready for submission to the minutes approval committee by the end of the meeting.

Action Log

In addition to the minutes, the organization may develop a system of recording actions taken, but which are separate from the minutes. This is called an *action log* and allows an organization to quickly review previous decisions. The need for this system often comes up when a motion is made that may or may not be in conflict with an action previously taken. It is not unusual, as an organization's leadership changes, to have a question about whether a proposed motion is in conflict with a past action. An action log provides a quick answer.

The log identifies all decisions of the organization. It is often a list of actions identified by subject and recorded by date for quick cross-reference to the minutes. Some organizations incorporate the total wording of the adopted motion because access to the minutes may not be readily available. Today, with computer access, the past minutes may quickly be retrieved. For an example of an action log, see Appendix H.

Chapter 26

GOVERNING DOCUMENTS: CHARTERS, BYLAWS, AND RULES

An organization may be governed by statutes, a charter, a constitution, bylaws, or standing rules or by two or more of these. If the organization is incorporated, the primary rules under which it operates are the corporate laws of the state in which it is incorporated. Next in rank are the rules included in its charter or constitution. Following in rank are the bylaws and standing rules. The parliamentary authority adopted by the organization controls all matters not covered by these governing documents.

Organizations that are not incorporated operate under any general laws that are applicable, and under their constitution, if any, as the next highest source of law. Next in rank are the bylaws. Many organizations prefer to consolidate in one document the provisions usually contained in the constitution and the bylaws, and the document is usually called *bylaws* or *constitution and bylaws*. One document is desirable since it is simpler and avoids confusion. Bylaws are rules adopted and maintained by an association to define and direct its internal structure and management. Bylaws may be thought of as terms of an agreement between members and their association. Members, once they have joined an organization, are legally bound by its bylaws. Rules relating to procedure particular to the organization are sometimes included in a group of rules known as *standing rules*.

Types of Charters

An organization looks to the law as its highest source of guidance on procedure and to its charters and bylaws as the next-ranking sources. Charters are of two types—charters of incorporation from the government and charters from a parent organization. Some organizations hold charters of both types. In this case, the charter from the government ranks above the charter from a parent organization.

The charter of an incorporated organization is a grant, usually by a state government, to a group of people who have the right to incorporate and to operate for specific purposes under the laws governing profit or nonprofit corporations. In some states, this charter is termed the *articles of incorporation*. The *corporate charter* of a nonprofit corporation usually contains its name and business address, a statement of the purposes of the organization, whether the organization is to be run as a membership organization or a board-only organization, and provisions relating to the organization's tax-exempt status.

Most state corporation statutes provide the method for amending the corporate charter. No amendment to the charter or articles of incorporation is effective until it has been approved in the manner prescribed by law and also by the governmental authority that granted the charter. Often state law provides the minimum requirements for amendments to corporate charters, but an organization can adopt provisions in its charter or bylaws making the charter amendment procedure stricter than the minimum statutory requirements. Organizations in such states should include charter provisions requiring amendments to their charters to be adopted by rules and procedures at least as strict as those required for amendments to the bylaws.

The charter from a parent organization (sometimes also called a superior or central organization) is a certificate issued to a group of people giving it the right to operate as a constituent or component unit of the parent organization. Typically, the constituent or component charter contains provisions regarding the relationship of the unit to the parent organization, often including provisions for parent organization approval of amendments to the constituent or component charter. Unless otherwise provided in its governing documents, the constituent or component unit is subject to the provisions in the charter or bylaws of the parent organization that relate to such component units.

Constitution and Bylaws

Some organizations adopt both a constitution and bylaws as two separate documents. The constitution establishes the fundamental framework of the organization, and its amendment should require a higher vote than amendment of the bylaws. In an unincorporated association with both constitution and bylaws, the constitution should address those issues usually addressed in a corporate charter, such as name, purpose, and requirements for tax-exempt status. The bylaws supplement these fundamental provisions and are usually easier to amend.

Bylaws

The function of the bylaws of an organization is to define the privileges secured and the duties assumed by the members and to set up the framework of the organization. An organization has the right to adopt such bylaws as the members may agree upon, so long as they are not contrary to the public policy, the law, or a higher level governing document.[1]

Drafting Bylaws

Drafting original bylaws should be done by a committee large enough to include those concerned with the creation of a new organization. The services of a parliamentarian are valuable in developing proper language and form. If the group plans on incorporating in the future, an attorney's advice would be invaluable. Accuracy is essential in writing bylaws with each section carefully thought out and stated clearly and concisely, using correct grammar and punctuation. When the final draft is developed, it should be agreed on by a majority of the committee. Adopted bylaws should be written so there is only one possible interpretation, since the bylaws will become a legal document.

The bylaws contain all the details necessary to make the organization function and are considered a contract between the organization and its members. Administrative details are enumerated in the standing rules. Bylaws are written to meet the needs of the particular organization. A provision that works well for one organization may be entirely unsuitable for another. Bylaws should be concise and are best arranged in outline form. All bylaws dealing with the same general subject are grouped together under one article, which in turn is divided into sections. (See Appendix I, Bylaws Template for Organizations.)

If not otherwise provided by state corporate statutes, provision for dissolution of the organization should be included in the bylaws to protect the assets of the organization. Not-for-profit, tax-exempt organizations cannot distribute profits to their members in the form of dividends and cannot distribute the assets to their members during the life of the organization. If the organization is incorporated, it dissolves under the laws of incorporation; if it is not incorporated, it dissolves by adoption of a resolution to do so, which should include how assets may be disposed of. A motion to dissolve is, in essence, a motion to rescind the bylaws, and, if not otherwise provided for by law or in the bylaws, should follow the same procedure as required for amendment of the bylaws.

Adoption of the Original Bylaws

When the presiding officer calls for the report of the committee appointed to draft the bylaws, the committee chair first moves the adoption of the proposed bylaws in order to bring them before the assembly for consideration and discussion. The presiding officer states the motion, "It has been moved that the bylaws be adopted. The committee chair will read the first section."

The committee chair reads the first section of the first article, and the presiding officer calls for discussion, questions, or amendments to it. If an amendment to the section is proposed, the presiding officer states it to the assembly, and after discussion it is voted on, but only the proposed subsidiary amendments, not articles or sections, are voted on at this time. The presiding officer then calls for the reading of the next section and follows the same procedure. When the reading and amendment of all the bylaw sections are completed, the presiding officer asks, "Are there any further amendments to the bylaws? Is there any further discussion?"

When all proposed amendments have been voted on and no one rises to discuss the bylaws further, the presiding officer takes the vote on the motion to adopt the bylaws. A majority vote is required for adoption of the original bylaws.

When Bylaws Go into Effect

The bylaws go into effect immediately with the announcement of the vote adopting them unless the motion to adopt provides that the bylaws, or some portion or provision in them, are not effective until a later date. For example, "I move that the bylaws be adopted as amended, with the proviso that Article VII, Section 8, which provides for a standing committee on strategic planning, not go into effect until September 1."

Provisions for Amending the Bylaws

It is good practice for an organization to include in its bylaws specific requirements that cover the following:

1. How and by whom amendments to bylaws may be initiated and proposed
2. The form in which proposed amendments should be stated

3. The date before which proposed amendments must be received by the organization
4. The required notice to members of proposed amendments
5. The vote required to adopt an amendment

Proposing Amendments to the Bylaws

An organization must be able to adapt to changing conditions by being able to amend its bylaws. However, to provide for stability and security in the purpose and function of the organization, it is recommended that the organization make changing the bylaws more difficult than amending standing rules or policies.

In many local groups, any member may rise while new business is being considered and offer an amendment to the bylaws simply by stating the proposed amendment and giving a copy of it to the secretary. In most groups, the amendment is then referred to the bylaws committee or reference committee, which studies it and reports its recommendation to the voting body. The bylaws of most organizations require previous notice for amendments, review by a bylaws or reference committee, and at least a two-thirds vote for adoption. Some groups also limit consideration of bylaw amendments to the annual meeting.

State, national, and international organizations ordinarily require that amendments be proposed by an elected delegate of the organization, a constituent or component unit, a committee, or a board of the parent organization. These organizations typically require that proposed amendments be sent to a reference committee or to the bylaws committee by a certain date preceding the convention. The reference or bylaws committee will consider all available information and should make recommendations on each amendment to the assembly of voting members. Reference committees, which are explained in Chapter 24, often hold hearings of the membership before making recommendations on amendments to the bylaws or standing rules. Notice of the time and date that the hearings are to be held, and when the recommendations are to be considered and voted on, should be included in the notice of proposed amendments to the bylaws and rules of the organization.

A notice of motion may be withdrawn up to and including the last date of the notice period. Beyond the notice period, a notice of motion may not be withdrawn. When a motion for which notice is required is pending, the mover of the motion may request of the assembly that the motion be withdrawn, just as any other motion may be requested to be withdrawn.

Form for Proposed Amendments to the Bylaws

Unless the bylaws provide differently, a proposed amendment should be stated in such language that, if adopted, it may be incorporated directly into the bylaws and should be sent in this form as a notice to all members.

The following is a simple method of stating a proposed amendment:

Proposed Amendment to Article VI, Section 1 of the Bylaws
    To Amend Article VI, Board of Trustees, Section 1, Membership, by striking out the words "three members elected by the house of delegates" and inserting in their place the words "five members elected by the general assembly."

If amended, the section will read:

Section 1, Membership. The board of trustees shall consist of the president, vice president, secretary, treasurer, and five members elected by the general assembly.

Considering Amendments to Bylaws

At a meeting or convention, when the time arrives for considering proposed amendments, the chair or some other member of the bylaws or reference committee reads the first proposed amendment as it is stated in the notice and moves its adoption. Since a proposed amendment to the bylaws is a specific main motion *to amend a previous action*, it may be amended, and an amendment to that amendment is also in order. (For more information on the specific main motion to amend a previous action, see Chapter 8.) These subsidiary amendments to the proposed amendment to the bylaws require no previous notice and require only a majority vote for their approval, even though the proposed motion to amend the bylaws may require previous notice and a higher vote.

When the required notice has been given concerning a proposed amendment to the bylaws, the law holds that the subject covered by the amendment has been opened to change and gives the assembly wide discretion in amending the proposed amendment. Parliamentary law, however, provides that:

1. The proposed amendment must be germane to the section to which it applies.
2. No amendments can be proposed that cannot reasonably be implied by the notice given on the proposed amendment of the bylaws.

If an organization wishes to restrict further the extent or type of amendments to proposed amendments to the bylaws, it must include provisions for the additional restrictions in the bylaws.

Since notice of the proposed amendment to the bylaws has been given, the members are aware that the particular amendment and the subject that it covers will be open to amendment without further notice at the meeting. For example, if a proposed amendment to a section of the bylaws titled Classes of Membership adds a new provision establishing an additional type of membership (for example, associate membership), members know that the proposed bylaw amendment may be amended by providing or changing the qualifications, rights, and privileges of the proposed class of associate members. Amendments pertaining to other classes of membership are not in order, since the notice does not state or imply amendments to any class of membership other than associate membership.

An amendment to another part of the bylaws not specified in the notice is admissible only if it is reasonably implied by the amendment as stated in the notice. Using the same example, if the original amendment provided for the creation of an associate membership class, the necessity of fixing the dues for associate members would reasonably be implied, although the subject of dues is covered in another part of the bylaws and might have been omitted unintentionally in the proposed amendment. An amendment providing the dues for associate members would therefore be admissible.

If a provision in a proposed amendment conflicts with a provision elsewhere in the bylaws, amendment to the conflicting provision in the bylaws should also be included in the original notice; however, if that is not done because of an oversight, the conflicting provision can also be amended to conform to the newly adopted amendment without additional notice.

No amendments to a pending proposed amendment are in order that propose a change greater or lesser than that of the existing bylaw in the opposite direction from the proposed amendment. As an example: The existing bylaw requires dues of $45. The proposed amendment is to raise the dues to $50. It is not in order to amend the bylaw amendment to an amount less than $45 or more than $50.

Vote Required on Amendments to Bylaws

The vote required to amend the bylaws should be stated in the bylaws. Because the adoption of the original bylaws requires only a majority of the legal votes cast, some organizations consider it logical to permit an amendment with the same majority vote, provided that there was advance notice of the proposed amendment. If this book is the parliamentary authority and the bylaws are silent on the vote required to amend or revise the bylaws, it requires a majority of the legal votes cast. If the bylaws are silent on the notice required to amend or revise the bylaws, advance notice is required at the previous meeting or with the notice for the meeting.

Revision of the Bylaws

After bylaws have been in place for a considerable period of time, it may be necessary to amend portions of them. When extensive changes are required, the simplest method is to establish a special committee for this purpose or instruct the bylaws committee to study the bylaws and submit a revision. The report of a special revision committee or of a bylaws committee is considered a revision when it proposes a substantial number of changes that may considerably affect the structure of the organization or a rewriting of the form of the bylaws for clarity or reorganization.

A copy of the proposed revision with notice of the date when it will be considered and voted on should be sent to each member in advance of the meeting or convention. Any necessary explanation should be inserted preceding the provision to which it applies.

A revision committee may be appointed or elected and should have the same qualifications stated for those creating new bylaws. The committee may hold hearings so that members have the opportunity to submit and justify suggested changes.

A revision proposes, in effect, a new set of bylaws, and the revision is presented and considered in the same manner as an amendment of the bylaws. A revision requires the same vote and advance notice that is required to amend the bylaws. The original bylaws, which are still in effect, are not before the assembly for consideration.

A revised set of bylaws automatically becomes effective immediately after the vote adopting the new revision. It is possible, however, to provide in the motion to adopt the revised bylaws that all, or certain portions, of them should not become effective until a later specified time.

Interpreting Bylaws and Rules

Organizations frequently have difficulty agreeing on the interpretation of their own bylaws and rules. It is wise to assign the duty of interpreting the bylaws and rules to the committee on bylaws or to the board of directors. The interpreting group may seek the advice of an attorney, a professional parliamentarian, or both. The final decision on an interpretation of the bylaws and rules, when they are ambiguous, rests with the membership, unless the bylaws assign this authority to another body.

Special and Standing Rules

Organizations sometimes adopt rules of procedure that add to or vary from the rules of parliamentary law as stated in their parliamentary authority. The rules that are temporary and intended to meet a current or special situation are termed *special rules*. The rules that are intended to stand until revoked are termed *standing rules*. Standing rules cover points of lesser importance than those contained in the bylaws.

Organizations have the right to adopt special or standing rules by majority vote without notice and to abolish or amend them by a two-thirds vote without notice. When a standing rule or special rule is abolished, the rule defaults to the rule contained in the *American Institute of Parliamentarians Standard Code of Parliamentary Procedure*.

Adopting a Parliamentary Authority

Every deliberative organization is presumed by law to be governed by the rules of parliamentary law. The charter, constitution, bylaws, and standing rules of the organization are its highest authority; but in all matters not covered by these rules, the organization is governed by parliamentary law.

An organization can adopt any code or book of rules on parliamentary procedure to govern it, and the name of the authority should be included in the bylaws or standing rules. This bylaw is usually stated in a form similar to the following:

> In all matters not covered by its constitution, bylaws, and standing rules, this organization shall be governed by the current edition of the *American Institute of Parliamentarians Standard Code of Parliamentary Procedure.*

Great care should be given to the selection of the parliamentary authority because the courts do not excuse any organization from its legal requirements because of errors, omissions, or ambiguities in the authority which may have been adopted. Ignorance of the correct rules of procedure is not a valid defense against legal entanglements or action.[2]

Detailed Procedures

There are many minor details of procedure that are necessary to carry out the provisions of the charter, bylaws, and adopted rules. These detailed procedures should not be included in the bylaws, as they will add length and confusion. These procedures adopted by an organization are called *adopted procedures.* They can be changed more frequently than the bylaws or more important rules and require only a majority vote to be adopted or changed. They should be classified under suitable headings–for example, "Convention Credentials Committee Procedures."

Supplementing Procedural Rules with Motions

An organization has the inherent power to take any action that is not in conflict with law or its charter, bylaws, or adopted rules. This includes the power to adopt motions regulating the conduct of its current business. Since many situations arise that are not covered by rules, it is essential that the details of transacting business be determined by motions. During the course of proceedings, motions are frequently necessary to facilitate the method, manner, or order of transacting business. For example, if a committee has submitted five recommendations relating to the same subject and the committee chair has moved that the first recommendation be adopted and it is being considered, some member might move that the fifth recommendation be considered and decided first because it states a general policy on which the other four recommendations depend.

The power of an organization to adopt any motions for the conduct of current business is particularly important during elections. For example, when there are several candidates for an office and no candidate receives the required majority vote, it is often impractical to require that successive votes be taken until one candidate receives the necessary majority. An organization has the power to adopt motions to enable it to complete the election within a reasonable amount of time. Organizations sometimes vote, for example, to drop the candidate having the lowest vote from the list of candidates after each successive vote. Or an organization may decide to reopen nominations for the office in order to secure a candidate on whom a majority can agree. Organizations have wide leeway in adopting motions to determine the conduct of pending business.

Adopted Policies

Policies define the beliefs and philosophy of an organization; bylaws define the structure. Both are equally binding on the organization. Organizations frequently adopt policies that are as important in determining the action of the group as are its bylaws or other rules. Policies are usually formulated to meet recurring problems that come up for decision. Most successful businesses have written policies that have developed from experience and that guide their operations. Many organizations develop policies that have an equally powerful influence on their effectiveness.

Once a policy has been developed and adopted, it sets a standard for judging and deciding all new proposals dealing with the subject or situation covered by the policy. If a proposal is contrary to an adopted policy of the organization, it should not be considered unless the policy is first amended to permit such a proposal.

Organizations that use policies as guiding principles should provide in their bylaws for their adoption, the vote required, and the method for amending and reviewing them. Some organizations review their policies each year or every several years to see whether changes or new policies are required. Many organizations provide for a standing committee on policies which maintains a list of currently effective policies, considers and makes recommendations on proposed policies, reviews all policies periodically, and interprets them when requested.

Other organizations may require committees to review periodically all policies that relate to their scope of work and determine whether they should be revised or allowed to sunset.

Policies should not be included in the bylaws but should be compiled separately and stated appropriately. The following are examples of policies:

1. This association believes that because its fundamental purpose is to educate senior citizens on proper use of medications, its programs should not include speakers on political topics.
2. This organization shall adhere to a policy of raising our professional standards by strict screening of applicants for membership. The professional character of our organization can best be advanced by gradually raising, but never lowering, the eligibility requirements of applicants for membership.
3. This organization believes that current services to members are its most important function. Our policy is that profit from convention registration fees should not be saved, accumulated, or invested for future use, but that all revenue from convention profits should be used to provide a constantly improving and expanding current program of services to our members.
4. To avoid any perception of a conflict of interest, this organization adheres strictly to the policy that no member may give gifts or gratuities to any employee of the organization, and that no employee or board member may receive gifts from a supplier of services to the organization.

Chapter 27

FINANCES

Every organization, large or small, should establish and maintain an appropriate accounting system for its funds. A good system for controlling finances saves time and money. Therefore, it is wise for even a small organization to consult an accountant when it is establishing or revising its financial records. If an organization expects to receive gifts or solicit contributions for specific causes, it should make sure to comply with laws regarding solicitation of funds (which may apply wherever funds are solicited, and not just in the jurisdiction of incorporation or the location of the organization's headquarters) and legal and accounting requirements to segregate funds whose use is intended by the donor to be restricted to particular purposes.

Report of the Treasurer

At each regular meeting, the treasurer should give a brief report or summary of the organization's revenues and expenses and call attention to any unusual items. The presiding officer should then inquire whether there are any questions about the treasurer's report.

The treasurer should make a complete report annually. All members should receive copies of this report, the auditor's certification, and any recommendations made by the treasurer or auditor. The treasurer's report should be filed for future reference.

If an organization has a finance committee, the committee should report at least quarterly, giving a realistic picture of the financial situation and problems of the organization and of any contemplated proposals or plans involving finances.

Report of the Auditor

Organizations should have an audit at least once a year. An auditing committee composed of members is helpful but is not the best financial safeguard of the organization's finances. Better results can be obtained if an independent audit is carried out. The auditor should be selected by vote of the governing board, the audit committee, or the membership. The treasurer, members involved in budgeting or the expenditure of funds, and staff members concerned with finances should have no voice or part in selecting the auditor or the type of audit.

Certified and licensed public accountants are authorized by law to express professional independent opinions on the financial statements of an organization. They may also be requested to provide comments on important financial expenditures, methods, and safeguards and on the integrity of the accounting system and practices.

An auditor's report is an opinion on the financial statements of the organization. There are two main types of report that auditors provide:

1. The standard *short-form report* consists of two paragraphs expressing the auditor's opinion of the financial statements. The short-form report usually is adequate for most organizations. The standard form, if no exceptions are indicated, means that in the auditor's opinion the financial statements reflect fairly the current financial condition and results of operations of the organization and conform with generally accepted accounting principles applied on a basis consistent with that of the preceding year. If an exception is expressed in the opinion, the reasons for the exception should be carefully investigated.

2. The *long-form report*, in addition to the contents of the short-form report, describes and explains in detail the significant items in the financial statements. It may also include further explanations of the audit procedures performed by the auditor. The long-form report is more expensive than the short-form report, and most organizations consider it unnecessary unless the board of directors or the management of the organization needs detailed financial information that is not otherwise available. State, provincial, or territorial law may require filing of short-form or long-form reports, depending on the size and nature of the organization.

Financial Safeguards

It is incumbent upon organizations to be aware of the various statutes, regulations, and tax laws that apply to their business in the jurisdictions in which they are incorporated or, if not incorporated, where they conduct business. This applies to audit requirements, appointment of auditors, financial record keeping, and other financial matters. To safeguard the integrity of the organization, the organization needs to consult with legal and accounting professionals for advice on setting up and maintaining its financial records and for advice on the reporting requirements and payment of taxes when applicable.

Among the financial safeguards set up by some organizations are: the adoption of a budget; the requirement of authorization for purchases; strict supervision of officers, committees, or employees who collect or expend funds or incur financial obligations; separation of the members or employees recording incoming funds and those recording outgoing expenditures; an annual audit; and a blanket bond (insurance) covering all members and employees who have access to organization's funds.

Most organizations prepare and adopt a budget of estimated revenues and expenses. A budget is an estimate only. Adoption of a budget does not mean that the organization must observe its provisions unless required to do so by the rules of the organization. More often, the budget is a financial guide. Some groups require the authorization of the governing board or the membership for any expenditure in excess of budgeted amounts. They also provide that any expenditure not included in the budget requires the same authorization.

A few organizations provide that proposed expenditures above a nominal amount require a purchase order or some other form of authorization, and some provide that unusual, and particularly large, expenditures require authorization by vote of the board of directors or of the membership.

Only members and employees specifically authorized to do so should be permitted to commit the organization to expenditures. Normally, expenditures above a certain amount must have an authorizing signature. If an authorized representative purchases goods or services in the name of the organization, the organization will be legally obligated to pay the bill, regardless of whether the members later vote to pay or not to pay it.

Instructions to any committee should state how much money, if any, it is authorized to spend. Unless a committee is authorized to collect, hold, or spend funds, all funds should be collected, held, and expended through the regular financial channels of the organization.

Chapter 28

TYPES OF ORGANIZATIONS

An organization can be organized in many different ways, depending on why it is created and its intended purposes and governance structure. This chapter discusses the typical ways that organizations are classified and the effects of those classifications on their structure.

Temporary and Permanent Organizations

An organization may be established as either temporary or permanent. A temporary organization may exist for a few meetings or even a single meeting. It dissolves automatically as soon as the members accomplish the purpose for which they organized. An example of a temporary organization is one created to accomplish a specific civic project, such as donating a statue or creating a park.

A permanent organization is one formed with the intention of functioning over a considerable period of time, indefinitely, in perpetuity, or until it is dissolved.

A temporary or permanent organization may choose any legal form of entity, but it is most common for temporary organizations to be created as unincorporated associations (sometimes called "voluntary associations").

Forms of Organizations

The founders of a new organization, or the members of an older organization who wish to reorganize, must decide on the type of entity that best suits their purpose. Most nonprofit membership organizations choose to organize either as unincorporated associations or as corporations. Nonprofit corporations may be organized as membership corporations or as board-only corporations. Business entities include partnerships and business corporations (where shareholders are similar to members in nonprofit corporations). Some nonprofits, typically those without individual members, and many businesses choose to organize as trusts (which may be governed by a board of trustees, but more frequently by a single trustee or a number of trustees who are required to act unanimously), or as limited liability companies (a relatively new form of entity which provides considerable governance flexibility, but requires consideration of tax-related concerns). (See Table 28.1.) In general, courts will apply basic principles of common parliamentary law to meetings of the members (or shareholders) and governing boards of all such entities, to the extent not otherwise provided for by the governing documents or applicable statutes,[1] with greater informality in the case of smaller bodies.

Business entities typically arrange their governance with considerable power concentrated in the hands of management and less member- (or shareholder-) based decision making, which is why it is somewhat less frequent for business entities to adopt a parliamentary authority.

Table 28.1 Common Forms of Business and Nonprofit Entities

	Unincorporated Association	Corporation	Trust	Limited Liability Company	Partnership
Nonprofit	Yes	Yes. Either a membership corporation or board-only corporation	Yes	Yes (occasionally)	No
Business	No	Yes. Shareholder corporation	Yes	Yes	Yes

It is difficult for a large assembly to formulate plans. When creating a new organization, a small group or committee of founders should meet to consider and decide on such questions as the purposes of the proposed organization, its legal form (temporary or permanent, profit or nonprofit, charitable or noncharitable, incorporated or unincorporated, and category of tax-exempt status), types of membership, financing, policies, temporary officers, and affiliation with other organizations. It may be helpful to seek legal advice regarding entity choice and formation, particularly if the choice is anything other than an unincorporated association.

Unincorporated Associations

Those unincorporated nonprofit entities that are rather loosely structured and operated only under a set of their own governing documents are termed *unincorporated associations*. Unions, political committees, homeowners associations, and local units of superior organizations are typical of the types of organizations often created as unincorporated associations.

Unincorporated associations may be somewhat limited with regard to the powers of property holding, employment, and receipt of charitable gifts.[2] Many jurisdictions, however, have adopted unincorporated nonprofit association acts that grant unincorporated associations powers similar to those of corporations, while allowing them much more flexibility over internal governance matters than corporations.[3] Review of the statutory code in the jurisdiction of the organization or consultation with a lawyer may be useful to see if such a statute is in effect and to ascertain its applicability to the proposed organization.

At the organizing meeting for an unincorporated association (sometimes referred to as a "mass meeting"), a member of the organizing group calls the meeting to order and nominates or calls for nominations for a temporary presiding officer.[4] If more than one person is nominated, a vote is taken on each until one candidate receives a majority vote. This nominee is then declared the temporary presiding officer who calls for nominations for a temporary secretary to be elected in the same manner. The presiding officer then requests a member of the organizing group to read the call of the meeting (the notice advertising the meeting) and to explain the purpose of the proposed organization.

If the new organization is forming as a unit of a superior organization, often the superior organization's charter has already been granted, and it constitutes the governing rules for the meetings creating the new organization. Otherwise, the call of the meeting and the rules of common parliamentary law govern the procedures of an organizing meeting, unless the body adopts a parliamentary authority, special rules, or both, which is advised if the formation process is expected to be long or complicated. Someone may then present a motion or resolution for forming the organization.

A resolution for forming a *temporary* organization might read:

> *Resolved*, That this assembly form a temporary organization, to be known as the Old Town Preservation Committee, for the purpose of promoting creation of a tax-free zone in the downtown area by the Milo City Council; and be it further

Resolved, That a committee consisting of five members elected by the assembly be formed to coordinate the efforts of the organization and to call further meetings if needed; and be it further

Resolved, That the members of the coordinating committee attend the next meeting of the Milo City Council to present a signed petition promoting creation of the zone; and be it further

Resolved, That a copy of this resolution with the reasons for our promotion and a list of members of the coordinating committee be sent to the news media located in this county.

A motion to form a *permanent* organization might read:

I move that we organize as the Woodford County Improvement Association, with the following purpose: To advocate for improved infrastructure and economic development of Woodford County.

If this motion is adopted, a member may move to appoint a committee to draft bylaws consistent with the stated purpose; or if the bylaws have already been prepared, they are presented, in which case the proposed purpose clause of the bylaws is sufficient and does not need to be repeated in the organizing motion. As soon as the bylaws have been adopted (which may need to be done at a continued meeting if they were not prepared in advance), permanent officers are elected, and the organization is complete. For more information on the adoption of original bylaws, see Chapter 26.

If the members decide to seek a charter as a unit of an already-existing superior organization and such a charter has not already been granted, they select or authorize the presiding officer to appoint a committee to follow through with obtaining a charter.

Corporations

Most nonprofit membership organizations, whether local, regional, national, or international in scope, are incorporated. The chief advantages of incorporation are:

1. The organization holds a charter from government, granted by the appropriate agency in the jurisdiction in which the organization incorporated. It operates under the guidance and protection of the applicable laws governing corporations.

2. The purposes of the organization and the powers necessary to carry out these purposes have legal recognition.
3. The individuals or member groups are able to work with greater effectiveness and scope by pooling their resources and efforts because of the greater formality afforded by corporate recognition.
4. The process for dissolution is generally more difficult than it is for unincorporated associations and must follow statutory formalities. Nevertheless, corporate statutes typically provide a method of dissolution when an organization is unable to function because it cannot obtain a quorum after a number of attempts, whereas dissolution of an unincorporated association in such circumstances may be difficult without a specific bylaw provision covering that situation.
5. The corporation is recognized as a legal entity apart from its individual members and thus can do business and hold property of any kind in its own right. Consequently, most jurisdictions require corporations to file contact and leadership information regularly with a government agency so that parties doing business with the corporation can locate the responsible individuals if necessary.
6. Officers, directors, and members are free from personal liability for the debts of the organization.
7. The name and seal of the organization are legally protected.

If an organization chooses to form as a corporation, it should consult legal counsel. Corporate formation must follow statutory requirements that vary with the jurisdiction. Generally, after formation, corporations may operate in any jurisdiction, possibly subject to local filing requirements. Nonprofits generally tend to incorporate in the jurisdiction where they are headquartered. If, however, the nonprofit corporation law of that jurisdiction contains onerous requirements incompatible with the intended governance structure of the organization, it may be useful for the organizers to consider incorporating in another jurisdiction.

One common way for individuals with common interests to form a corporation is to create a temporary organization in the form of an unincorporated association in order to assist in the creation and registration of the corporation. In such cases, the temporary organization's formation resolution should state the intended name and purposes of

the corporation and authorize the organizing or coordinating committee to take the steps that are necessary to incorporate the organization.

Statutory Requirements

If a nonprofit organization is incorporated, members should be aware
that in addition to having their bylaws and practices comply with their
corporate charter (sometimes called "articles of incorporation"), they
also must comply with applicable corporation codes. Many of these
codes set specific guidelines for such things as quorum requirements,
election procedures, notice required for meetings, and proxy voting.
An attorney should be consulted when a corporation is established to
ensure that the charter and bylaws conform to applicable statutes and
to any requirements for tax-exempt status.

Most corporation codes do not provide detailed guidance on the
conduct of meetings. The codes permit the organization to adopt
its own procedural guide, such as this book, and to establish its own
bylaws and rules as long as these do not conflict with the corporate
charter or with statutory or common law.[5]

Private-sector labor unions in the United States should be aware
that their bylaws must conform to provisions of federal law, particularly
the Labor-Management Reporting and Disclosure Act of 1959, better
known as the Landrum-Griffin Act.[6] Public-sector labor unions in the
United States are typically covered by similar statutory requirements
of the applicable jurisdiction. On procedural matters not covered by
these acts, the union should be guided by the basic principles of common parliamentary law and should adopt a parliamentary authority
to resolve questions not dealt with in the act or in the union's bylaws.
Similarly, other organizations, such as political committees, homeowners associations, and public charities, may be subject to statutory
governance and filing requirements based on their substantive work,
regardless of their form of organization.

Differences among Nonprofit, Tax-Exempt, and Charitable Organizations

Almost all voluntary membership organizations are *nonprofit groups*
(sometimes also called "not-for-profit" organizations, although any
distinction between the terms is largely theoretical). Applicable law
will determine what purposes of the organization qualify as nonprofit.

In many jurisdictions, special nonprofit corporation statutes may make formation of a nonprofit corporation easier.[7] Nonprofit organizations, whether or not organized as corporations, may have certain advantages or privileges under applicable law. Typical permissible purposes for a nonprofit corporation may be charitable, political, social, governmental, or educational in nature. The main requirement is that any income or profit of the organization must be used solely to carry out its legal purposes and cannot be distributed as profit to its members. The organization cannot pay dividends or other remuneration to its members. It can, however, pay reasonable compensation or salaries for services rendered, and in some cases, such as some mutual benefit organizations, it may be able to distribute certain assets to members upon dissolution, but this would be the exception.[8]

Some nonprofit organizations are *charities*. The test to determine whether an organization is charitable depends on applicable law and may vary somewhat from jurisdiction to jurisdiction. Generally, organizations with purposes related to healthcare; education; service to the poor; and advancement of science, sports, the arts, and culture qualify as charitable in most jurisdictions. Charitable nonprofits may have additional filing requirements not applicable to other nonprofits, for example, in regard to charitable solicitation.

A nonprofit organization may receive profit incidental to its operations, but that profit must be used for the purposes for which the organization exists. For example, a regional medical association might receive considerable profit from some of its activities; this money could not be distributed as pecuniary gain to its members, but it could be expended for educational or other purposes that would benefit its members and the public.

A nonprofit organization, whether incorporated or not, may be treated by both the federal and state, territorial, or provincial government as a *tax-exempt entity*. Tax-exempt status is accorded on the basis of specific statutory and regulatory provisions. While most nonprofit organizations will qualify as tax-exempt, the particular category of exemption (and the consequent benefits and compliance requirements) may not be obvious. Consultation with a lawyer or tax professional is advisable when asserting tax-exempt status. If an organization asserts tax-exempt status, it is important that it comply with applicable filing requirements in order not to jeopardize that status.

Chapter 29

RIGHTS OF MEMBERS AND OF ORGANIZATIONS

When a member joins an organization, an implicit relationship is formed between the member and the organization. No particular procedure is necessary to establish this relationship as long as a mutual understanding as to membership is reached. Most often it is outlined in the bylaws of the organization. Some organizations require members to sign the bylaws or go through an initiation ceremony to emphasize their relative rights and responsibilities. An organization may have prerequisites that a potential member has to meet before receiving full benefits. Membership orientation or initiation ceremonies may be a required part of acceptance as a new member. A person who joins an organization accepts the organization as it exists at that time. The current charter, bylaws, and other rules of the organization are a part of the implicit contract binding the members and the organization.

A member's rights do not necessarily remain unchanged forever. Privileges of membership may be taken away by decision of the voting body, or privileges may be added. Fees and dues can be changed, and assessments may be levied if provided for in the bylaws. However, vested rights, those that have been acquired as a result of the fundamental agreement between the member and the organization, cannot be taken away.

All adjustments in the rights and privileges of members and all changes in the rules of the organization must be made according to the provisions for making such changes contained in the bylaws or parliamentary authority.

Rights of Members

In addition to the rights a member has as a person, there are rights related to being a member of an association, property rights, and parliamentary rights, all of which are protected by law. A member's associational rights stem from membership in the organization. For example, a member has the right to fair and equitable treatment from the other members of the organization.

Property rights also may be involved with membership in the organization, such as an interest in a clubhouse, boat dock, a cemetery plot, or other assets owned by the group.

All members have the following fundamental rights under common parliamentary law, subject only to any specific limitations contained in the bylaws:

- To be notified of meetings
- To attend meetings
- To make motions
- To speak on and debate matters
- To vote
- To run for office, and to nominate and elect officers and directors of the organization
- To propose and vote on amendments to the governing documents
- To insist on the enforcement of the rules of the organization and of parliamentary law
- To resign from an office or from the organization itself
- To remain in the organization even when on the losing side of a particular proposition
- To have a fair hearing before expulsion or other penalties are applied
- To receive or have the right to inspect copies of the bylaws, charter, rules, minutes, or other official records of the organization
- To exercise any other rights or privileges given to the members by the law, by the bylaws, or by the rules of the organization

The rights of membership may vary depending on the bylaws. An organization may have different classifications of membership, which may have different rights that should be delineated in the bylaws.

If any of the associational, property, or parliamentary rights of a member are violated, legal action may be taken against the organization or its representatives.[1] As a general rule, however, courts will not adjudicate such actions until the member has exhausted the means provided for enforcing such rights under the rules of parliamentary procedure and the bylaws of the organization.[2]

Member in Good Standing

Organizations often use the term "member in good standing" and variations of it in their documents of authority. A member in good standing can usually exercise all the rights of membership, while loss of good standing may result in loss of one or more rights of membership. Loss of good standing usually differs from suspension or expulsion, in that it often may occur or terminate automatically or through administrative steps, rather than through consideration of charges against the member as described below under "Discipline and Expulsion of Members."

The term has some basis in law, but each organization should provide its own definition, which should clearly describe (1) the events that lead to loss of good standing and the particular conditions, if any, that must be met to maintain good standing, (2) the consequences of the loss of good standing, and (3) the conditions that must be met to restore good standing.

A common condition for maintaining good standing is payment of financial obligations to the organization such as dues and assessments. Loss of good standing might occur automatically at a given interval after such obligations are due, or such arrears may cause some other process to occur, which, if carried to completion, will then lead to a loss of good standing. A less common condition leading to loss of good standing might be failure to meet a meeting attendance requirement.

Consequences of loss of good standing might include the loss of some or all of the rights of membership. For this reason, these details should be placed in the bylaws or in another document or set of rules authorized by the bylaws.

Restoration of good standing might occur automatically upon removal of the conditions leading to the loss, such as payment of financial arrears, or additional steps might be required to restore good standing. Usually action by the full assembly is not required for loss of good standing to occur or for it to be restored.

Rights of Organizations

The implicit agreement between the organization and its members is not a one-way street. An organization also has rights, which are exercised by the decision of the organization as provided in its governing documents. Some of the fundamental rights of an organization are:

- To carry out its mission and to exercise any of the rights or authority granted it by law
- To change its purpose, if permitted by law and its charter, to merge with another organization, or to dissolve
- To establish eligibility requirements and procedures governing the admission of members and to grant or refuse membership according to its adopted rules and within the law
- To establish and to amend, through changes in its bylaws, the rights, privileges, and obligations of its members either by extension or by limitation
- To delegate authority, within legal limits, to officers, boards, committees, and employees
- To select its officers, directors, and committee members and to suspend or remove them as prescribed by the bylaws or the law
- To discipline or expel members, directors, and officers in accordance with its bylaws and within the law
- To purchase and hold property and to defend against or enter into litigation in its own name, if permitted by applicable law

Relationship of Individual and Organizational Rights

The rights of each member should be definite, and to the extent they are definite, they are protected by law.[3] However, they must be regarded in relation to the rights of other members and of the organization. In order to successfully assert the rights of membership, the member must choose the appropriate time and forum.[4] The member must also follow the proper procedures. For example, a member has the right to have correct procedure followed; however, the demand for this enforcement must be made in a timely and appropriate manner. Also, a member has the right to present any proposal within the organization's purposes to the assembly, but this right cannot be exercised at a special meeting by proposing a motion that is not stated in the call for the special meeting.

Similarly, a member has the fundamental right to speak on any debatable question before the assembly. However, if the member attempts to discuss the question when it has not yet been presented by the presiding officer, attempts to discuss it for a second time when others desire to speak, when another member has the floor, or after debate has been terminated by a motion to vote immediately, the member's right to discuss gives way to the organization's right to set its own rules. If the rights of an individual member or a minority of members conflict with the rights of the majority of the assembly, the rights of the majority ultimately must prevail unless the governing documents protect the minority. For example, a minority has the right to be heard, but if the minority attempts to be heard when a majority wishes to adjourn, the minority's right must give way to that of the majority. Yet, some member rights are so fundamental that they cannot be overridden by the majority. Rules denying some of these rights require a higher vote, such as the rule for stopping debate. Other rights cannot be overridden by any vote—for example, notice requirements. This second kind cannot be superseded even by unanimous vote.

The right of members to oppose ideas and candidates does not extend to the right to undermine the organization itself. If, after the majority has made a decision, some members continue to oppose that decision to the point where the organization has difficulty in functioning or is in danger of being destroyed, the governing board or the membership should protect the organization by taking proper disciplinary action. This does not mean, however, that a member does not have the right to attempt to influence fellow members to change policy, thereby creating a new majority.

Discipline and Expulsion of Members

Procedures for the discipline and expulsion of members should be included in the bylaws. However, every organization has the inherent right to discipline, suspend, or expel a member regardless of whether this is covered in the bylaws.[5] Membership can be terminated and a member expelled because of violation of an important duty to the organization, a breach of a fundamental rule or principle of the organization, or for any violation stated in the bylaws as grounds for expulsion.[6] However, even if rules for discipline are not included in the bylaws, action can be taken against a member who has breached important duties, fundamental rules, or the principles of an organization.

For example, discipline may consist of requiring a member to appear before the governing board and explain certain actions or pay a fine (but only if the bylaws permit imposition of a fine), or a member may be reprimanded or suspended from membership for a limited time.

In addition, an organization has the implied power to expel a member for violation of duties as a citizen.[7] For example, a member may be expelled upon being convicted of a criminal offense that would discredit the organization.

All these powers must be exercised in the context of fairness. A proceeding to expel a member must not violate any rule of the organization or any of the member's rights under the law. The primary requisites for expulsion proceedings are due notice and a fair hearing.[8]

The essential steps for imposing severe discipline or expelling a member are:

1. *Charges.* Charges made by a member in an affidavit stating the alleged violations and preliminary proof should be filed with the secretary. An organization may provide in its bylaws that a member's rights may be suspended, either automatically or pursuant to a vote of the board, from the time that charges are served until completion of the disciplinary action.

   In organizations adopting this book as their parliamentary authority, an officer of the organization who has been charged on a disciplinary matter may be suspended temporarily from office by a majority vote of the board.

2. *Investigation.* A disinterested committee should be appointed to investigate the charges thoroughly and promptly, and if it decides that a hearing is warranted, it should set a date for the hearing and notify the secretary.

3. *Notification.* The secretary should send the accused member a registered or certified letter at least 15 days before the date of the hearing. The letter should contain a copy of the charges, the time and place of the hearing, and a statement of the member's right to be present at the hearing to present a defense, to be represented by an attorney or other party, and to receive a copy of any record of the proceedings.

4. *Hearing.* A hearing should then be held either at a closed membership meeting or by a hearing committee composed of disinterested members other than those on the investigating committee. In conducting the hearing, the committee should preserve decorum and fair play; restrict evidence and

testimony to the written charges; and uphold the right of the accused member to present a defense, to cross-examine witnesses, and to refute the charges that have been made.

5. *Decision.* The hearing committee or membership meeting should, within a reasonable time, make findings of fact on the essential points at issue. If the hearing is held before a committee, it should recommend a decision of guilt or innocence and send a copy of the recommended decision and findings of fact to the accused member and to the secretary.

6. *Penalty.* If the member is found guilty of the charges, the hearing committee should recommend a penalty to the membership meeting. The decision may be approved by a majority of the legal votes cast at the meeting. The authority to impose penalties can be delegated to the hearing committee by the membership as stated in the bylaws or standing rules.

Some organizations permit a member who has been expelled to apply for readmission after a certain period of time.

Resignations

A member has the absolute right to resign from an organization at any time. A provision in the bylaws that a member's dues must be paid up before the member resigns cannot prevent a resignation. There is no practical way in which an ordinary society can compel a delinquent member to continue as a member, nor can it persist in assessing and collecting dues. There are exceptions in law to this rule, such as property ownership where there is a need to maintain ownership.

The bylaws, when addressing discipline, should also address the situation in which a member resigns, but does so with disciplinary charges pending and before the applicable disciplinary process has been completed. If the bylaws are silent, the organization may decide, by motion, whether the process should continue.

A resignation becomes effective immediately, unless some future time is specified by the resigning member, and no acceptance of it is necessary to make it effective unless the bylaws say otherwise.

An officer or director may resign from office at any time. A resignation need not be written, and it may be implied or automatic, as when a member moves out of the jurisdiction of the organization and is no longer eligible for membership. A bylaws provision that an officer shall hold office "until a successor is elected" does not prevent the officer from resigning, nor can it be used to force a person to remain in office.

A resignation effective at some future date may be withdrawn until it has been accepted, or until the effective date of the resignation. If, however, the resignation is intended to become effective immediately, it cannot be withdrawn.

After the effective date has passed, an officer or director who has resigned either orally or in writing cannot simply resume office because of a change of mind. A person who has resigned from office can be restored to that office only pursuant to the applicable vacancy-filling provision. After resigning, an officer or director continues to be liable for acts committed or agreed to before the resignation.

Chapter 30

STAFF AND CONSULTANTS

Staff and consultants are generally nonmembers who provide management guidance for the organization. They often provide expertise at various levels of management.

The Executive Director

While many small organizations operate solely with volunteers, a governing board, or with some part-time staff, many organizations, both large and small, employ a chief administrator who is known by various titles: the executive director, executive secretary, executive officer, chief executive officer, administrative officer, or manager. This person is usually chosen by the governing board or executive committee and is responsible to the selecting body.

The executive director, along with the elected leadership, is often the "face" of the organization to the public. The executive director needs an extensive knowledge of planning for, and managing of membership organizations; experience with business practices; and the skill and willingness to assist officers, committees, and members.

The executive director, usually under supervision of the governing board, directs the administration of the organization, employs staff members, and performs any other duties assigned by the voting body, the governing board, the executive committee, or the president.

An executive director will focus on doing things for the overall good of the organization. The executive director, although given a lot of responsibilities within the organization, is usually most effective when working quietly behind the scenes, avoiding the limelight, and letting the elected officers receive the credit and appreciation. The executive director will often be the person who can be the intermediary in interpersonal and political differences among leaders and thus, provide a solid leadership foundation for the organization as a whole. A competent and loyal executive director is a great asset to any organization, providing continuity within an association whose leaders are changing frequently and whose members are busy with their own occupations.

Typically, the executive director is the primary supervisor of all staff employees, except in large organizations that have a chief financial officer. The executive director is the liaison between the staff and the board.

The Accountant or Chief Financial Officer

An organization may find it advantageous to hire a full-time chief financial officer (CFO), who is often an accountant. Some such organizations also appoint the employed chief financial officer as the organization's treasurer with oversight by a finance committee. In a large organization, an employed chief financial officer can save the organization time and money by establishing or revising its accounting system to meet the particular needs of the group.

An organization with an employed financial officer should also have an audit provided by an outside auditor at the close of the fiscal year to validate the reports of the officer. An employed financial officer, working with an outside auditing firm, plays a key role in closing the books and relieving the treasurer of liability.

Small organizations often hire an accountant on a limited basis to provide input as a consultant, to prepare tax reports, and provide auditing services on a yearly basis. The organization may elect a treasurer or have a finance committee to oversee and review the accountant's work. An accountant can be invaluable in keeping any size organization informed of current government regulations and provide the resources for the organization to maintain approved accounting records. In a smaller organization, an accountant may work with an audit committee to close the books at the end of the fiscal year and present an audit for approval.

A Consultant to Nonprofit Organizations

Nonprofit organizations often work almost entirely with unpaid volunteers; therefore, they may benefit from the services of management and business consultants who are experienced in working with such groups. A consultant is often hired on a temporary basis to perform a specific task, such as strategic planning facilitation, program development, fund-raising, or membership recruitment.

An Attorney

An organization needs the assistance of an attorney on legal matters. The organization's needs for legal counsel will be determined by the size and focus of the organization. An attorney should be involved in the creation of a new organization (if it is organized as a corporation or trust), the filing of legal documents, and the review of proposed organizational documents.

An attorney should be available to assist the organization on any legal matters relating to the organization. There are many situations in which the attorney must become an active participant. These situations include incorporating the organization, creating a foundation, developing contracts, taking disciplinary actions, or pursuing litigation. The attorney should also be involved in preparing legal documents relating to employment, mergers, consolidations, dissolution, the purchase or sale of property, and any other major purchases.

The Parliamentarian

A professional parliamentarian can be helpful to both small and large organizations. In large organizations, a parliamentarian's services are often essential to maintain effective operation.

The parliamentarian is usually chosen by, and works under, the direction of the presiding officer. The parliamentarian may also aid and advise the governing board, committees—especially committees with an active role in the organization's annual meeting or convention—and staff members. In many large organizations, a professional parliamentarian is retained on an annual basis and therefore is available to members who need consultations on parliamentary questions or assistance in planning for a meeting or convention. Best practices are for a parliamentarian to meet with the presiding officer to determine the method of communication between them before and during meetings, to review the meeting script, and to discuss any "what ifs" that may come up during the meeting.

At a meeting or convention, the parliamentarian should sit next to the presiding officer. The parliamentarian does not make rulings but advises the presiding officer on procedures. The presiding officer may or may not follow the advice and is responsible for the final ruling, based on the officer's knowledge of the organization, assembly, and procedures. The parliamentarian should be alert to any problems that are developing and advise the presiding officer on proper procedures.

If a serious mistake is being made, the parliamentarian unobtrusively calls it to the attention of the presiding officer, who then decides what action to take. At the request of the presiding officer, the parliamentarian may explain a procedure to the members.

The more capable a presiding officer, the better he or she understands the value and importance of a good parliamentarian. An experienced presiding officer understands that a parliamentarian brings to the table a professional attitude and an excellent knowledge of the details of the procedures so that the presiding officer is free to concentrate on the agenda and the overall progress and tone of the meeting. This enables the presiding officer to focus on the assembly and proceed with confidence and poise.

The parliamentarian is responsible for seeing that no procedural details are overlooked, for anticipating procedural strategy, and for being certain that all parliamentary requirements are observed. The parliamentarian is not an advocate of causes or a representative of any group or individual within the organization, but is retained to help the members accomplish the legitimate purposes of the organization.

Often parliamentary problems involve several rules and principles. A parliamentarian must be able to reconcile the principles and rules of parliamentary law that may be involved in a particular situation with the documents of the organization. When asked a question, the parliamentarian must give a considered opinion as to how the rules and principles apply. Having been retained as an authority, the parliamentarian should be familiar with the organization's parliamentary authority and governing documents to the degree that it is generally unnecessary to research the documents during a meeting. If requested to quote a specific passage, the parliamentarian should be familiar enough with the documents to find quickly the appropriate citations in the parliamentary authority or governing documents.

In addition to serving an organization as a consultant, a parliamentarian may also serve an organization with expertise in a variety of other services, including working with the board, drafting and reviewing bylaws, preparing scripts and convention rules, and presenting seminars and workshops for the membership on parliamentary procedures.

A parliamentary situation may be so complex that the presiding officer relinquishes the chair temporarily to the parliamentarian until the problem is explained or resolved—or until the pending motion has been disposed of. The parliamentarian then presides only with the assembly's permission, which is usually granted by general consent.

There also may be times when it may be advantageous for the parliamentarian to preside over the business portion of a meeting or convention, or when a part of the meeting may be controversial and the assembly would welcome a neutral party to preside. This can be prearranged, but it still requires permission from the assembly. When this occurs, only those duties associated with the business of the meeting are assumed by the parliamentarian. All the other powers, rights, duties, and responsibilities of the presiding officer enumerated in the bylaws remain with that officer. For example, the parliamentarian would not be able to vote or appoint members to committees when he or she presides over the meeting.[1]

Following the close of a meeting or convention, the parliamentarian should follow up with the organization on the items of business acted upon during the meeting. The parliamentarian has the opportunity at this time to provide input to the leadership on any procedures that should be changed for the next meeting or problems that need to be addressed.

Chapter 31

FREQUENTLY ASKED QUESTIONS

Organization's Governing Documents

When an organization's bylaws or its own adopted rules of order disagree or are inconsistent with its parliamentary authority, which should it follow?

The organization follows its own bylaws. If it has adopted its own standing or special rules of order, it also follows those before the parliamentary authority. The parliamentary authority always takes lesser precedence than the organization's bylaws and its specifically adopted rules of order.

The bylaws state that the **American Institute of Parliamentarians Standard Code of Parliamentary Procedure** *is the parliamentary authority. However, the bylaws do not contain any provisions for amending the bylaws. What vote will be required to adopt an article on Amendments? Will we need to give notice to all the members before the new article can be adopted?*

If the *AIP Standard Code of Parliamentary Procedure* is the parliamentary authority and the bylaws are silent on the vote required to amend or revise the bylaws, a majority of the legal votes cast is required. If the bylaws are silent on the notice required to amend or revise the bylaws, advance notice at the previous meeting or with the notice for the meeting is required.

Procedures

Can we send out our notice of meetings by e-mail?

The association may send notices using e-mail, or other electronic means, if the association's bylaws provide specific authority to use this method of notification. Rules for implementation should include a method for keeping e-mail addresses current and providing alternative methods of notice for members who do not have e-mail or Internet access, thus ensuring that all members receive the required notice.

Why follow parliamentary procedure in a meeting rather than conduct business informally?

The degree to which formal parliamentary procedure is used will be determined by the type of meeting and its size. In small meetings, informality is often very desirable; however, as the meeting size increases, the degree to which parliamentary procedure should be used increases. The key concept is for the presiding officer to use the amount of formality necessary to maintain control of the meeting.

Does a board of directors operate as an assembly or a committee?

It depends on the size of the board. A small board, such as one with nine or fewer members, will operate much like a committee. As the board increases in size, the degree of formality increases proportionately in order to maintain order and get the business done in a timely manner. Boards have to find their own level of formality and increase it or decrease it from time to time to ensure that meetings are conducted efficiently and effectively.

In order to ensure being the next person to speak when the current speaker is finished, may a member remain standing during another person's remarks?

No. Members should remain seated while someone else has the floor. This rule should be enforced by the presiding officer. In a large assembly, using a recognition system that involves queuing at microphones, the member may remain in the line, but should step back from the microphone while others are speaking. In a board meeting, the presiding officer often keeps a list of the order of speakers.

What should the presiding officer do if he or she is uncertain of how to proceed?

The presiding officer can seek help from the assembly by saying, "The chair is unsure of how to proceed. The chair will accept advice from the meeting participants." In addition if the matter is important enough, the presiding officer may also take a recess to confer with other leaders or members. Asking the assembly for assistance or taking a break will often result in a consensus on how the presiding officer should proceed, which can then be explained to the assembly. If options are available, a formal vote can be taken on the options.

Motions

Why does a motion need to be made before discussion in regular meetings?

The key concept is focus. If unfocused discussion is permitted in a large group, people tend to go off in different directions, and there is no way to determine what the scope of the discussion should be. A motion provides a way of focusing attention on specific points in order to reach a concrete decision.

In a small committee, however, it is not always necessary or even desirable, in some circumstances, to have a specific motion on the floor before discussion occurs because the small group is often striving to frame a motion or a solution to a problem.

When someone moves to amend a motion, should the presiding officer check to see if the amendment is acceptable to the maker of the motion?

No. The presiding officer should seek a second and then state the amendment. It would be inappropriate for the presiding officer, both before and after the motion has been stated, to check with the person whose motion is the subject of the amendment. If a noncontroversial amendment is made, even if the motion has been stated, the presiding officer may ask the assembly for general consent to adopt the change.

What is a friendly amendment?

A friendly amendment is an amendment made by a member who believes that the change will be acceptable to the maker of the motion or the assembly and that the amendment could be incorporated into the motion by general consent (without a formal vote). However, an amendment's "friendliness" is often in the eyes of the beholder, and, after the motion has been stated by the presiding officer, any member (including the presiding officer) may object to the proposed friendly amendment. On hearing an objection, the presiding officer should seek a second for the amendment, call for discussion, and take a vote on the amendment.

Can the mover of a motion speak against and vote against his or her own motion?

Yes. The maker of a motion has the right to speak for or against and vote against his or her own motion.

Voting

When a member is elected or appointed to more than one position on a board, should that member be allowed to cast multiple votes in relation to the number of positions he or she holds?

No. A basic principle of parliamentary procedure is that, in a deliberative assembly, each member's opinion as expressed by vote has the same weight as any other member's. If the bylaws allow a member to be elected to multiple positions, the member has the obligation to meet the duties of each position, but is still only allotted one vote on any issue.

How does the presiding officer determine the form for taking a vote?

Each form of voting fills a specific purpose. The most common method is a voice vote—calling for the ayes and noes. To verify an indecisive voice vote, the presiding officer should take a standing vote. If a two-thirds vote is required, a standing vote, or show of hands in a small group, generally is used because of the difficulty in measuring a two-thirds voice vote. The presiding officer may also take a vote by general consent if the motion is noncontroversial. A ballot vote is used when required by the bylaws, by a standing rule, or when the assembly, by motion, decides on a ballot vote. A roll call vote is most commonly used in conventions of delegates when required by the bylaws or by vote of the assembly.

Any member may move that a particular method be used for voting, provided the bylaws do not specifically state what type or method of vote is required in certain instances. This is an incidental motion, which requires a majority vote for adoption.

What is cumulative voting?

Cumulative voting is a method that allows a member to place multiple votes for a single candidate instead of the casting of single votes for a number of different candidates. This form of voting must be authorized in the bylaws.

What is bullet voting?

Bullet voting is a method of focusing your voting power on a single candidate by choosing to place a single vote for a single candidate and to abstain from using any additional votes for anyone else. Bullet voting is permitted unless it is prohibited by the bylaws because a member has a right to abstain.

What is a Texas ballot?

A Texas ballot is a method of voting in which voters indicate the candidate that they do *not* wish to be elected. It can be efficiently used when there are a large number of positions open for a specific office, and there are slightly more candidates than the number of positions open.

General

What is the difference between the terms question and motion? Sometimes the presiding officer will refer to a motion as a question, as in "... are you ready to vote on the question?"

This question is answered in Demeter's *Manual of Parliamentary Law and Procedure* on page 57: "Strictly speaking, a motion is correctly referred to as a 'question' after the Chair has stated it to the body; before it is fully stated, it is properly known as 'motion.' But in practice they are synonymous terms and are used interchangeably."

Why should our association use the American Institute of Parliamentarians Standard Code of Parliamentary Procedure?

The *American Institute of Parliamentarians Standard Code of Parliamentary Procedure* is intended to present the principles of procedure in modern terms, reflecting the usage encountered in a typical gathering today. The procedures are established to accomplish the business in a meeting in a simple and straightforward way. The *AIP Standard Code of Parliamentary Procedure* is intended to provide a complete reference manual for parliamentary questions that might arise in an organization, relying on long-standing approaches that work and on case law as appropriate.

The parliamentary authority should be identified in the organization's bylaws. To change or add a parliamentary authority requires an amendment to the bylaws. If no parliamentary authority is identified, the current edition of the *American Institute of Parliamentarians Standard Code of Parliamentary Procedure* may be added in an article titled Parliamentary Authority. A parliamentary authority may also be adopted by a standing rule, although a bylaw provision is preferable.

What should I do if I have a question about parliamentary procedure that is not answered directly in the AIP Standard Code of Parliamentary Procedure?

Many times unique circumstances arise that are not directly addressed in the text of the *American Institute of Parliamentarians Standard Code of Parliamentary Procedure*. In such cases, the answer to the question may lie in an analogy to another similar situation covered by the text, or it may be found by relying on the fundamental principles detailed in Chapter 2. When no answer is otherwise clear, provisions found in other respected parliamentary authorities may provide persuasive authority on how to address a situation not directly covered by the *AIP Standard Code of Parliamentary Procedure* if such authorities are consistent with the simplified and modernized approach of the *AIP Standard Code of Parliamentary Procedure*. If none of these approaches yields a clear answer, inquirers who are members of the American Institute of Parliamentarians (AIP) may submit questions to the Opinions Committee, reachable through AIP Headquarters.

Where can I obtain information about the American Institute of Parliamentarians, such as its other publications, correspondence courses, educational opportunities, referral to its member professional parliamentarians, and addresses of local organizations of parliamentarians?

Contact the organization at this address:

American Institute of Parliamentarians
550M Ritchie Highway, #271
Severna Park, MD 21146
Phone: 888-664-0428
E-mail: aip@AIPparl.org
Website address: http://www.aipparl.org

Appendix A

FLAG ETIQUETTE

This section on flag etiquette is intended to increase the knowledge of parliamentarians and meeting planners in proper display and respect for the flags of the United States of America and Canada.

U.S. Flag Etiquette

This appendix about the proper etiquette concerning the U.S. flag will assist the presiding officer and other officers in preparing for a large meeting. The following information highlights many important parts of the U.S. Flag Code found in Title 4, U.S. Code, Chapter 1. The Flag Code codifies the existing customs and rules governing the display and use of the flag of the United States by civilians or civilian groups and organizations.

The national flag of the United States should be displayed in a manner befitting this national symbol. It should not be subjected to indignity or displayed in a position inferior to any other flag. It should never have placed upon it, or on any part of it, nor attached to it any mark, insignia, letter, word, figure, design, picture, or drawing of any kind. The flag, when it is in such poor condition that it is no longer a fitting emblem for display, should be destroyed in a dignified way, preferably by burning. Many civilian clubs like the American Legion will usually respectfully dispose of used flags for others if they are asked.

There are many customs and rules pertaining to displaying the flag. This appendix provides the rules that relate particularly to large meetings and conventions.

Position and Manner of Display

1. The U. S. flag, when carried in a procession with another flag or other flags, should be either on the marching right; that is,

the flag's own right, or if there is a line of other flags, in front of the center of that line.

2. The U.S. flag, when displayed with another flag against a wall from crossed staffs should be on the right, the flag's own right, and its staff should be in front of the staff of the other flag.

3. The U.S. flag should be at the center and at the highest point of the group when a number of flags of states or localities are grouped and displayed from staffs.

4. No flags of states, cities, or localities may be placed above the flag of the United States or to the U.S. flag's right.

5. When flags of two or more nations are displayed, they are to be flown from separate staffs of the same height. The flags should be approximately of equal size. International usage forbids the display of the flag of one nation above that of another nation in peacetime.

6. When the U.S. flag is used on a speaker's platform, the flag, if displayed flat, should be displayed above and behind the speaker. When displayed from a staff in an auditorium, the U.S. flag should hold a position of superior prominence in front of the audience and in a position of honor at the speaker's right as he or she faces the audience. Any other flag should be to the left of the speaker or to the right of the audience. If a U.S. civilian organization meeting in a foreign country for predominantly U.S. citizens in a leased facility, the U.S. flag would take the same position as it would if the meeting were held on U.S. soil. If the meeting is an international meeting, then the flags would be arranged according to the custom of the host country.

7. When the U.S. flag is passing in a parade or in review, all persons present should face the flag and stand at attention with their right hand over the heart, or if applicable, remove their headdress with their right hand and hold it at the left shoulder, the hand being over the heart. Citizens of other countries who are present should stand at attention.

Order of Precedence in Opening Ceremonies

1. Invocation
2. Pledge of allegiance to the flag of the United States of America
3. National anthem
4. Inspiration

Pledge of Allegiance

The pledge of allegiance to the flag should be rendered by people standing at attention facing the flag with their right hand over their heart.

When not in uniform, men should remove their hats with their right hand and hold them at the left shoulder, the hand being over the heart. People in uniform should remain silent, face the flag, and render a military salute for the duration of the pledge.

National Anthem

When the flag is displayed during the national anthem:

1. All present, except those in uniform, should stand at attention facing the flag with the right hand over the heart.
2. Men not in uniform should remove their hats with their right hand and hold the hat at the left shoulder, their hand being over their heart.
3. Individuals in uniform give the military salute at the first note of the anthem and maintain that position until the last note.

When the flag is not displayed during the national anthem, all present should face toward where the music is coming from and act in the same manner they would if the flag were being displayed.

Canadian Flag Etiquette

The national flag of Canada and the flags of Canadian provinces and territories are symbols of honor and pride. They should be treated with respect. The manner in which flags are displayed in Canada is not governed by any legislation but has been established by practice and customs as listed below.

1. When flown in Canada, the national flag always takes precedence over all other national flags.
2. The national flag of Canada should always be flown on its own mast.
3. When the national flag of Canada is raised or lowered, or when it is carried past in a parade, all people present should face the flag, men should remove their hats, and all should remain silent. Those in uniform should salute.

4. When the national flag of Canada is in combination with a provincial or territorial flag, a municipal flag, or an organization banner, it should be in the center with the provincial or territorial flag to the left and the municipal flag to the right as an observer facing the flag sees it.

5. The location of the position of honor depends on the number of flags flown and the chosen configuration. When two flags, or more than three flags, are displayed, the position of honor is farthest to the left of the observer facing the flag. When three flags are flown, the position of honor is in the center.

6. The order of precedence for flags is:
   a. National flag of Canada
   b. Flags of other sovereign nations in alphabetical order
   c. Flags of Canadian provinces
   d. Flags of Canadian territories
   e. Flags of municipalities or cities
   f. Banners of organizations

7. When the national flag of Canada is displayed on a speaker's platform, it should be against the wall or on a flagpole at the left from the point of view of the audience facing the speaker.

8. When used in an auditorium, the national flag of Canada should be to the right of the spectator facing the flag.

9. When displayed with the flag of another nation, the national flag of Canada should be on the left of the observer facing the flags and both should be at the same height.

10. When crossed with the flag of another sovereign nation, the national flag of Canada should be on the left of the observer facing the flags with the flagpole bearing the national flag of Canada in front of the pole of the other flag.

11. When a flag becomes tattered and is no longer in a suitable condition for use, it should be destroyed in a dignified way by being burned.

12. When used in the body of a place of worship or auditorium, the national flag of Canada should be to the right of the congregation or spectators facing the flag.

The preceding information on Canadian flag etiquette was taken from Canadianflags.com/Canadianflagetiquette.htm

Appendix B

PROTOCOL AT CONVENTIONS

The following meeting protocol for conventions and annual meetings explains principles and usual practice and is offered as a suggestion or guideline. Organizations should establish their own protocol based on customs and practices that would make the meeting function most effectively.

Many organizations have a formal opening for annual meetings or conventions. It is the universal custom in the United States to have an invocation before the pledge of allegiance or the singing of the national anthem.

Seating at the Head Table

The seating at the head table of an annual meeting or convention can vary depending on the type of program, customs, or the need of the president or presiding officer. The head table always faces the assembly and may have more than one tier, depending on the need of the organization. The seating at the head table where there is a speaker and no business to be conducted is as follows:

1. The president sits at the right of the lectern.
2. The highest-ranking guest sits to the right of the president.
3. The remaining guests alternate left and right of the lectern according to rank.
4. The president introduces the guests at the head table.
5. Usually the program chair introduces the speaker and would sit to the left of the speaker unless the speaker is the highest-ranking guest. Then the president may opt to introduce the speaker.
6. Notable guests are introduced immediately after the guest of honor. If distinguished guests are present, they should be introduced before the speaker even if the speaker is the guest of honor.

7. The installing officer or leader of the pledge of allegiance sits at either end of the table unless the duty is performed by the president.

8. The president introduces the guests at the head table unless it is the custom for someone else to carry out the introductions.

9. There may be multiple-tier seating arrangements with various customs for seating guests, so the protocol should be flexible.

Seating at the head table may differ when business is to be conducted at the meeting. The president or presiding officer should have the parliamentarian and the secretary seated next to him or her, usually to his or her left. It is important for the parliamentarian to be seated next to the presiding officer either on the left or right depending on his or her preference in order to provide adequate communication and advice in facilitating the organization's business. When an organization is conducting business, there are usually no guests seated at the head table. Many organizations, when conducting business, will have their officers and executive director seated at the head table. Customarily the president is seated to the right of the lectern.

Introductions

When introducing guests or speakers, the presiding officer should start with the one of lowest rank and end with the one of highest rank. A speaker who is well known should be presented, while a speaker who is not well known is introduced. When introducing the speaker, the president should state the qualifications first, withholding the name until last. Then the presiding officer should call the speaker to the podium by name and title.

A man should always stand up when he is introduced to someone. A woman should rise if she is introduced to someone of higher rank, an older person, or to the host or hostess.

Receiving Lines

1. The first person in a receiving line is the president and everyone else stands to his or her right. The president's spouse may opt to stand in the line at his or her partner's left.

2. The guest of honor stands next to the president on the right unless the guest of honor's spouse opts to stand in the line at his or her partner's left.

3. The other guests stand in the receiving line in order of rank from the highest to the lowest.
4. The official host or hostess greets guests as they arrive, escorts them to the receiving line, and introduces them to the president.
5. The name and title of each guest should be clearly stated when being introduced to the president.
6. Each person in line should introduce the guest to the next person in line.
7. Conversation in line should be brief in order to keep the line moving.
8. Socially, one refers to a spouse by first name when introducing the spouse at the receiving line.
9. Receiving lines should be as short as possible.

Toasts

1. The toastmaster asks everyone to rise and says, "Ladies and gentlemen, I propose a toast to … "
2. Glasses may be slightly filled, but should never be empty, and they are raised to eye level.
3. Each person takes a sip and says, "To the president" or whoever is being toasted.
4. Glasses are never clinked.

The above information was taken from an American Institute of Parliamentarians publication titled *Manners and Protocol,* Second Edition.

Appendix C

SAMPLE PROXY FORM

A. Proxy giver identification
   Name _____ Membership No. _____
   Address _____
B. Proxy holder identification
   Name _____,
   Membership No. _____ (if applicable)
   Address _____
C. Authority to act as proxy
   I,_____, the undersigned, hereby appoint
   the above-named proxy holder to attend, act, and vote in my
   place at the meeting of members of the _____
   (association name) to be held on the _____ day of
   _____ (month and year), and at any continuation
   or adjournments of said meeting. This proxy may be revoked
   by me at any time by notice in writing to the proxy holder
   and to the secretary of _____ (association name).
   The proxy holder may not further assign the rights and duties
   detailed in this proxy to another. The proxy holder may act in
   the same manner and to the same extent, and with the same
   power as I, the proxy giver, could act if I were personally present at the meeting, subject to the following instructions or
   restrictions:
D. Instructions and restrictions
   (The proxy giver may include any instructions or restrictions
   below as to how the proxy holder may act and vote at the
   meeting.)
   1. *Example:* The proxy holder shall vote in favor of the pro-
      posal to amend Bylaw VII.
   2. *Example:* The proxy holder shall only vote for candidates
      nominated by the nominations committee.

3. *Example:* The proxy holder may vote in my place but may
   not make motions or participate in debate.
4. (To be filled in by proxy giver if necessary.)
5.

E. Signature of proxy giver

Signature _____ Date _____

Appendix D

TELLERS' REPORT—ELECTIONS

Office _Vice President_

Eligible voters ___ _345_ ___
Legal votes cast ___ _341_ ___
Vote required for election (circle one) <u>Majority</u> Plurality Other
Votes required to elect (if majority) ___ _171_ ___
        John Smith _195_
        Jeff Jones ___ _141_ ___
        Bob Wright (write-in) ___ _5_ ___
        Illegal votes _2 (ineligible candidate)_

Date ___ _(current date)_ ___

Signatures of tellers
         Nancy Norton
         Robert Roark
         Tom Tuttle

Appendix E

MODEL MINUTES

Call to Order
The regular meeting of the AB Association was called to order at 5:00 p.m., on July 25, 20___, at headquarters by President Ann Anderson. Secretary Richard Recorder was present.

Opening Ceremonies
Invocation was given by Sally Wright.
Pledge of Allegiance to the Flag of the United States of America was lead by Helen Honor.
Inspiration was given by Hillary Hearing.

Roll Call
Members in attendance: President Ann Anderson, Vice President John Jones, Secretary Richard Recorder, Treasurer Milly Mooney, members; Molly Stone, Helen Honor, Sally Wright, Hillary Hearing, Mary Member
Parliamentarian: Kate Karing
Members absent: David Dodger, Milly Mentor
Guest present: Susan Samuel

Quorum
A quorum was present.

Minutes
The minutes of the June 18, 20___, meeting were approved as presented.

Reports of Officers
President Anderson reported.
Vice President Jones reported.
Secretary Recorder read correspondence from AB Association National Headquarters concerning the dates for the convention in January.

Treasurer Mooney reported as follows:

Opening balance as of (date)	$ 1,898.50
Income	$ 500.00
(donation)	
Disbursements (expenses)	$ 200.00
(printing)	
Closing balance as of (date)	$ 2,198.50

The report of the treasurer was filed.
Bills for deposit for meeting room and office supplies were approved for payment.

Report of the Board
The secretary presented the report of the AB board as follows:
The board met by teleconference on July 4, 20___, and took the following actions:

• Approved the appointment of Johnny Green as chair for the Spring Fling
• Approved the application for the *American Institute of Parliamentarians Standard Code of Parliamentary Procedure* to be sold in the AB bookstore
• Reviewed the AB insurance documents

Reports of Standing Committees
The membership committee report was presented by Chairman Mary Member. The chair reported (add information here).
The scholarship committee report was presented by Chairman Helen Honor. The chair reported (add information here).

Report of Special Committees
The report of the planning task force was presented by Chairman Hillary Hearing. The chair reported (add information here).

Unfinished Business
The motion relating to the fall fair, which was pending at adjournment of the previous meeting, was adopted as amended to read, "That the AB Association hold a potluck dinner on the first Thursday in September at 6:30 p.m. in the community center to welcome this year's new members."

New Business
Molly Stone moved that the AB Association sponsor a student to the AB National Training Conference in the spring at the cost of $500. The motion was adopted.

John Jones moved, "That the president appoint a committee of three to explore the cost of purchasing a computer for the secretary." The motion was adopted as amended to read, "That the president appoint a committee of three to explore the cost of purchasing a computer and printer for the secretary and report back at the next meeting."

Announcements
The next meeting will be held at the fairgrounds on August 18, 20___.

Program
The program was presented by Susan Samuel, consultant for setting personal goals.

Adjournment
There being no further business to come before the meeting, the meeting was adjourned at 8:52 p.m.

_____
Richard Recorder
Secretary

Approval
Minutes approved this ____ day of _____, 20___

(Date minutes were approved)

_____
Secretary (initials or signature)

Appendix F

MINUTES TEMPLATE—COLUMN FORMAT

The (regular, special, annual) meeting of the (name of organization) was called to order at (time), on (date), at (location) by (name and title of presiding officer). The secretary (or secretary pro tem) was present.	CALL TO ORDER
Invocation was given by (if applicable) Pledge of allegiance (if applicable) was led by (name). Inspiration was given by (if applicable).	OPENING CEREMONIES (if applicable)
Members in attendance: (list members). Parliamentarian: (if not a member). Members absent: (if applicable). Guests present: (if applicable).	ROLL CALL (if roll call taken)
A quorum was (was not) present.	QUORUM
The minutes of the (previous or date) meeting were (approved, not approved) as (presented, read, amended, etc). (Note: corrections are entered in the final draft of the minutes.)	MINUTES
(Elected officers—president, vice president, other elected officers) (last names) reported (only actions or informational items that apply to the organization. One paragraph per officer.)	REPORTS OF OFFICERS
Secretary (last name) read correspondence from (identify source, basic information) and (action taken or to be taken, if applicable).	SECRETARY

Treasurer (last name) reported as follows:

Opening balance $ 0,000.00
  Income $ 000.00
   (may identify sources of new income)
  Disbursements (expenses) $ 00.00
   (may identify new disbursements)
Closing balance $ 0,000.00

The report of the treasurer was filed.
Bills (identify the bills) were approved for
payment (if applicable).

The secretary presented the report of the
(organization) board as follows: (summarize
actions taken).

The (standing committee name) report was
presented by (name, title if chair). (Give
a brief summary of information and/or
action taken based on recommendations
from the report. No opinion or discussion.
Use one paragraph per report.)

The (special/ad hoc committee/task force
name) report was presented by (name,
title if chair). (Give a brief summary of
information and/or action taken based
on recommendations from the report. No
opinion or discussion. Use one paragraph
per report.)

The motion relating to (subject), which
was (pending at adjournment, noticed,
referred, etc.), at the previous meeting was
(adopted, adopted as amended, defeated,
referred, etc.). (If amended, use the wording as adopted. If votes were counted, state
the number of votes for and against. One
paragraph per motion.)

TREASURER

REPORT OF
THE BOARD
(if applicable)

STANDING
COMMITTEES

SPECIAL
COMMITTEES

UNFINISHED
BUSINESS

(Name) moved that (exact wording of the motion as stated by the chair: "It was moved and seconded ..."). The motion was (action taken). (If amended, use the wording of the motion as adopted with the notation that it was amended.)	NEW BUSINESS
(Announcements of information pertaining to the whole organization.)	ANNOUNCE-MENTS
The program was presented by (name of presenter and title of subject). (No personal comments.) (Note: the program may be prior to adjournment or at other times as determined by the organization.)	PROGRAM (if applicable)
(If by motion) (Name) moved that the meeting be adjourned.	ADJOURNMENT
(If by the chair) The meeting was adjourned at (time). (*Or*, The meeting was adjourned by the presiding officer at (time)	
_____	
Secretary (or Secretary pro tem)	
Minutes approved this ___ day of _____, 20___	APPROVAL
(Date minutes were approved)	
_____	
Secretary (initials or signature)	

Appendix G

MINUTES TEMPLATE—SUBJECT FORMAT

Call to Order
The (regular, special, annual) meeting of the (name of organization) was called to order at (time), on (date), at (location) by (name and title of presiding officer). The secretary (or secretary pro tem) was present.

Opening Ceremonies (if applicable)
Invocation was given by (if applicable).
Pledge of allegiance (if applicable) was lead by____.
Inspiration was given by (if applicable).

Roll Call (if roll call generally taken)
Members in attendance: (names).
Parliamentarian: (if not a member).
Members absent: (if applicable).
Guests present: (if applicable).

Quorum
A quorum was (was not) present.

Minutes
The minutes of the (previous or date) meeting were (approved, not approved) as (presented, read, amended, corrected, etc).

Reports of Officers
(Elected officers—president, vice president, other elected officers) (title, last name) reported (only actions or informational items that apply to the organization. One paragraph per officer.)

Secretary (last name) read correspondence from (identify source, basic information) and (action taken or to be taken, if applicable).

Treasurer (last name) reported as follows:

Opening balance $ 0,000.00
    Income $ 000.00
    (May identify sources of new income)
    Disbursements (expenses) $ 00.00
    (May identify new disbursements)
Closing balance $ 0,000.00
The report of the treasurer was filed.
Bills (identify) were approved for payment (if applicable).

Report of the Board (if applicable)
The secretary presented the report of the (identify organization) board as follows: (summarize actions taken).

Standing Committee
The (standing committee name) report was presented by (name, title if chair). (Give a brief summary of information and/or action taken on recommendations based on the report. No opinion or discussion. Use one paragraph per report.)

Special Committees
The (special/ad hoc committee/task force name) report was presented by (name, title if chair). (Give a brief summary of information and action taken based on recommendations from the report. No opinion or discussion. Use one paragraph per report.)

Unfinished Business
The motion relating to (subject), which was (pending at adjournment, noticed, etc.) at the previous meeting, was (adopted, adopted as amended, defeated, referred, etc.). (If amended, use the wording as adopted. If the vote was counted, state the number of votes for and against. One paragraph per motion.)

New Business
(Name, title) moved that (exact wording of the motion as stated by the chair: "It was moved and seconded ...."). The motion was (action taken). (If amended, use the wording of the motion as adopted with the notation that it was amended.)

Announcements
(Announcements of information pertaining to the whole organization.)

Program (if applicable presented before adjournment)
The program was presented by (name of presenter and title of subject).
(No personal and comments.)

Adjournment
(If by motion) (name) moved that the meeting be adjourned. The
motion was adopted. (Or if adjourned by the chair.) The meeting was
adjourned at (time).

_____

Secretary (or Secretary pro tem)

Approval
Minutes approved this ____ day of _____, 20___

(Date minutes were approved)

_____

Secretary (initials or signature)

Appendix H

SAMPLE ACTION LOG

Administrative
Date   *Action*
1/01/2011   Reports shall be submitted 30 days in advance of the
                     meeting.
2/12/2008   The secretary shall notify all members who are more
                     than 30 days delinquent in their dues.

Annual Meeting
Date   *Action*
1/12/1999   Registration for the annual meeting shall include all
                     meals.

Documents of Authority
Date   *Action*
1/12/2000   The bylaw committee shall submit standing orders
                     to headquarters and place them in the online docu-
                     ments within 30 days of adoption.
6/27/1991   ~~Standing orders shall be printed on green paper and
                     mailed to all members~~. Removed August 1998.

Financial
Date   *Action*
5/15/1999   The Lost One accounting firm is hired to audit the
                     organization books on an annual basis.

Membership
Date   *Action*
2/12/2011   The membership committee shall provide computers
                     to all members who have given 25 years of service.

9/20/1956   ~~The membership committee shall provide watches~~
              ~~to all members who have given 25 years of service~~.
              Removed 1 Feb 2005.

Program

Date   *Action*
10/10/2007   All programs shall be no longer than 30 minutes.

Appendix I

BYLAWS TEMPLATE FOR ORGANIZATIONS

Article I. Name

Article II. Purpose
(If the purposes are stated in a charter, they need not be repeated in the bylaws.)

Article III. Membership

    A. Classes of membership with eligibility requirements, rights, and privileges of each class (active, associate, honorary, etc.)

    B. Requirements of parent organization if group holds a charter from a higher organization

    C. Procedure for membership application and certification (many organizations place procedures in a lower category of governing document such as "organizational policy and procedure")

Article IV. Officers

    A. List of officers of the organization
    B. Method of selection
    C. Duties of each officer
    D. Method of filling vacancies
    E. Removal of officers

Article V. Board of directors (or another name for the governing board)

    A. Membership
        1. Ex officio members (usually the officers of the organization)
        2. Elected and appointed members: qualifications, vacancies, removal

B. Officers of the board
  1. Qualifications
  2. Selection
C. Duties and responsibilities of board (often the duty and power to act for the organization between meetings of the organization)
D. Executive committee of board
  1. Membership
  2. Duties
E. Meetings of the board, including requirements for special meetings
F. Quorum requirements for board meetings often included in this article
G. Requirements for reports of board and executive committee

Article VI. Meetings

A. Annual: notice requirements, business to be conducted
B. Regular: notice requirements
C. Special: how called, who has power to call, notice requirements
D. Quorum: requirement for organization meetings often found here

Article VII. Committees

A. Standing committees: list of standing committees, number of members, method of selection, duties, powers, meetings, reports
B. Special committees: provisions for selection

Article VIII. Finances

A. Budget preparation and adoption
B. Dues: how determined, when delinquent
C. Auditor: when and how selected, type of report, if report is approved by governing board or membership
D. Surety bond for officers and employees
E. Requirements of organization to provide directors' and officers' insurance

Article IX. Terms of office

A. Length of term of officers and board members
B. Staggering of terms

Article X. Elections

  A. Time and method of nominating

  B. Nominating committee: duties and report

  C. Time and method of election

  D. Vote necessary to elect

Article XI. Quorum

  A. Meetings of the organization

  B. Meetings of the board

Article XII. Discipline and expulsion of members

  A. Grounds for action

  B. Investigation, hearing, final decision

  C. Vote requirements for disciplinary actions

  D. Reinstatement

Article XIII. Parliamentary authority
(To adopt this book as the parliamentary authority, see Chapter 26 for the wording to be used in the bylaws.)

  A. Provision for adoption

  B. Scope of application

Article XIV. Policies

  A. Provisions of adoption

  B. Vote required for adoption and amendment

Article XV. Amendments

  A. Notice, form

  B. Who may submit

  C. Method of consideration, vote required

Article XVI. Dissolution

DEFINITIONS OF PARLIAMENTARY TERMS

ad hoc committee. See *special committee.*

adhere. To be attached to and dependent on; pending amendments
· *adhere* to the motion to which they are applied.

adjourned meeting. See *continued meeting.*

adjournment sine die (without day). The final adjournment termi-
nating a convention or series of meetings.

administrative duty. A duty requiring only the faithful performance
of acts or functions already determined; administrative duties
include both discretionary and ministerial duties. See also *discretionary duty.*

adopt. To approve by vote and give effect to a motion or a report.

affirmative vote. The yes or aye vote supporting a motion as stated.

agenda. The official list of items of business planned for consideration during a meeting or convention.

apply. A motion is said to *apply* to another motion when it may be
used to alter, dispose of, or affect the first motion.

approval of minutes. Formal acceptance, by vote of the members or
by general consent, of the secretary's record of a meeting, thus
making the record the official minutes of the organization.

assembly. A meeting of the members of a deliberative body.

ballot vote. The expression or casting by ballot, voting machine, or
otherwise of a choice with regard to an election or vote taken on
a matter; the casting of such a vote is most often to maintain the
privacy and secrecy of the members' votes. See Chapter 18 for the
concept of a signed ballot.

bylaws. The set of rules adopted by an organization defining its structure and governing its functions.

call of a meeting. The written notice distributed to members prior to
a meeting indicating the time and place of the meeting and stating the business that is to be brought up at the meeting.

chair. The presiding officer of a deliberative body or committee.

challenging a vote. Objecting to a vote on the ground that the voter does not have the right to vote. Often confused with *challenging an election* (see below).

challenging an election. Objecting to an election on the ground that it is not being, or has not been, conducted properly.

charter. An official grant from government of the right to operate as an incorporated organization, or an official grant from a parent organization of the right to operate as a constituent or component group of the parent organization.

closed meeting. A meeting of an assembly, board, or committee, which only members of the particular group may attend unless the attendance of others is requested by the body; the discussions held or actions taken are considered confidential. Sometimes called *executive session.*

common parliamentary law. The body of rules and principles that is applied by the courts in deciding litigation involving the procedures of organizations. It does not include statutory law or particular rules adopted by an organization.

constituent or component groups. Subordinate groups making up a superior parent state, national, or international organization and chartered by it.

continued meeting. A meeting that is a continuation at a later specified time of an earlier regular or special meeting. The continued meeting is legally a part of the original meeting. It is sometimes called an *adjourned meeting.*

convene. To open a meeting or convention, usually a large and formal one.

debate. Formal discussion of a motion or proposal by members under the rules of parliamentary law.

delegation of authority. An assignment by one person or group to another person or group of the authority to act for the first person or group in certain matters that are lawful and capable of being delegated.

demand. An assertion of a parliamentary right by a member.

dilatory tactics. Misuse of procedures with the intent to delay or prevent progress in a meeting.

discretionary duty. A duty that usually cannot be delegated to another because members rely on the special intelligence, skill, or ability of the person chosen to perform the duty. See *administrative duty.*

disposition of a motion. Action on a motion by voting on it, referring, postponing, tabling, withdrawing, or in some way removing it from the consideration of the assembly.

entity. A particular and discrete unit that is recognized as having a separate legal existence, as distinct from individuals and other similar units, with certain legally recognized rights appropriate to its form. As used in this book, it is a comprehensive term for recognized organizational forms, as distinct from individual persons, that includes corporations, partnerships, limited liability companies, unincorporated associations, trusts, estates, and governmental units.

ex officio member. One who is a member of a committee or board by reason of holding another office; a treasurer is often an *ex officio member* of the finance committee.

executive session. See *closed meeting.*

floor (as in *have the floor***).** When a member receives formal recognition from the presiding officer, that member *has the floor* and is the only member entitled to make a motion or to speak.

general consent. An informal method of approving routine motions by assuming unanimous approval unless objection is raised. Also called *unanimous consent.*

germane amendment. An amendment relating directly to the subject of the motion to which it is applied.

hearing. A meeting of an authorized group for the purpose of listening to the views of members or others on a particular subject.

hostile amendment. An amendment that is opposed to the spirit or purpose of the motion to which it is applied.

illegal ballot. A ballot that cannot be counted because it does not conform to the rules governing ballot voting.

immediately pending question. The last-proposed of several pending motions and therefore open for immediate consideration.

in order. Permissible and correct from a parliamentary standpoint at a particular time.

incorporate. To form a group into a legal entity chartered by the government as a corporation. The group is recognized by law as having special rights, duties, and liabilities distinct from those of its members.

informal consideration. Consideration and discussion of a problem or motion without the usual restrictions on debate.

inherent right. A right or power that is possessed without being derived from another source.

main motion. A motion that brings business before the assembly.

majority. A number that is more than half of any given total.

majority rule. Rule by decision of the majority of those who actually vote, regardless of whether a majority of those entitled to vote do so.

majority vote. More than half of the number of legal votes cast for a particular motion or candidate, unless a different basis for determining the majority is required.

mass meeting. See *organizing meeting.*

meeting. An official assembly of the members of an organization during which there is no separation of the members, except for a recess, and which continues until adjournment.

member in good standing. See the section "Member in Good Standing" in Chapter 29.

minority. Any number that is less than half of any given total.

minutes. The legal history and record of official actions of an organization.

motion. A proposal submitted to an assembly for its consideration and decision; it is introduced by the words, "I move ..."

multiple slate. A list of offices and candidates containing the names of more than one nominee for an office or offices. See also *single slate.*

nomination. The formal proposal to an assembly of a person as a candidate for an office.

nonprofit corporation. A corporation whose basic and dominant purposes are ethical, moral, educational, or social, and which distributes no profit to its members.

objection. The formal expression of opposition to a proposed action.

official year. Commences at the time that an event, such as the commencement of an officer's term or annual meeting, is scheduled pursuant to a rule (including a rule permitting such an event to be scheduled within a limited timeframe by a specific body or individual) and runs until the time scheduled for the next such event, when the next such event is approximately one year from the original event. When procedural rules refer to a year and the context does not clearly refer to a calendar year, the year referred to is an official year.

order of business. The adopted order in which the various classifications of business are presented to the meetings of an assembly.

organizing meeting. The initial meeting of a group that does not have an established membership roster or rules, sometimes called a *mass meeting.*

out of order. Not correct, from a parliamentary standpoint, at the particular time.

parliamentary authority. The code or rulebook specified in an organization's bylaws as its authority in matters not covered by its bylaws or standing rules.

pending question. Any motion that has been proposed and stated to the assembly for consideration and that is awaiting decision by vote.

plurality vote. A larger vote than that received by any opposing candidate or alternative measure.

policy. An adopted statement of a belief, philosophy, or practice of an organization.

precedence. The rank or priority governing a proposal, consideration, and disposal of motions.

precedent. A course of action or decision that may serve as a guide or rule for future similar situations in the particular organization.

procedural motion. A motion that is not directly related to the business of the organization such as a motion to recess or close debate. See *substantive motion.*

proposal or proposition. A statement of a motion of any kind for consideration and action.

proviso. A temporary or conditional stipulation in the bylaws, motion, rule, usually indicating the date or time the bylaws, motion, or rule goes into effect.

proxy. A written authorization empowering another person to act in a meeting for the member who signs the proxy. This includes voting. *Proxy* may also refer to the person who casts the vote.

putting the question. The statement, by the presiding officer, of a motion to the assembly for the purpose of taking a vote on it.

qualified motion. A motion that is limited or modified in some way in its effect by additional words or provisions; for example, "I move we adjourn *at four o'clock.*"

question. Any proposal submitted to an assembly for decision.

quorum. The number or proportion of members that must be present at a meeting of an organization to enable it to act legally on business.

railroading. To push a motion through so rapidly that members do not have opportunity to exercise their parliamentary rights.

recognition. Formal acknowledgment by the presiding officer of a particular member, giving that member the sole right to speak or to present a motion.

renew a motion. To present again a motion previously defeated at the same meeting or convention.

request. A statement to the presiding officer expressing a desire that something be done. It is usually decided by the presiding officer. The request may also be expressed as a motion.

resolution. A formal motion, usually in writing, and introduced by the word "Resolved" that is presented to an assembly for decision.

restricted debate. Debate on certain motions in which discussion is restricted to a few specified points.

ruling. Any decision of the presiding officer that relates to the procedure of the assembly. An opinion of the presiding officer is not a ruling.

second. After a motion has been proposed, the statement "I second the motion" by another member who thus indicates willingness to have the motion considered.

seriatim. Consideration by sections or paragraphs.

single slate. A list of offices and candidates containing the name of only one candidate for each office.

special committee. A committee that is selected to carry out a particular task and that ceases to exist once the task is completed. Also called an *ad hoc committee.*

special meeting. A meeting held at a time other than that at which the organization normally meets. It is called to handle one or more specific matters, which must be noted in the call to the meeting and must be called in accordance with the bylaw provisions governing special meetings or in accordance with applicable statutory requirements.

specific main motion. A main motion that is so frequently used that it has acquired a specific name to distinguish it from the general main motion; for example, the motion to rescind.

standing committee. A committee that has a fixed term of office and that performs any work in its field assigned to it by the bylaws or referred to it by the organization or the governing board.

statute. A law passed by a legislative body.

statutory law. Law that is enacted by legislative bodies.

substantive motion. A motion that states a concrete proposal of business as opposed to a procedural matter.

substitute motion. A form of amendment that offers a new motion on the same subject as an alternative to the original motion.

table. To dispose of a main motion without a direct vote.

teller. A member appointed to help conduct an election and help count the votes.

term of office. The duration of service for which a member is elected or appointed to an office.

tie vote. A vote in which the affirmative and negative votes are equal on a motion, or a vote in an election in which two or more candidates receive the same number of votes. A motion receiving a tie vote is lost, since a majority vote is required to take an action. Candidates receiving a tie vote may be voted on again until one is elected or the assembly votes to break the tie in some other way.

two-thirds vote. Two-thirds of all legal votes cast.

unanimous consent. See *general consent.*

unanimous vote. A vote without any dissenting vote. One adverse vote prevents a unanimous vote.

unfinished business. Any business that is postponed to the next meeting or that was pending and interrupted by adjournment of the previous meeting.

voice vote. A vote taken by calling for "those in favor say aye" and "those against say no," and judged by volume of voice response; sometimes called a *viva voce vote.*

waiver of notice. Act of relinquishing the right to have had notice of a proposal or meeting. Also may refer to the statement proving the relinquishment of notice.

write-in vote. A vote for someone who has not been nominated, cast by voters writing on the ballot the name of the person.

NOTES AND CITATIONS

Chapter 2: Fundamental Principles of Parliamentary Law

1. "[A] town meeting would very soon find itself entangled in the complicated meshes of parliamentary rules, which would effectually stop all proceedings ...." *Hill v. Goodwin,* 56 N. H. 441 (1876), quoted in *Bullard v. Allen,* 124 Me. 251, 127 A. 722, 727 (1925).

2. "Among the rights protected by the First Amendment [of the U.S. Constitution] is the right of individuals to associate to further their personal beliefs." *Healy v. James,* 408 U.S. 169, 181 (1972).

3. "In the absence of any statutory provisions controlling the matter ... a decision of the majority will be valid and binding." *Norfolk & W. Ry. Co. v. Virginian Ry. Co.,* 110 Va. 631, 66 S.E. 863, 868 (1910).

4. "The fundamental rule is that all who are entitled to take part shall be treated with fairness and good faith." *In re Election of Directors of Bushwick S.&L. Assn.,* 189 Misc. 316, 318–19, 70 N.Y.S.2d 478, 481 (Sup. Ct. 1947).

Chapter 5: Rules Governing Motions

1. "Whether these forms be in all cases the most rational or not is really not of so great importance. It is much more material that there should be a rule to go by, than what the rule is; that there may be an uniformity of proceeding in business, not subject to the caprice of the Speaker, or captiousness of the members." Thomas Jefferson, *Manual of Parliamentary Practice* § 1 (1801).

2. "[W]here there is no special rule on the subject, a motion to reconsider may be made at any time, or by any member, precisely like any other motion, and subject to no other rules." Luther Stearns Cushing, *Lex Parliamentaria Americana* §1266, p. 506 (1856). See George Demeter, *Demeter's Manual of Parliamentary Law and Procedure* p. 153 (Blue Book ed. 1969); Richard B. Johnson et al., *Town Meeting Time* (3rd ed. 2001) § 32, p. 78; Paul Mason, *Mason's Manual of Legislative Procedure* § 464.3–5 (2010 ed.).

3. Paul Mason, *Mason's Manual of Legislative Procedure* §§ 62, 157 (2010 ed.) (provides reasons why seconds are not required in legislative bodies).

4. American Bar Association, Revised Model Nonprofit Corporation Act § 12.02 (1988).

5. Longstanding common law supports rescission of earlier enactments by implication when directly contradicted by subsequent enactments. See Theodore Sedgwick, *A Treatise of the Rules which Govern the Interpretation of Statutory and Constitutional Law*, pp. 97–107 (2nd ed., 1874).

Chapter 7: Main Motions

1. Paul Mason, *Mason's Manual of Legislative Procedure* (2010 ed.) § 56.

Chapter 8: Specific Main Motions

1. "The policy having been determined, and the action taken and carried out under authority of law, the power to change or rescind does not exist." *Schiefelin v. Hylan*, 106 Misc. 347, 355, 174 N.Y.S. 506, 511 (Sup. Ct.), aff'd, 188 A.D. 192, 176 N.Y.S. 809, aff'd, 227 N.Y. 593, 125 N.E. 925 (1919).

Chapter 9: Subsidiary Motions

1. Paul Mason, *Mason's Manual of Legislative Procedure* § 402.1 (2010 ed.).

2. "It [the amendment] may entirely change the effect of or be in conflict with the spirit of the original motion ...." Paul Mason, *Mason's Manual of Legislative Procedure* § 402.3 (2010 ed.).

3. "[I]t may be adopted by a majority vote, even when the motion to which it is applied requires more than a majority." Howard L. Oleck and Cami Green, *Parliamentary Law and Practice for Nonprofit Organizations* § 27, p. 56 (2nd ed., 1991).

Chapter 10: Privileged Motions

1. Paul Mason, *Mason's Manual of Legislative Procedure* § 201 (2010 ed.).

Chapter 11: Incidental Motions

1. "[I]t is always the duty of the presiding officer [at council meetings] to enforce the law or rules applicable to the body ...." *Arrington v. Moore*, 31 Md. App. 448, 456, 358 A.2d 909, 914 (citations omitted) (quoting McQuillin's *The Law of Municipal Corporations*), *cert. denied*, 278 Md. 729 (1976).

2. "No presiding officer should be permitted to arbitrarily or fraudulently defeat the will of the majority of any deliberative assembly by making a knowingly false announcement of the result of a vote ...." *Gipson v. Morris*, 31 Tex. Civ. App. 645, 649, 73 S.W. 85, 88 (1903).

Chapter 12: Types of Meetings

1. "No action can be taken which will be binding upon the corporation unless every stockholder has notice ...." *Asbury v. Mauney*, 173 N.C. 454, 92 S.E. 267, 268 (1917) (citation omitted).

Chapter 13: Notice of Meetings and Proposals

1. "If the notice failed to comply with the statutory and ... by-law requirements, such omission is ground for voiding the election unless there is a clear waiver on [the] part [of the complaining member] .... Where insufficient notice of an election is given 'there is no election and justice requires no further showing." *Election of Directors of FDR-Woodrow Wilson Democrats, Inc.*, 57 Misc. 2d 743, 746–47, 293 N.Y.S.2d 463, 466–67 (Sup. Ct., 1968) (citations omitted).

2. "[T]he attempt ... to oust [the member] from his positions as vice president and director, without notice to him and without a vacancy having been created, in the directors' meeting of June was void." *Piedmont Press Assn. v. Record Pub. Co.*, 156 S.C. 43, 152 S.E. 721, 726 (1930).

3. "There can be modifications and supplementations [to the proposal as stated in the notice of the meeting] provided that the Notice has fairly apprised its recipients of the scope of the action to be taken." *Nigro v. English*, 59 Misc. 2d 193, 196, 298 N.Y.S.2d 438, 441–42 (N.Y. Sup. Ct., 1969) (citations omitted).

Chapter 15: Quorum

1. "It is a fundamental rule of parliamentary procedure ... that a majority of the members of a body consisting of a *definite* number constitutes a quorum for the transaction of business ...." (citations omitted) (emphasis added). *Hill v. Ponder*, 221 N.C. 58, 19 S.E.2d 5, 8 (1942).

2. "[A] quorum of any body of an *indefinite* number for purposes of elections and voting upon questions ... consists of those who assemble at any meeting regularly called ...." (citation omitted) (emphasis added). *In re Havender*, 181 Misc. 989, 992, 44 N.Y.S.2d 213, 215 (Sup. Ct., 1943).

3. *In re Application of Gilmore*, 340 N.J. Super. 303, 310, 774 A.2d 576, 580 (App. Div. 2001) (citing Paul Mason, *Mason's Manual of Legislative Procedure* § 504).

Chapter 16: Debate

1. The presiding officer "must relinquish the chair and should not return until after disposition of the pending question." Howard L. Oleck and Cami Green, *Parliamentary Law and Practice for Nonprofit Organizations* § 39, p. 77 (2nd ed., 1991).

Chapter 17: Votes Required for Valid Actions

1. *Hascard v. Somany*, 1 Freeman 504, 89 E.R. 380 (K.B. 1693).

Chapter 18: Methods of Voting

1. "The requirement of secrecy would seem to include not only the right to vote in secret but also the right to secrecy after the ballots are cast." *Bachowski v. Brennan*, 413 F. Supp. 147, 150 (W.D. Pa.1976), appeal dismissed, 545 F. 2d 363 (3rd Cir. 1976), quoted in *Donovan v. CSEA Local Union 1000*, 594 F. Supp. 188, 196–97 (N.D.N.Y. 1984), aff'd in part, rev'd in part on other grounds, 761 F.2d 870 (2nd Cir. 1985).

2. Benjamin I. Sachs, "Enabling Employee Choice: A Structural Approach to Union Organizing," 123 *Harv. L. Rev.* 655, 720–23 (2010) (proposal on confidential telephone or Internet voting).

3. "A member may be 'present' in person or by proxy ...." *Herning v. Eason,* 739 P.2d 167, 169 (Alaska, 1987).

Chapter 19: Nominations and Elections

1. "We reject plaintiffs' arguments that calling for nominations from the floor at the time of an election is not a fair and effective method for nominating Board managers ...." *Liberty Court Condominium Residential Unit Owners Coalition v. Board of Managers of Liberty Court Condominium,* 3 A.D.3d 443, 444, 772 N.Y.S.2d 6, 7 (2004).

2. "If the by-law was intended to mean that no member should be eligible for the office of director, unless nominated as prescribed in [the provision on nominations], such a regulation would be unreasonable." *In re Farrell,* 205 A.D. 443, 445, 200 N.Y.S. 95, 96, aff'd, 236 N.Y. 603, 142 N.E. 301 (1923).

3. "Even when one is elected, there is no restriction upon his right to decline the office ...." *Black v. Board of Supervisors of Elections,* 232 Md. 74, 79, 191 A.2d 580, 582–83 (1963).

4. See 29 U.S.C. § 482 (c) (union elections not to be set aside unless errors could have affected the election).

5. "Because [the] nominees did not receive the required number of votes, its nominees cannot be seated as members of [the] Board of Directors." *Badlands Trust Co. v. First Financial Fund, Inc.,* 65 Fed. Appx. 876, 880 (4th Cir., 2003) (bylaw upheld despite the fact that the bylaw requirement resulted in a failed election).

Chapter 20: Officers

1. Felix Frankfurter, *Of Law and Men,* p. 119 (1956).

2. The "right and duty [of the vice-president acting on behalf of the president] devolved upon him from the very nature of his office." *Francis v. Blair,* 89 Mo. 291, 1 S.W. 297, 300 (1886).

3. See Parliamentary Opinion 2009–532, *Vice-Presidential Succession, Numbered Vice-Presidents,* 50 (2) P.J. 68 (April 2009).

4. See Model Nonprofit Corporation Act (3rd ed. 2008) § 1.40 (55).

5. "The act of delegation, however, does not relieve the delegant of the ultimate responsibility to see that the obligation is performed." *Contemporary Mission, Inc. v. Famous Music Corp.,* 557 F.2d 918, 924 (2nd Cir., 1977) (footnote omitted).

6. "The law is settled that a corporation possesses the inherent power to remove a member, officer or director for cause …." *Grace v. Grace Institute,* 19 N.Y.2d 307, 313, 226 N.E.2d 531, 533, 279 N.Y.S.2d 721, 724 (1967).

7. Opinion 2009–535, *Default Procedure for Officer Discipline under* The Standard Code, 50 (3) P.J. 100 (July 2009).

8. "It is the general and well established jurisdictional rule that a plaintiff who seeks judicial relief against an organization of which he is a member must first invoke and exhaust the remedies provided by that organization …." *Holderby v. International Union,* 45 Cal.2d 843, 846, 291 P.2d 463, 466 (1955).

Chapter 21: Committees and Boards

1. "The Directors are … but the agents of the corporation, and where their authority is limited by the act of incorporation, have clearly no power to bind their principal beyond it. If the general power of making bylaws regulating the transactions of the corporation remain in the body at large, the power of the directors may be circumscribed by them ." Joseph K. Angell and Samuel Ames, *Treatise on the Law of Private Corporations Aggregate* § 299, at p. 316 (4th ed., 1852).

2. "It is a well settled principle that the power to appoint generally includes the power to dismiss ." *Myers v. Hartnett,* 153 Pa. Super. 228, 231, 33 A.2d 512, 513 (1943).

3. "An individual director … has no power of his own to act on the corporation's behalf, but only as one of the body of directors acting as a board." *Fleet Bank of Maine v. Druce,* 791 F. Supp. 14, 17 n.6 (D. Me., 1992) [quoting *Restatement (Second) of Agency* § 14C (1958)].

4. "The requirement that a director or officer disclose to shareholders all material facts bearing upon a particular transaction arises under the duties of care and loyalty." William Meade Fletcher, *Fletcher Cyclopedia of the Law of Corporations* § 837.70 (2011 ed.).

5. "[T]he Church failed to carry its burden of proof in a situation where 'the potential for abuse … required open and candid disclosure of facts bearing on the exemption application.'" *Church of Scientology v. Commissioner,* 823 F.2d 1310, 1318 (9th Cir., 1987), cert. denied, 486 U.S. 1015 (1988).

Chapter 22: Committee Reports and Recommendations

1. See James J. Fishman, *Stealth Preemption: The IRS's Nonprofit Corporate Governance Initiative,* 29 Va. Tax Rev. 545, 573–74 (2010); 18 U.S.C. § 1519 (provision of Sarbanes-Oxley Act of 2002, Pub. L. 107–204, 116 Stat. 745 (July 30, 2002) (applying document destruction liability on nonprofit organizations).

2. "Newt Gingrich ... promised that all congressional documents ... would be filed electronically so that they would be 'available to any citizen in the country at the same moment it is available to the highest-paid Washington lobbyist.'" David S. Levine, *Secrecy and Unaccountability: Trade Secrets in Our Public Infrastructure,* 59 Fla. L. Rev. 135, 161 (2007).

Chapter 25: Minutes

1. Henry Campbell Black, *Black's Law Dictionary,* p. 1087 (Bryan A. Garner, ed., 9th ed., 2009) [citing Ray Keesey, *Modern Parliamentary Procedure* (rev. ed. 1994) and RONR].

2. "Corporate books and records generally subject to inspection include the transcript of charter and by-laws, minutes of meetings ...." *Morton v. Rogers,* 20 Ariz. App. 581, 586, 514 P.2d 752, 757 (1973).

3. "A nonprofit corporation must keep as permanent records minutes of all meetings of its members, board of directors, and any designated body ...." American Bar Association, *Model Nonprofit Corporation Act* § 16.01 (a) (3rd ed., 2008).

Chapter 26: Governing Documents: Charters, Bylaws, and Rules

1. "It is well established that 'the constitution, rules and bylaws of an unincorporated association if they are not immoral, contrary to public policy or the law of the land, or unreasonable, constitute a contract between the members which the courts will enforce.'" *Casumpang v. ILWU Local 142,* 108 Haw. 411, 422, 121 P.3d 391, 402 (2005) [quoting *Martinez v. Parado,* 35 Haw. 149, 153 (1939)] (footnote omitted).

2. See *In re Koliba,* 338 B.R. 48, 50 (Bkrtcy. N.D. Ohio 2006) (in the absence of extenuating circumstances, an attorney may not plead

ignorance of procedural rules as a defense in proceeding to sanction him for violating such rules).

Chapter 28: Types of Organizations

1. "Common parliamentary rules, in use by all deliberative assemblies in this country, may also be resorted to, in the absence of any made by the association itself, in considering the regularity of its proceedings." *Ostrom v. Greene,* 161 N.Y. 353, 362, 55 N.E. 919, 922 (1900).

2. "A nonprofit voluntary association ... seems to occupy an anomalous position in the law. It is not a partnership, yet, in reference to the rights of the members in the property owned by it, they are to be determined to a large extent by the application of the principles of law peculiar to partnerships." *Bentley v. Hurley,* 222 Mo. App. 51, 299 S.W. 604, 606 (1927).

3. National Conference of Commissioners on Uniform State Laws, Revised Uniform Unincorporated Nonprofit Associations Act (2008).

4. *Kansas City Power & Light Co. v. NLRB,* 137 F.2d 77, 81 (8th Cir. C.A.8, 1943).

5. See D.C. Code § 29–401.50 (e).

6. Codified at 29 U.S.C. §§ 401 et seq.

7. American Bar Association, Revised Model Nonprofit Corporation Act (1988); American Bar Association, Model Nonprofit Corporation Act (3rd ed., 2008).

8. American Bar Association, Revised Model Nonprofit Corporation Act § 13.02 (1988); American Bar Association, Model Nonprofit Corporation Act §§ 6.22, 6.41 (3rd ed., 2008).

Chapter 29: Rights of Members and Organizations

1. *Baron v. Fontes,* 311 Mass. 473, 42 N.E.2d 280 (1942) (former officers of an organization were entitled to injunctive relief when offices were usurped, and there were no means in the bylaws to challenge such action).

2. *Snay v. Lovely,* 276 Mass. 159, 176 N.E. 791 (1931).

3. "It is essential that the associates shall each be able to learn from the charter ... his rights in the corporation, and the extent to

which his interests are involved in it." *In re National Literary Ass'n,* 30 Pa. 150 (1858).

4. "It is well established that members of voluntary associations are required to exhaust their internal remedies prior to instituting legal action to enforce certain rights." *Logan v. 3750 North Lake Shore Drive, Inc.,* 17 Ill. App. 3d 584, 587 308 N.E.2d 278, 280–81 (1974) (citation omitted).

5. "[M]embership corporation[s] ... possess inherent power to expel or suspend members for good cause, provided ... that the member is notified of the charges and there is a hearing and an opportunity to defend." *Chisholm v. Hyattstown Volunteer Fire Dept., Inc.,* 115 Md. App. 58, 71, 691 A.2d 776, 782 (1997) [quoting 18A Am. Jur. 2d *Corporations* § 935 (1997)].

6. "[I]n every contract of association there inheres a term binding members to loyal support of the society in the attainment of its proper purposes, and that for a gross breach of this obligation the power of expulsion is impliedly conferred upon the association." *Polin v. Kaplan,* 257 N.Y. 277, 282–83, 177 N.E. 833, 834 (1931).

7. "[T]here was an inherent right of expulsion for the crime of perjury." *Cunningham v. Supreme Council of Royal Arcanum,* 165 A.D. 52, 53–54, 151 N.Y.S. 83, 84 (1914).

8. *Davenport v. Society of Cincinnati,* 46 Conn. Supp. 411, 441, 754 A.2d 225, 241 (Super. Ct., 1999). ("The accused must have notice of the charges, notice of the time and place of the hearing, and a full and fair opportunity to be present and present a defense.")

Chapter 30: Staff and Consultants

1. See Parliamentary Opinion 2009–550, *The Role of the Professional Parliamentarian when Serving as Professional Presider,* 51 (3) P.J. 18 (July 2010).

INDEX